SO WHAT ARE YOU ABOUT, THEN, "AGENT GRAVES"?

100 BULLETS: HANG UP ON THE HANG LOW

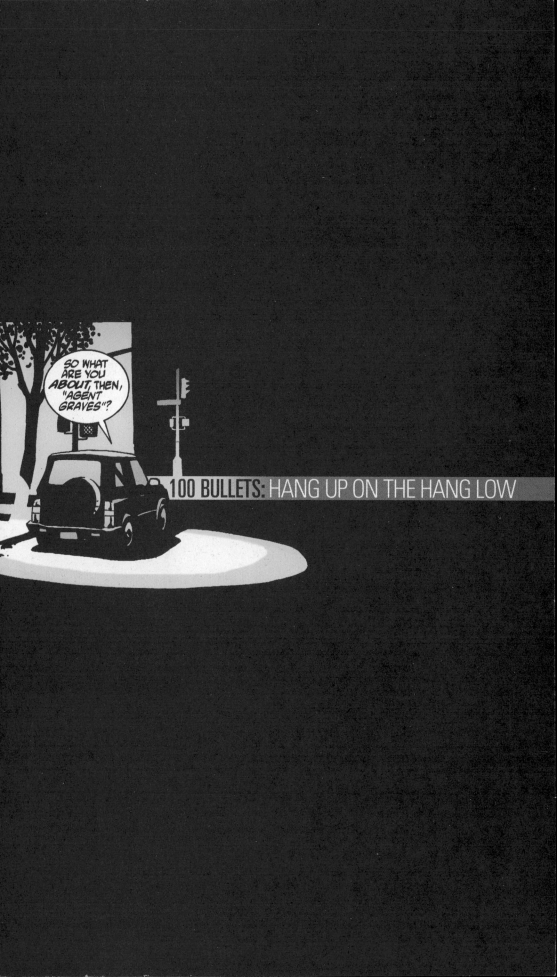

100 BULLETS:

HANG UP ON THE HANG LOW

Brian Azzarello Writer **Eduardo Risso** Artist **Patricia Mulvihill** Colorist **Digital Chameleon** Separator
Clem Robins Letterer **Dave Johnson** Covers 100 BULLETS created by Brian Azzarello and Eduardo Risso

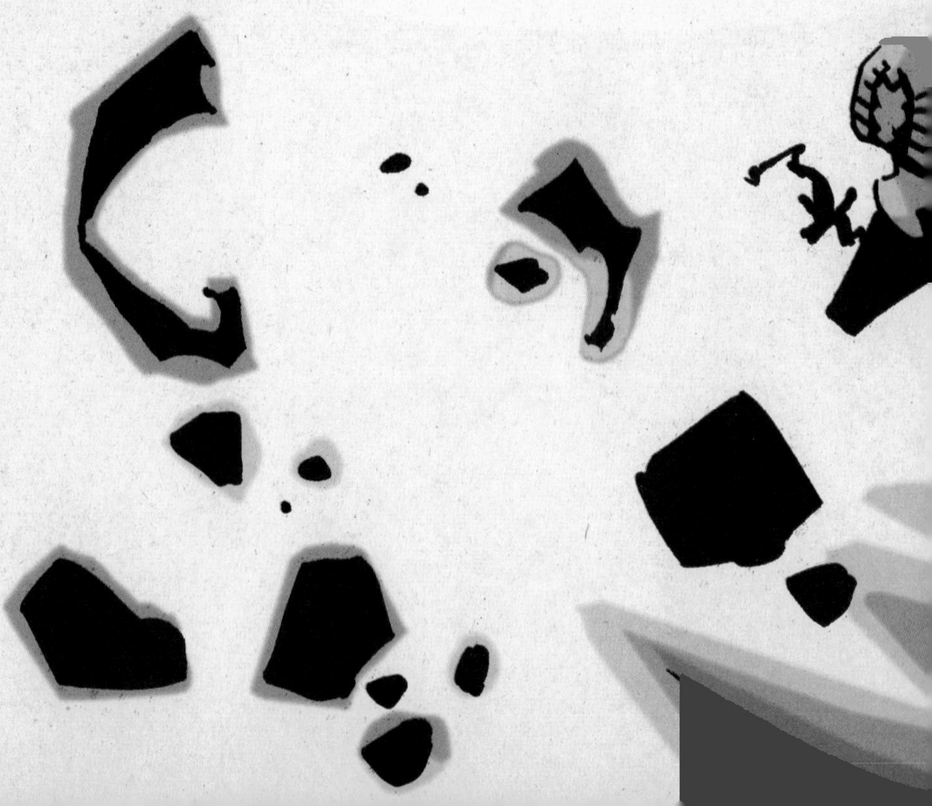

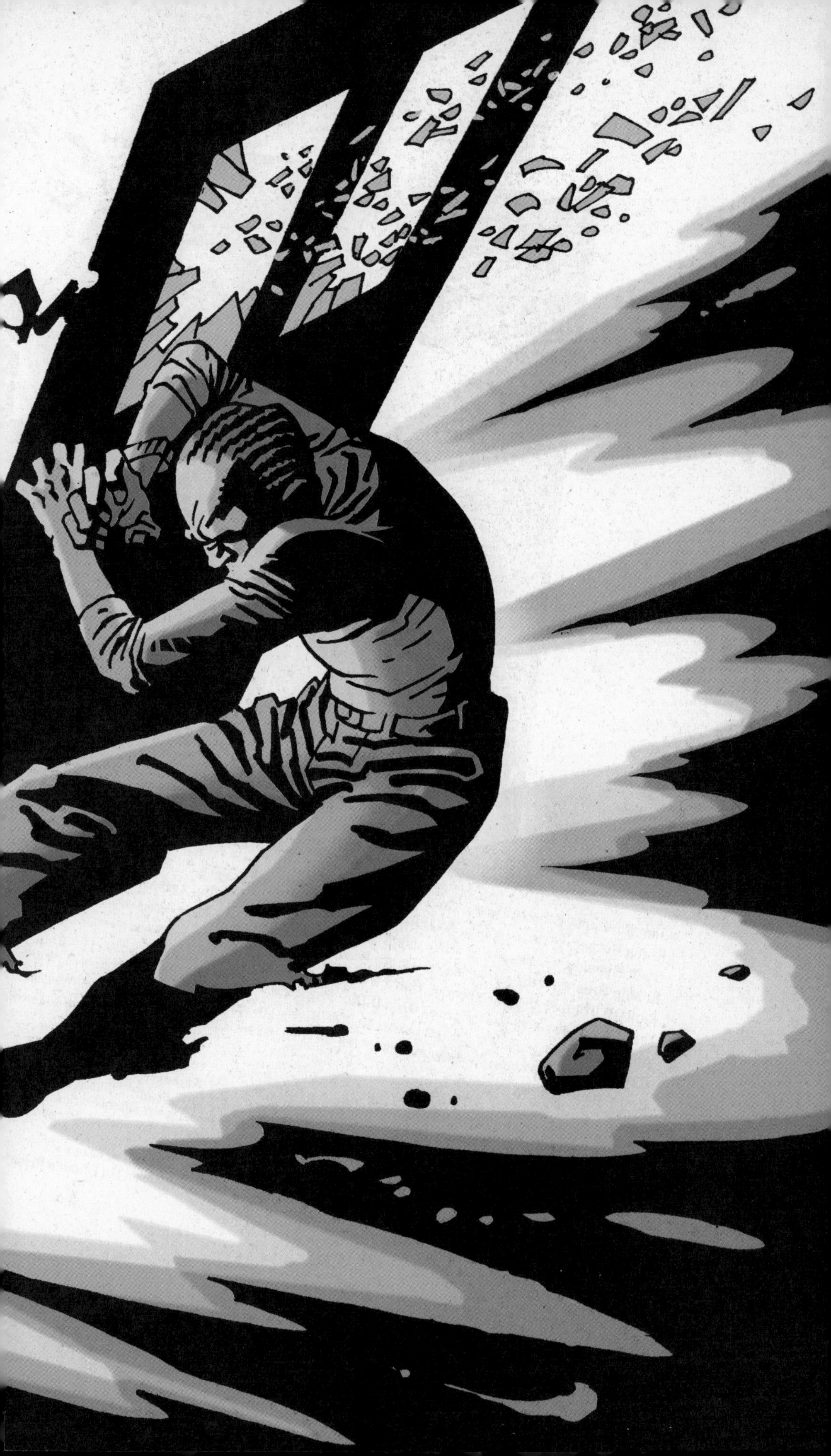

Jenette Kahn President & Editor-in-Chief **Paul Levitz** Executive Vice President & Publisher
Karen Berger VP-Executive Editor **Axel Alonso** Editor-original series **Jennifer Lee** Assistant Editor-original series
Scott Nybakken Editor-collected edition **Nick J. Napolitano** Associate Editor-collected edition
Robbin Brosterman Senior Art Director **Georg Brewer** VP-Design & Retail Product Development
Richard Bruning VP-Creative Director **Patrick Caldon** Senior VP-Finance & Operations
Terri Cunningham VP-Managing Editor **Dan DiDio** VP-Editorial **Joel Ehrlich** Senior VP-Advertising & Promotions
Alison Gill VP-Manufacturing **Lillian Laserson** VP & General Counsel **Jim Lee** Editorial Director-WildStorm
David McKillips VP-Advertising **John Nee** VP-Business Development **Cheryl Rubin** VP-Licensing & Merchandising
Bob Wayne VP-Sales & Marketing

100 BULLETS: HANG UP ON THE HANG LOW Published by DC Comics. Cover and compilation copyright © 2001 DC Comics.
All Rights Reserved. Originally published in single magazine form as 100 BULLETS 15-19. Copyright © 2000, 2001 Brian
Azzarello and DC Comics. All Rights Reserved. All characters, their distinctive likenesses and related indicia featured in
this publication are trademarks of DC Comics. The stories, characters, and incidents featured in this publication are entirely
fictional. DC Comics does not read or accept unsolicited submissions of ideas, stories or artwork.
DC Comics, 1700 Broadway, New York, NY 10019. A division of Warner Bros. - An AOL Time Warner Company.
Printed in Canada. Second Printing. ISBN: 1-56389-855-1. Cover illustration by **Dave Johnson** and **Eduardo Risso**.
Publication design by **Louis Prandi**.

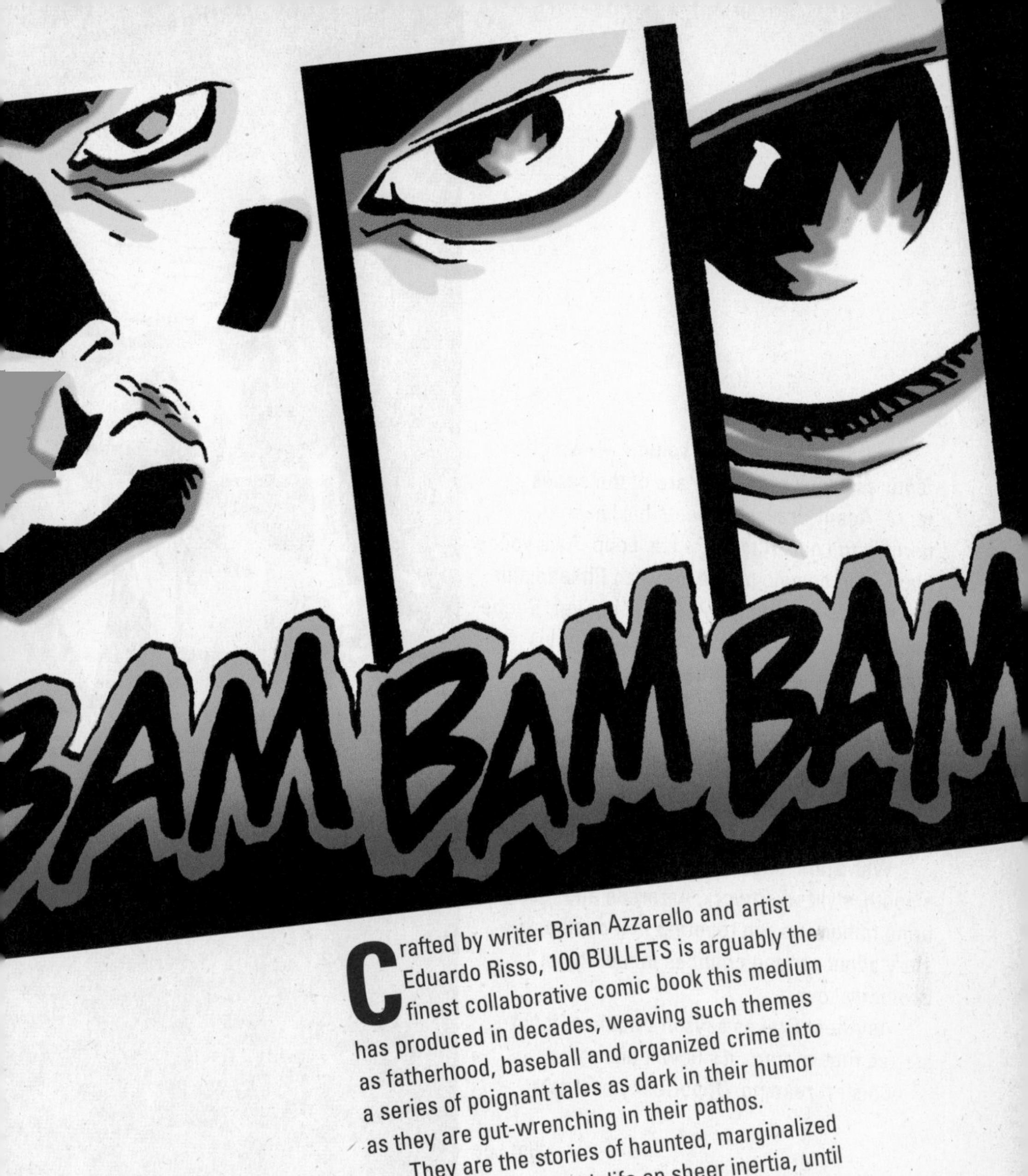
BAM BAM BAM

INTRODUCTION

Crafted by writer Brian Azzarello and artist Eduardo Risso, 100 BULLETS is arguably the finest collaborative comic book this medium has produced in decades, weaving such themes as fatherhood, baseball and organized crime into a series of poignant tales as dark in their humor as they are gut-wrenching in their pathos.

They are the stories of haunted, marginalized people who slip through life on sheer inertia, until their destinies are irrevocably changed by a man known only as Agent Graves. A cross between the archangel Gabriel and an old-fashioned G-man, the ghostlike Graves comes into their lives with a powerful handgun and 100 untraceable bullets. His offer? *Opportunity.*

The opportunity to exact vengeance — or the opportunity to make amends.

It is the dichotomy between these two choices which makes 100 BULLETS so engaging. While the untraceable bullets offer immunity from the law, the characters find that they cannot shield themselves from the moral consequences of their actions.

In this third collected volume — which features my favorite story arc of the series so far — Agent Graves presents his Faustian bargain to Louis Hughes, a.k.a. Loop. As a young black man coming of age in urban Philadelphia, Loop isn't a gangbanger. At least not yet. But he does have a chip on his shoulder about his absentee father — a father he both resents and yearns for at the same time. Fate has it that Curtis Hughes, Loop's father, is as rudderless as his son, wasting his days away collecting debts for a creepy Mister Magoo loanshark — until the day Graves appears.

With stark, dead-on dialogue punctuating smooth, stylized artwork, Azzarello and Risso bring father and son together in a combustive story about second chances in the City of Brotherly Love.

As Agent Graves says, it's not how it got started that matters, it's how it ends.

So start reading. Opportunity awaits!

— Jim Lee

One of contemporary comics' most popular creators, Jim Lee has been writing and drawing in the medium for almost fifteen years. Along the way, he co-founded Image Comics, created WildStorm Productions, and transformed himself into a Vegas-grade card shark.

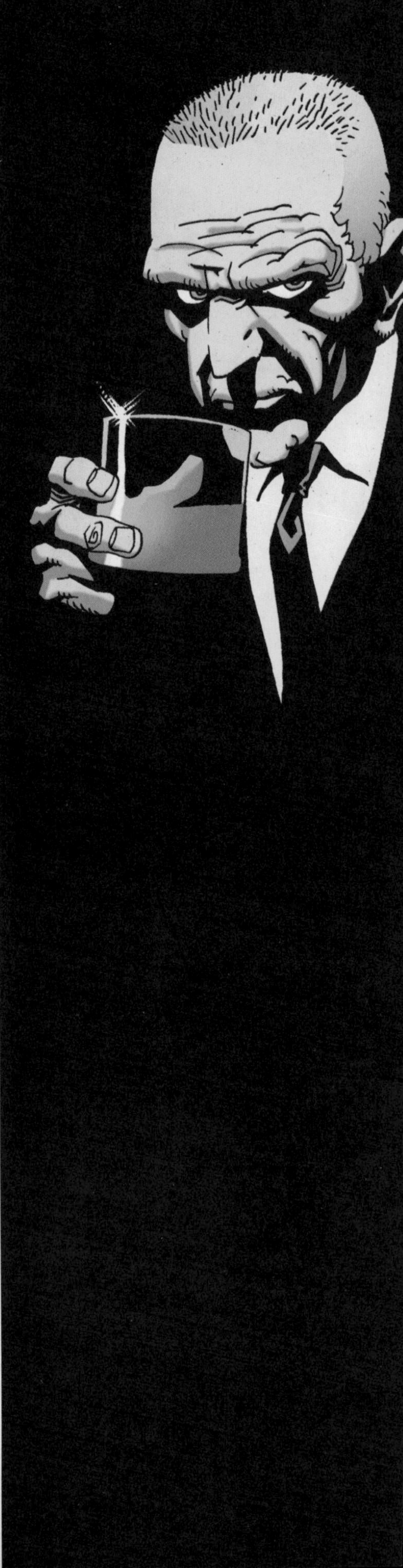

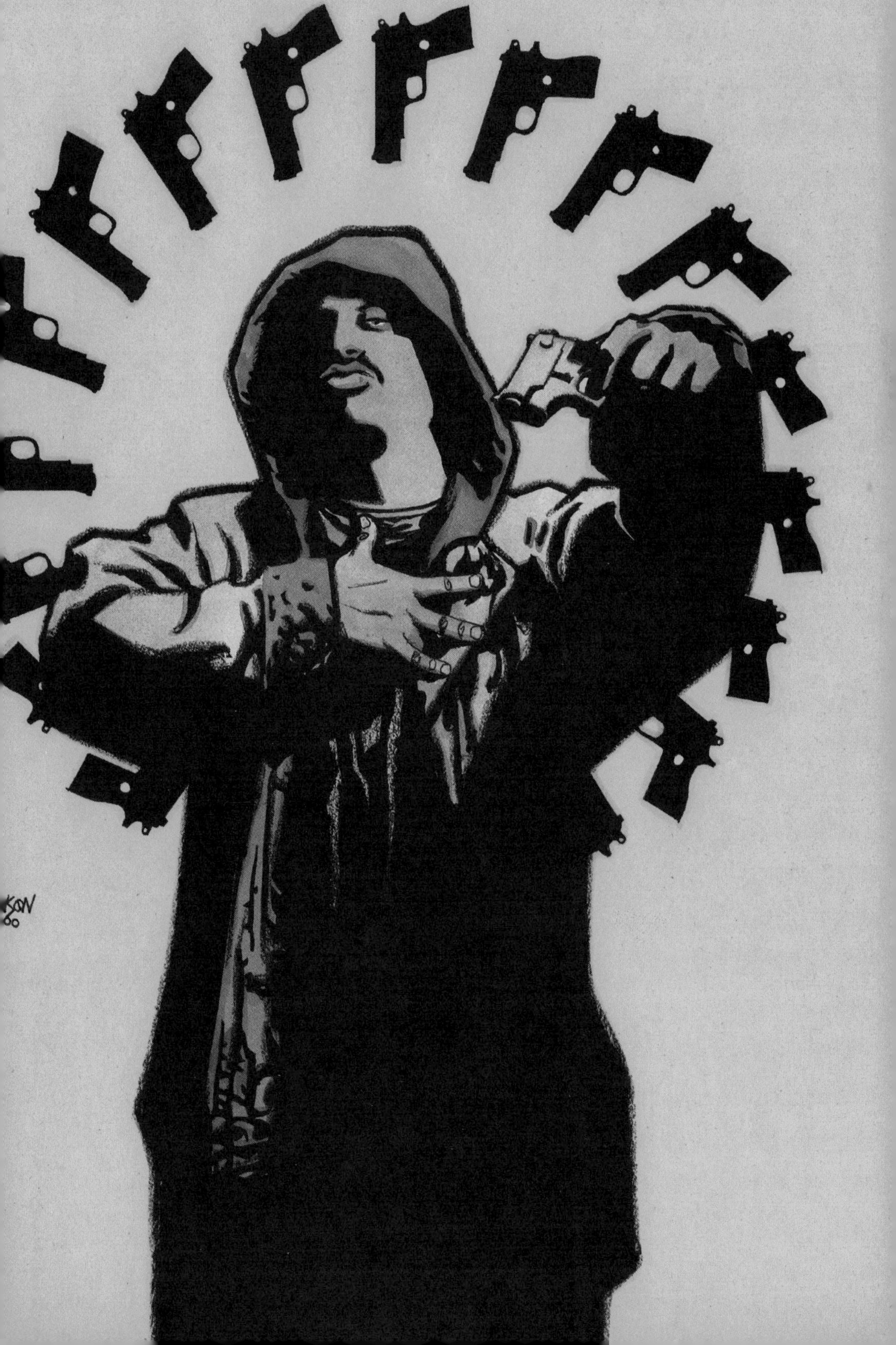

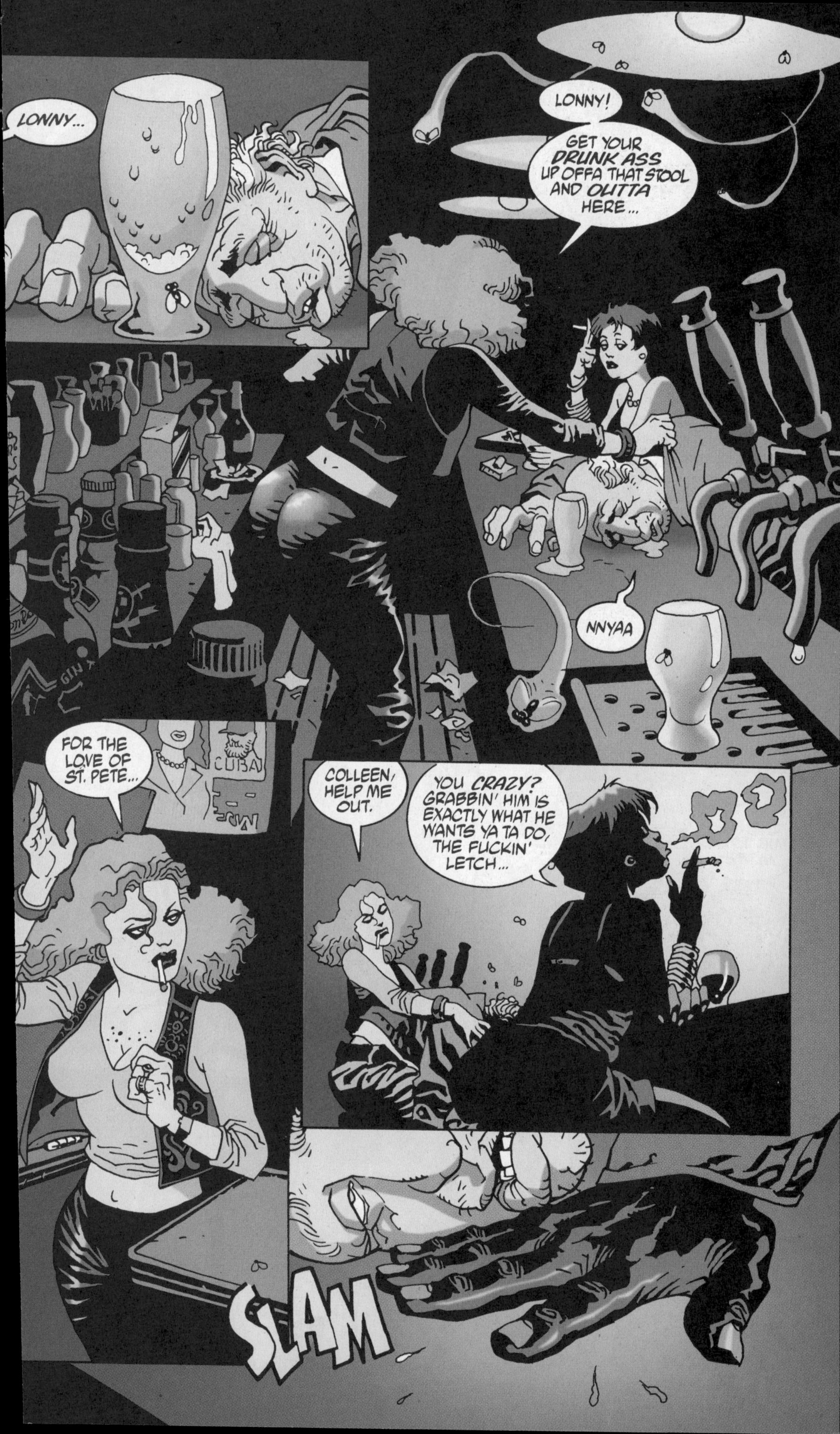
LONNY...
LONNY!
GET YOUR DRUNK ASS UP OFFA THAT STOOL AND OUTTA HERE...
NNYAA
FOR THE LOVE OF ST. PETE...
CUBA
COLLEEN, HELP ME OUT.
YOU CRAZY? GRABBIN' HIM IS EXACTLY WHAT HE WANTS YA TA DO, THE FUCKIN' LETCH...
SLAM

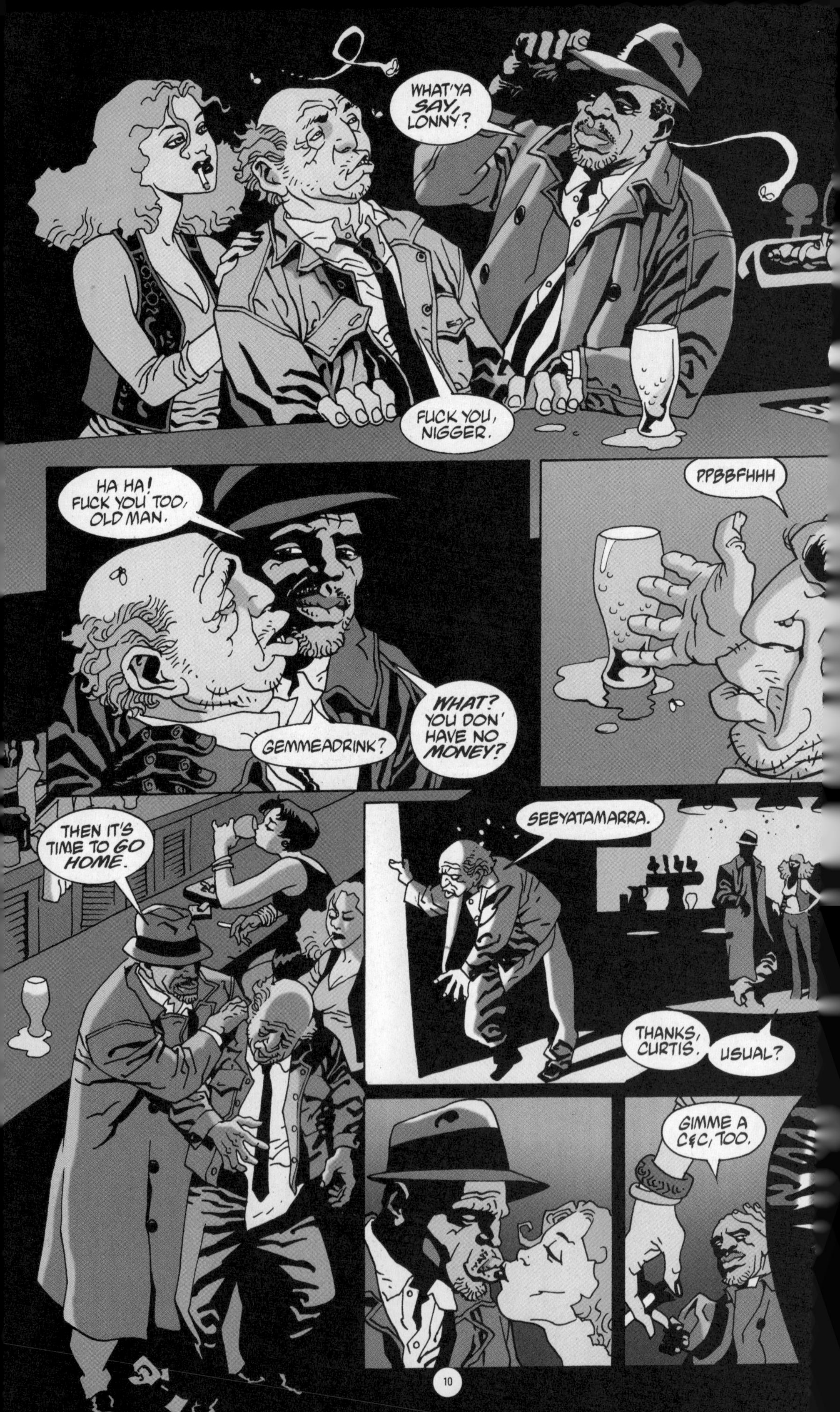
WHAT'YA SAY, LONNY?
FUCK YOU, NIGGER.
HA HA! FUCK YOU TOO, OLD MAN.
GEMMEADRINK?
WHAT? YOU DON' HAVE NO MONEY?
PPBBFHHH
THEN IT'S TIME TO GO HOME.
SEEYATAMARRA.
THANKS, CURTIS.
USUAL?
GIMME A C&C, TOO.

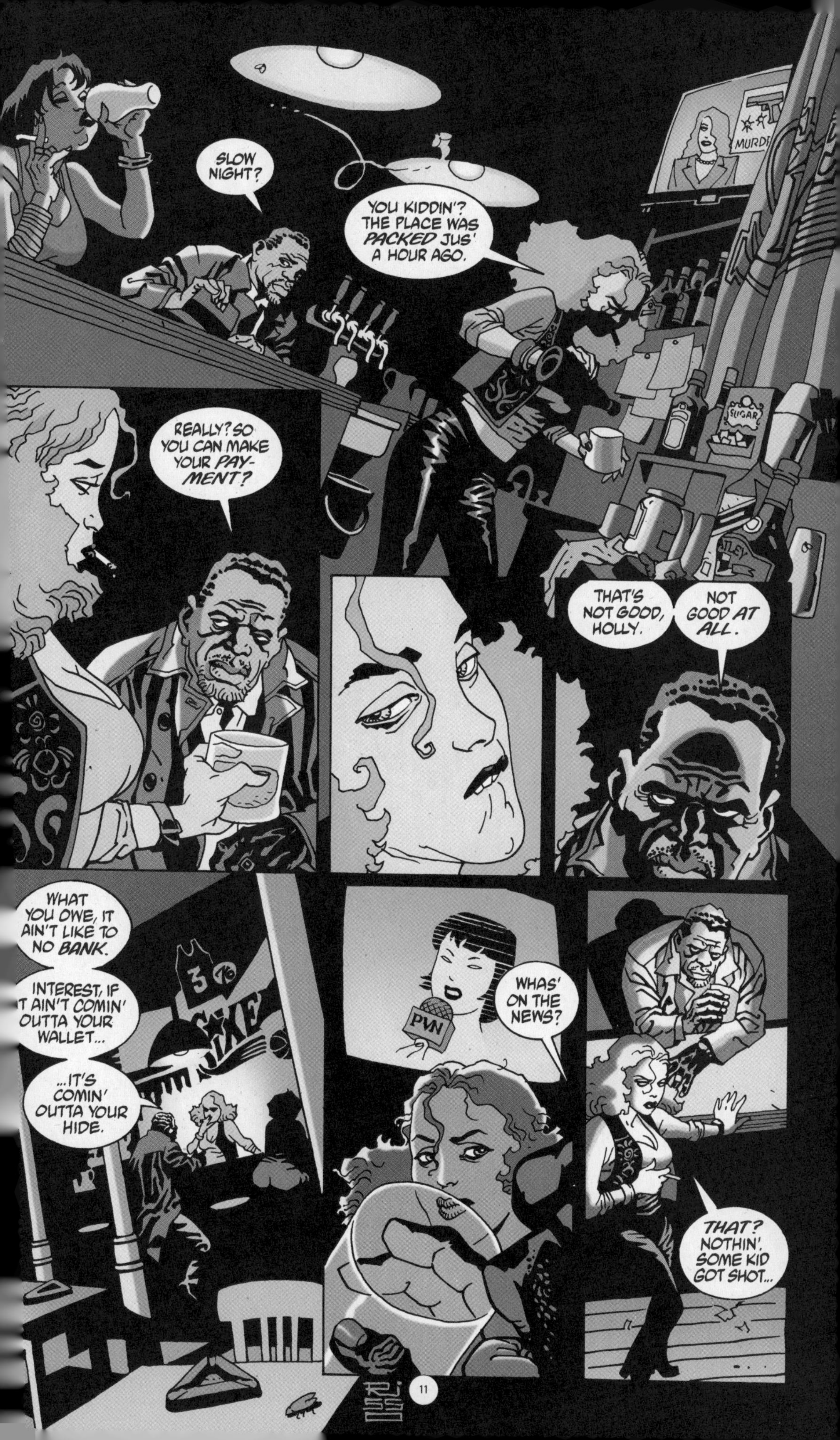
SLOW NIGHT?
YOU KIDDIN'? THE PLACE WAS PACKED JUS' A HOUR AGO.
MURDE
REALLY? SO YOU CAN MAKE YOUR PAY-MENT?
SUGAR
THAT'S NOT GOOD, HOLLY.
NOT GOOD AT ALL.
WHAT YOU OWE, IT AIN'T LIKE TO NO BANK.
INTEREST, IF IT AIN'T COMIN' OUTTA YOUR WALLET...
...IT'S COMIN' OUTTA YOUR HIDE.
PVN
WHAS' ON THE NEWS?
THAT? NOTHIN'. SOME KID GOT SHOT...

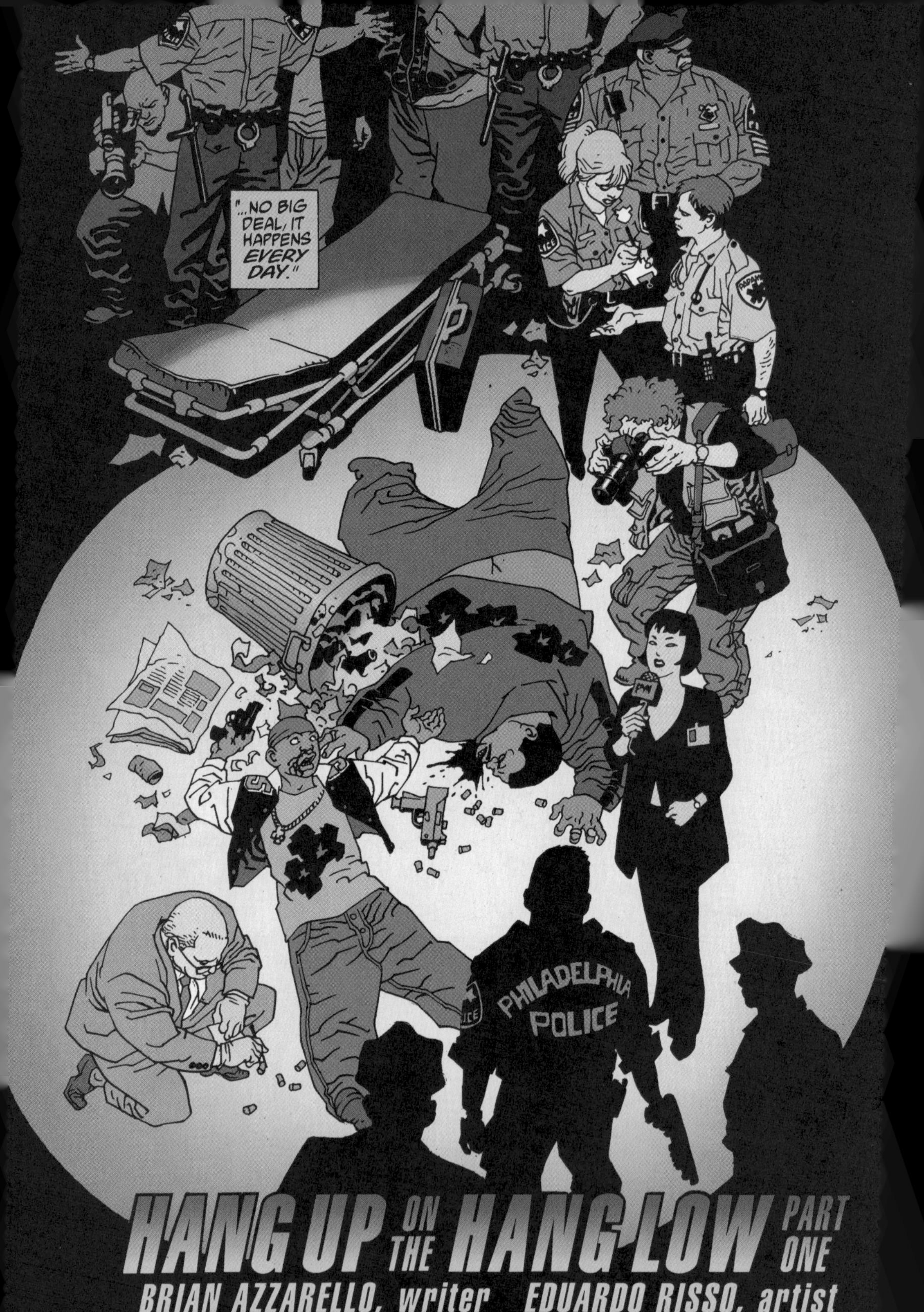
"...NO BIG DEAL, IT HAPPENS EVERY DAY."
PHILADELPHIA POLICE

HANG UP ON THE HANG LOW PART ONE

BRIAN AZZARELLO, writer EDUARDO RISSO, artist

PATRICIA MULVIHILL, colorist DIGITAL CHAMELEON, separations CLEM ROBINS, letters

DAVE JOHNSON, cover JENNIFER LEE, asst. editor AXEL ALONSO, editor

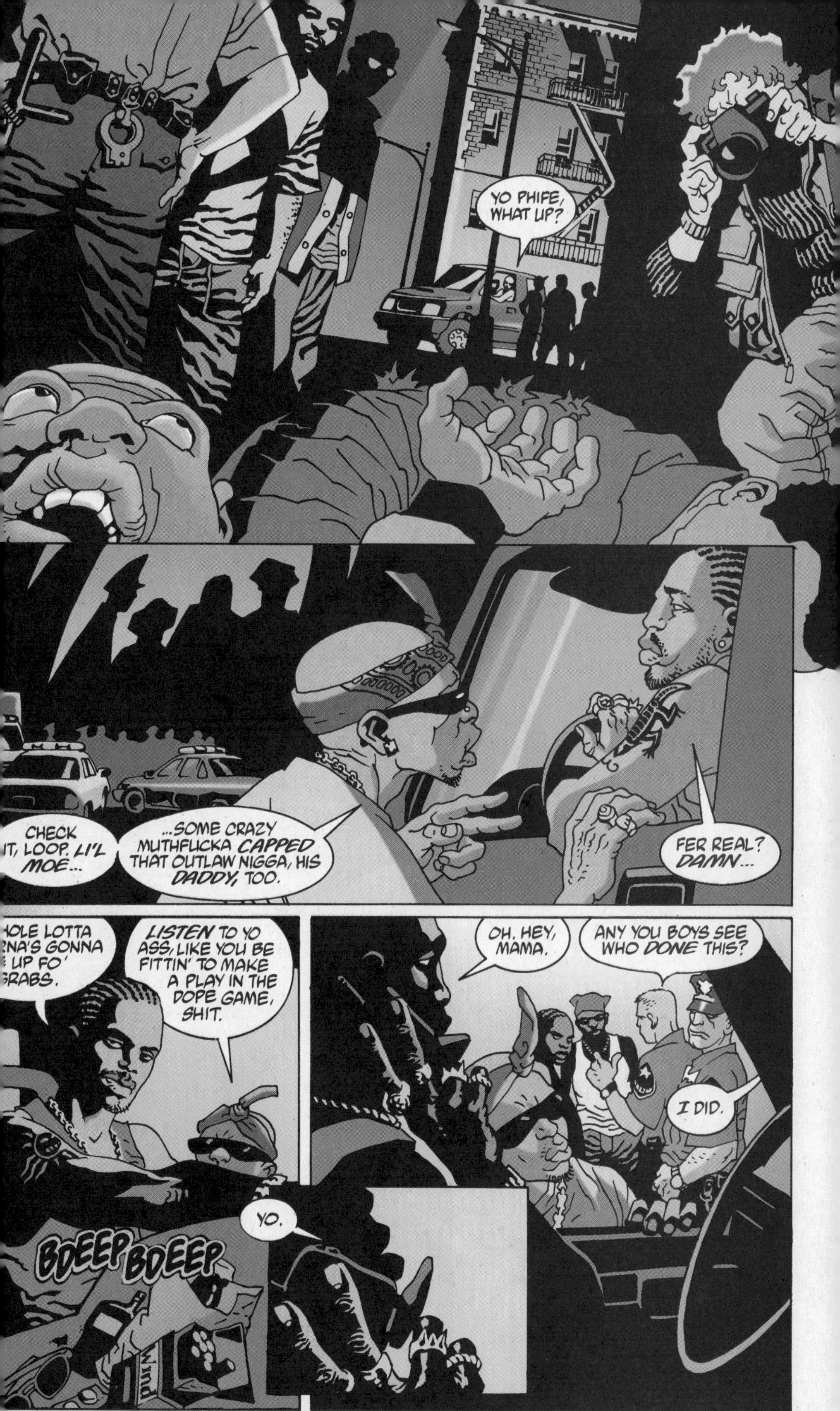
YO PHIFE, WHAT UP?
CHECK IT, LOOP. LI'L MOE...
...SOME CRAZY MUTHFUCKA CAPPED THAT OUTLAW NIGGA, HIS DADDY, TOO.
FER REAL? DAMN...
HOLE LOTTA RNA'S GONNA E UP FO' GRABS.
LISTEN TO YO ASS, LIKE YOU BE FITTIN' TO MAKE A PLAY IN THE DOPE GAME, SHIT.
OH, HEY, MAMA.
ANY YOU BOYS SEE WHO DONE THIS?
I DID.
YO.
BDEEP BDEEP

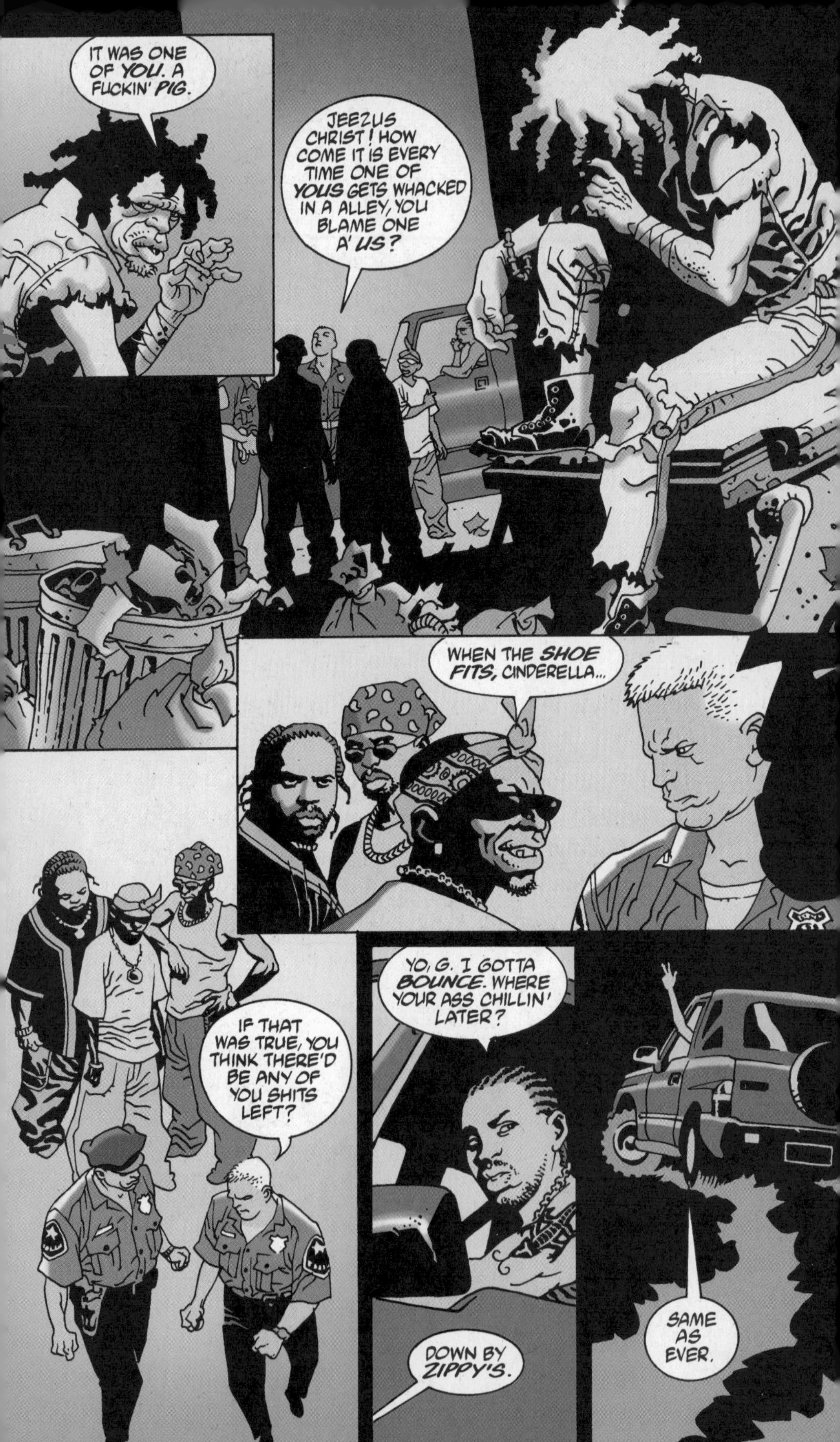
IT WAS ONE OF YOU. A FUCKIN' PIG.
JEEZUS CHRIST! HOW COME IT IS EVERY TIME ONE OF YOUS GETS WHACKED IN A ALLEY, YOU BLAME ONE A' US?
WHEN THE SHOE FITS, CINDERELLA...
IF THAT WAS TRUE, YOU THINK THERE'D BE ANY OF YOU SHITS LEFT?
YO, G. I GOTTA BOUNCE. WHERE YOUR ASS CHILLIN' LATER?
DOWN BY ZIPPY'S.
SAME AS EVER.

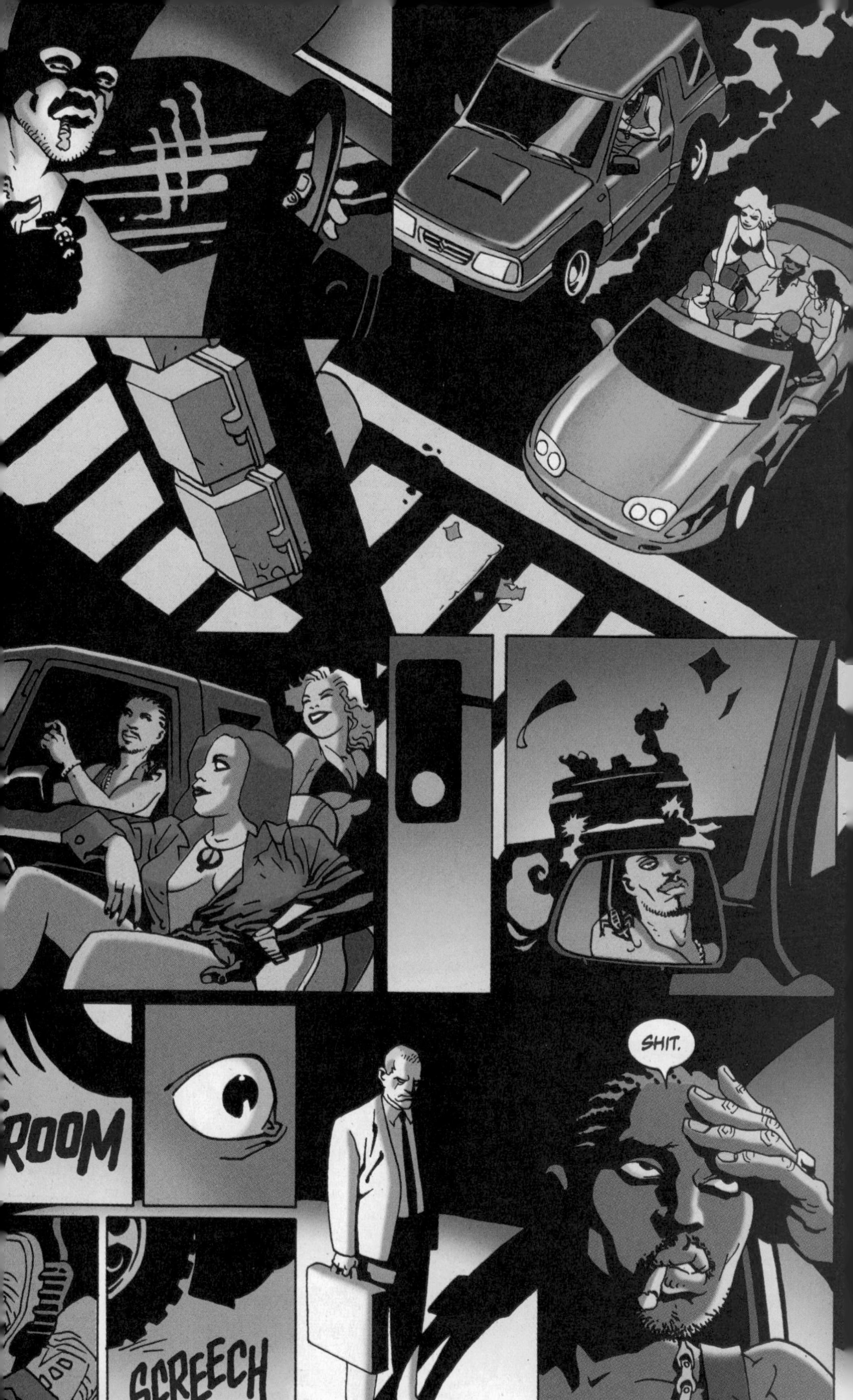
ROOM
SCREECH
SHIT.

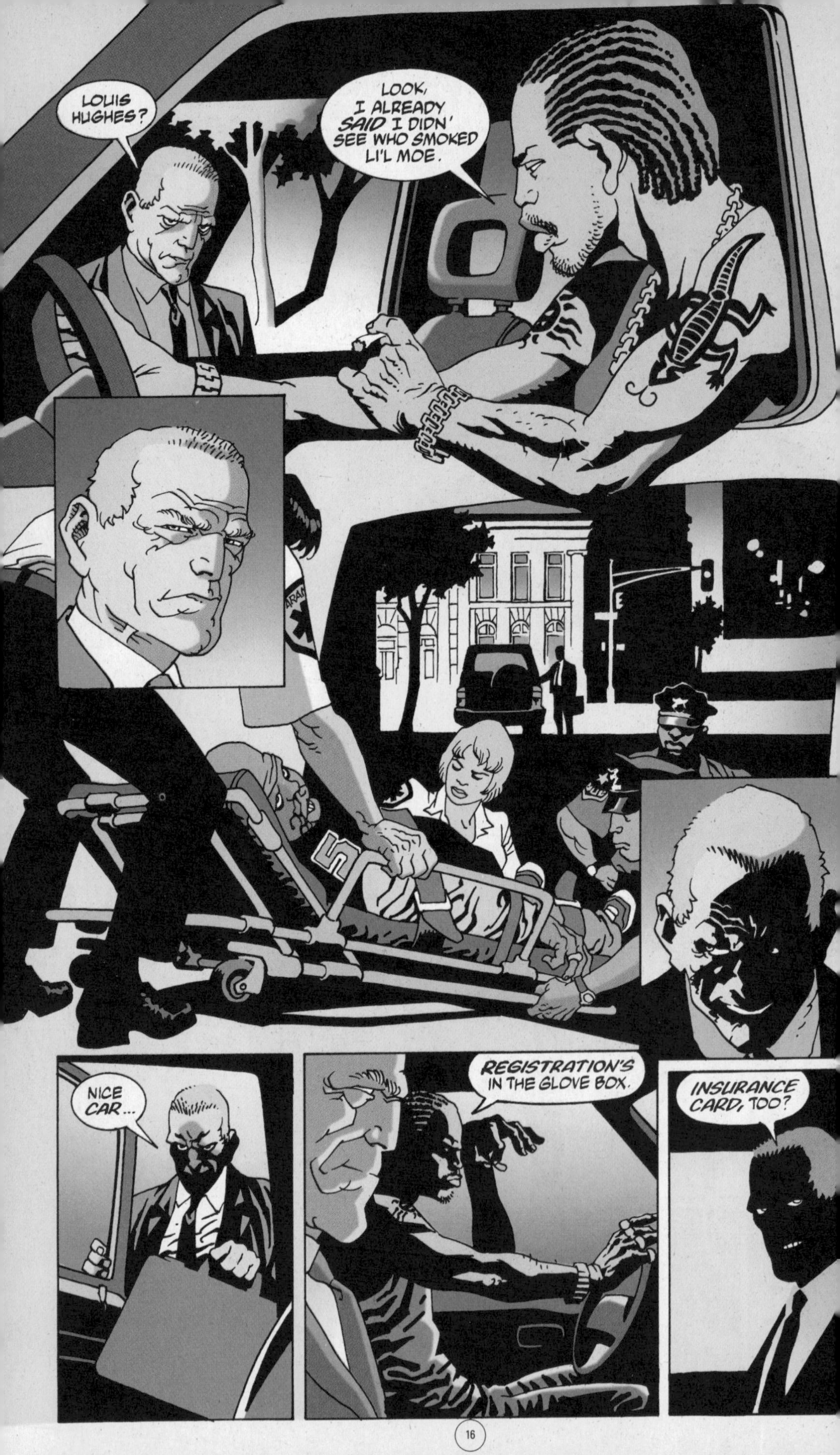
LOUIS HUGHES?
LOOK, I ALREADY SAID I DIDN' SEE WHO SMOKED LI'L MOE.
NICE CAR...
REGISTRATION'S IN THE GLOVE BOX.
INSURANCE CARD, TOO?

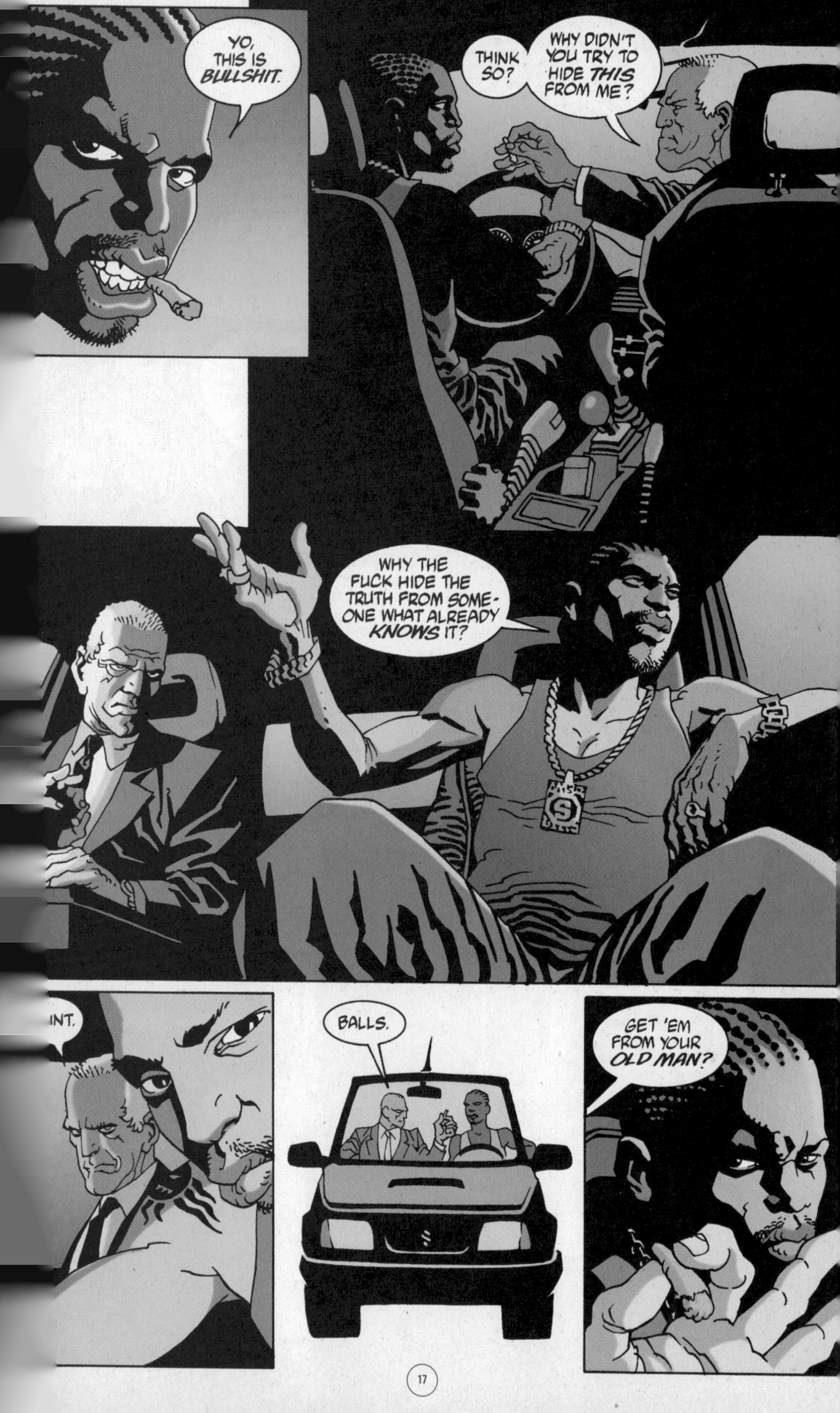
YO, THIS IS BULLSHIT.
THINK SO?
WHY DIDN'T YOU TRY TO HIDE THIS FROM ME?
WHY THE FUCK HIDE THE TRUTH FROM SOME-ONE WHAT ALREADY KNOWS IT?
INT.
BALLS.
GET 'EM FROM YOUR OLD MAN?

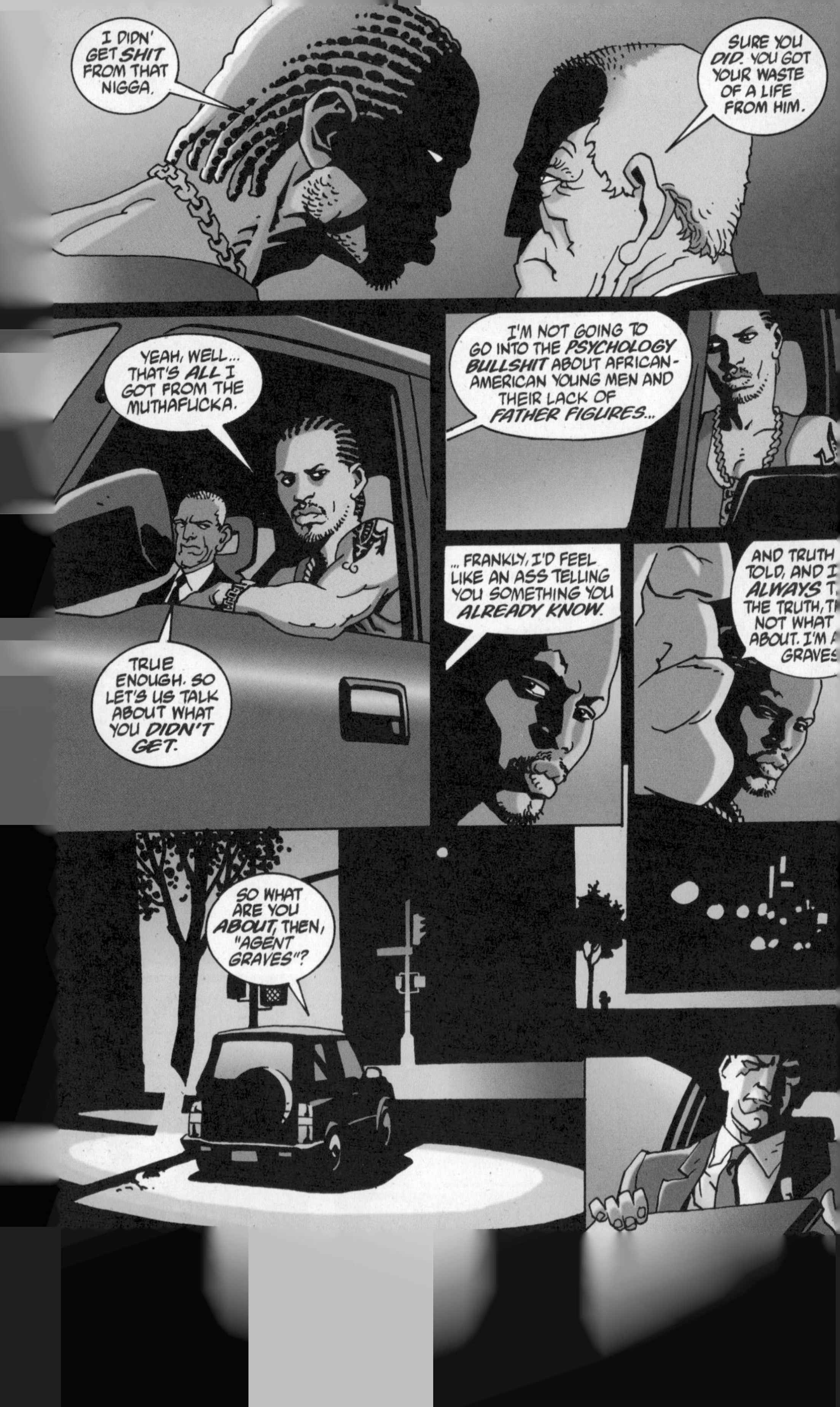

I DIDN' GET SHIT FROM THAT NIGGA.
SURE YOU DID. YOU GOT YOUR WASTE OF A LIFE FROM HIM.
YEAH, WELL... THAT'S ALL I GOT FROM THE MUTHAFUCKA.
TRUE ENOUGH. SO LET'S US TALK ABOUT WHAT YOU DIDN'T GET.
I'M NOT GOING TO GO INTO THE PSYCHOLOGY BULLSHIT ABOUT AFRICAN-AMERICAN YOUNG MEN AND THEIR LACK OF FATHER FIGURES...
...FRANKLY, I'D FEEL LIKE AN ASS TELLING YOU SOMETHING YOU ALREADY KNOW.
SO WHAT ARE YOU ABOUT, THEN, "AGENT GRAVES"?

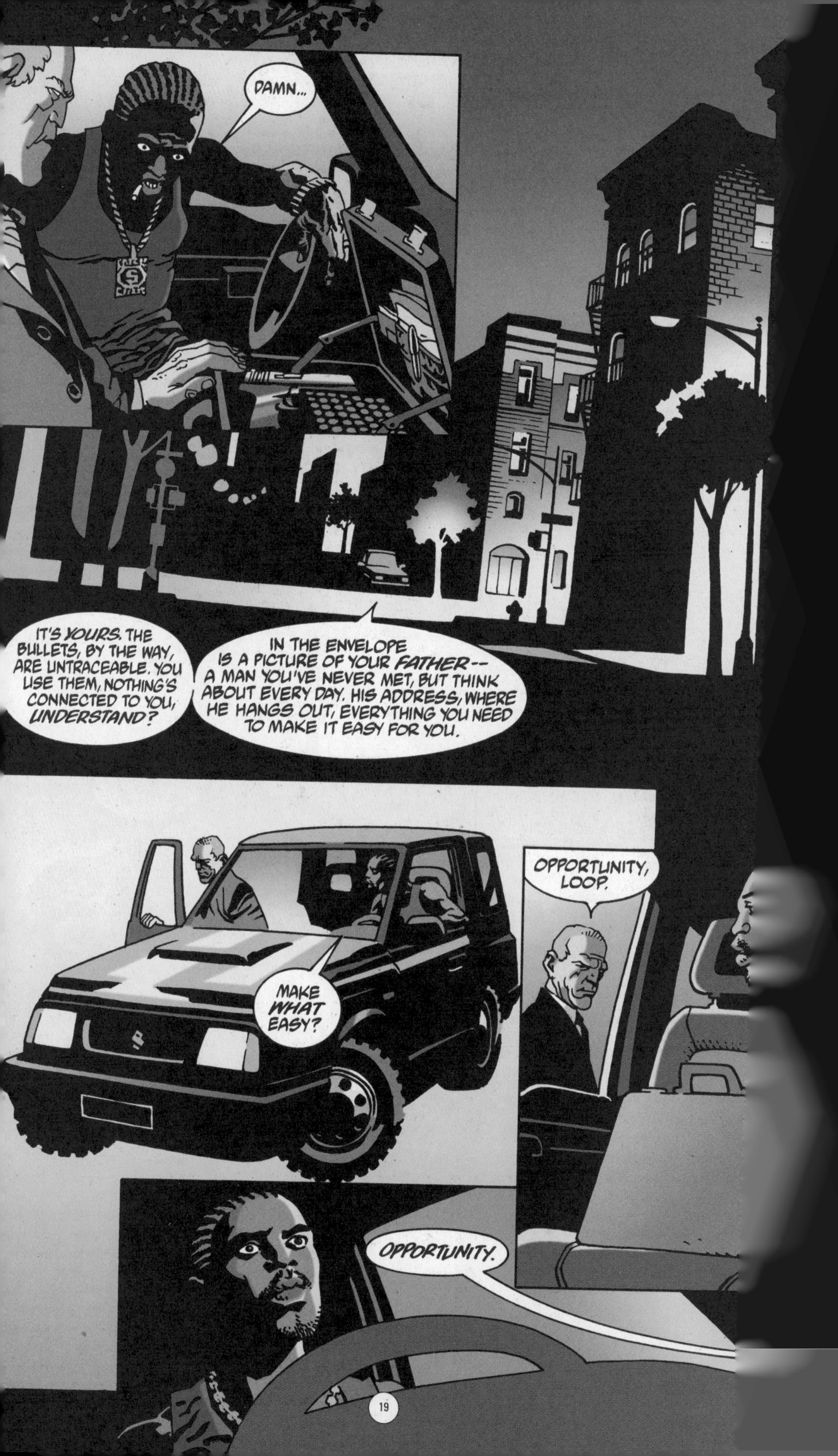
DAMN...
IT'S YOURS. THE BULLETS, BY THE WAY, ARE UNTRACEABLE. YOU USE THEM, NOTHING'S CONNECTED TO YOU, UNDERSTAND?
IN THE ENVELOPE IS A PICTURE OF YOUR FATHER-- A MAN YOU'VE NEVER MET, BUT THINK ABOUT EVERY DAY. HIS ADDRESS, WHERE HE HANGS OUT, EVERYTHING YOU NEED TO MAKE IT EASY FOR YOU.
MAKE WHAT EASY?
OPPORTUNITY, LOOP.
OPPORTUNITY.

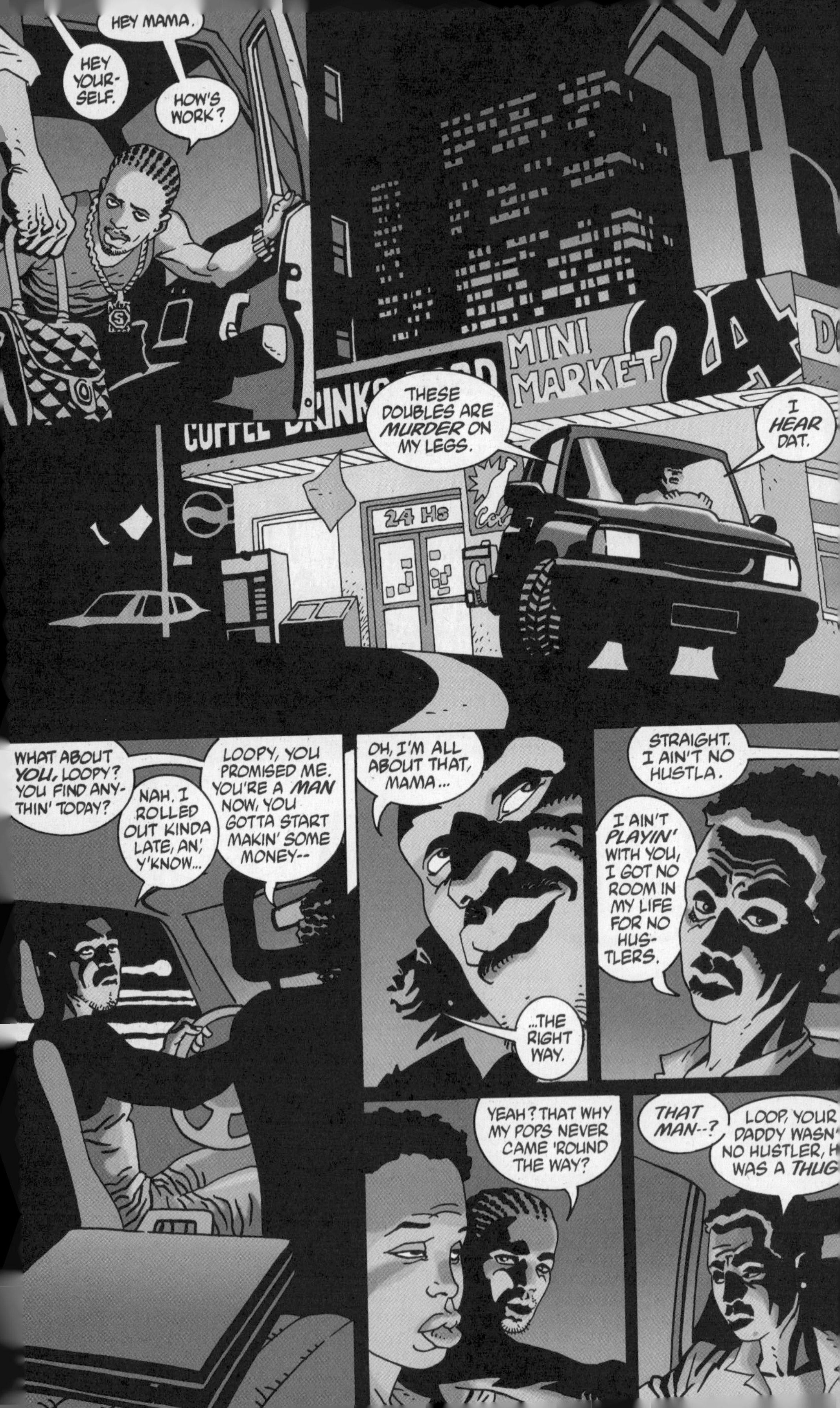
HEY MAMA.
HEY YOURSELF.
HOW'S WORK?
MINI MARKET
COFFEE DRINKS
24 Hs
THESE DOUBLES ARE MURDER ON MY LEGS.
I HEAR DAT.
WHAT ABOUT YOU, LOOPY? YOU FIND ANYTHIN' TODAY?
NAH, I ROLLED OUT KINDA LATE, AN', Y'KNOW...
LOOPY, YOU PROMISED ME. YOU'RE A MAN NOW, YOU GOTTA START MAKIN' SOME MONEY--
OH, I'M ALL ABOUT THAT, MAMA...
...THE RIGHT WAY.
STRAIGHT. I AIN'T NO HUSTLA.
I AIN'T PLAYIN' WITH YOU, I GOT NO ROOM IN MY LIFE FOR NO HUSTLERS.
YEAH? THAT WHY MY POPS NEVER CAME 'ROUND THE WAY?
THAT MAN--?
LOOP, YOUR DADDY WASN' NO HUSTLER, H WAS A THUG

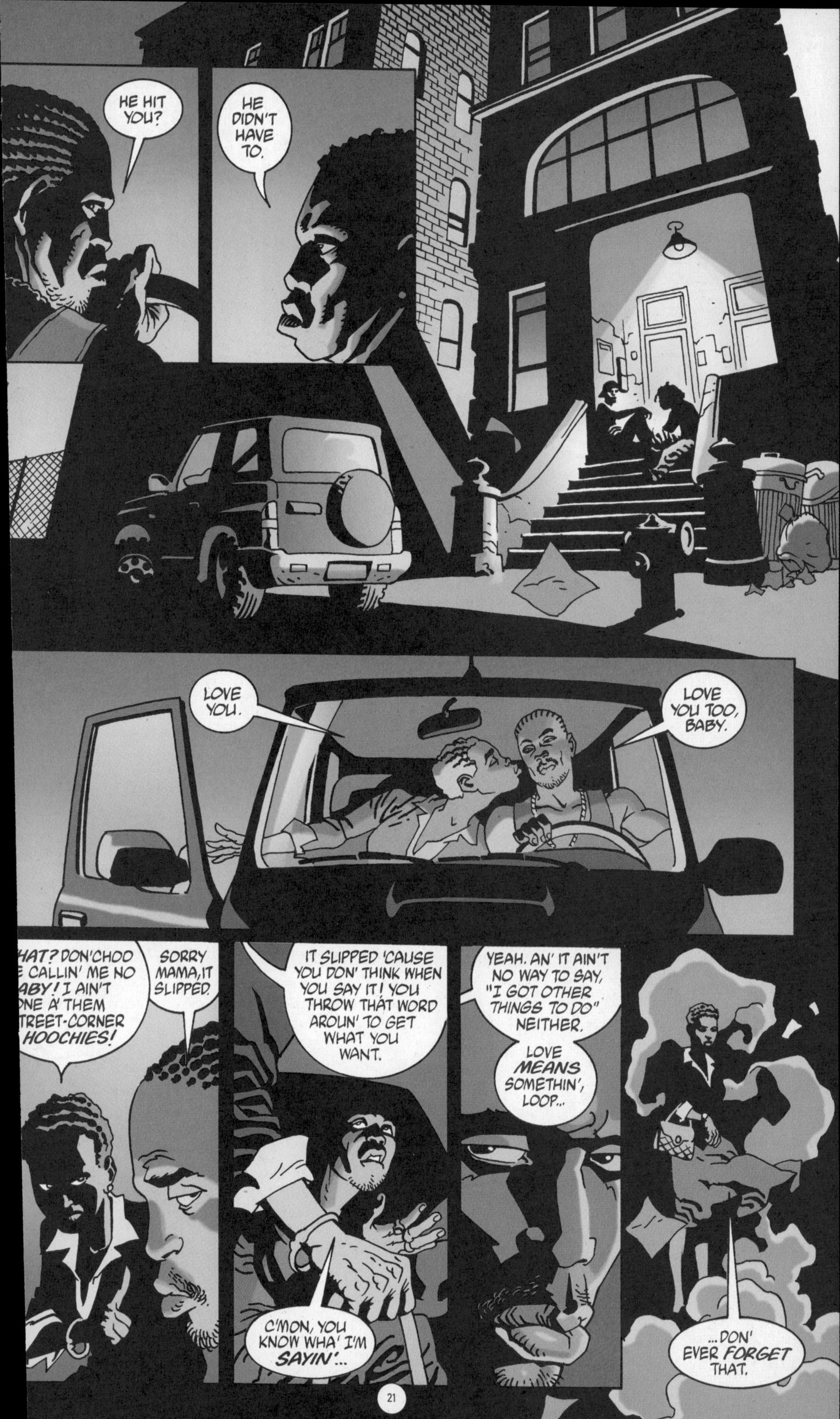
HE HIT YOU?
HE DIDN'T HAVE TO.
LOVE YOU.
LOVE YOU TOO, BABY.
HAT? DON'CHOO
E CALLIN' ME NO
ABY! I AIN'T
ONE A' THEM
TREET-CORNER
HOOCHIES!
SORRY MAMA, IT SLIPPED.
IT SLIPPED 'CAUSE YOU DON' THINK WHEN YOU SAY IT! YOU THROW THAT WORD AROUN' TO GET WHAT YOU WANT.
C'MON, YOU KNOW WHA' I'M SAYIN'...
YEAH. AN' IT AIN'T NO WAY TO SAY, "I GOT OTHER THINGS TO DO" NEITHER.
LOVE MEANS SOMETHIN', LOOP...
...DON' EVER FORGET THAT.

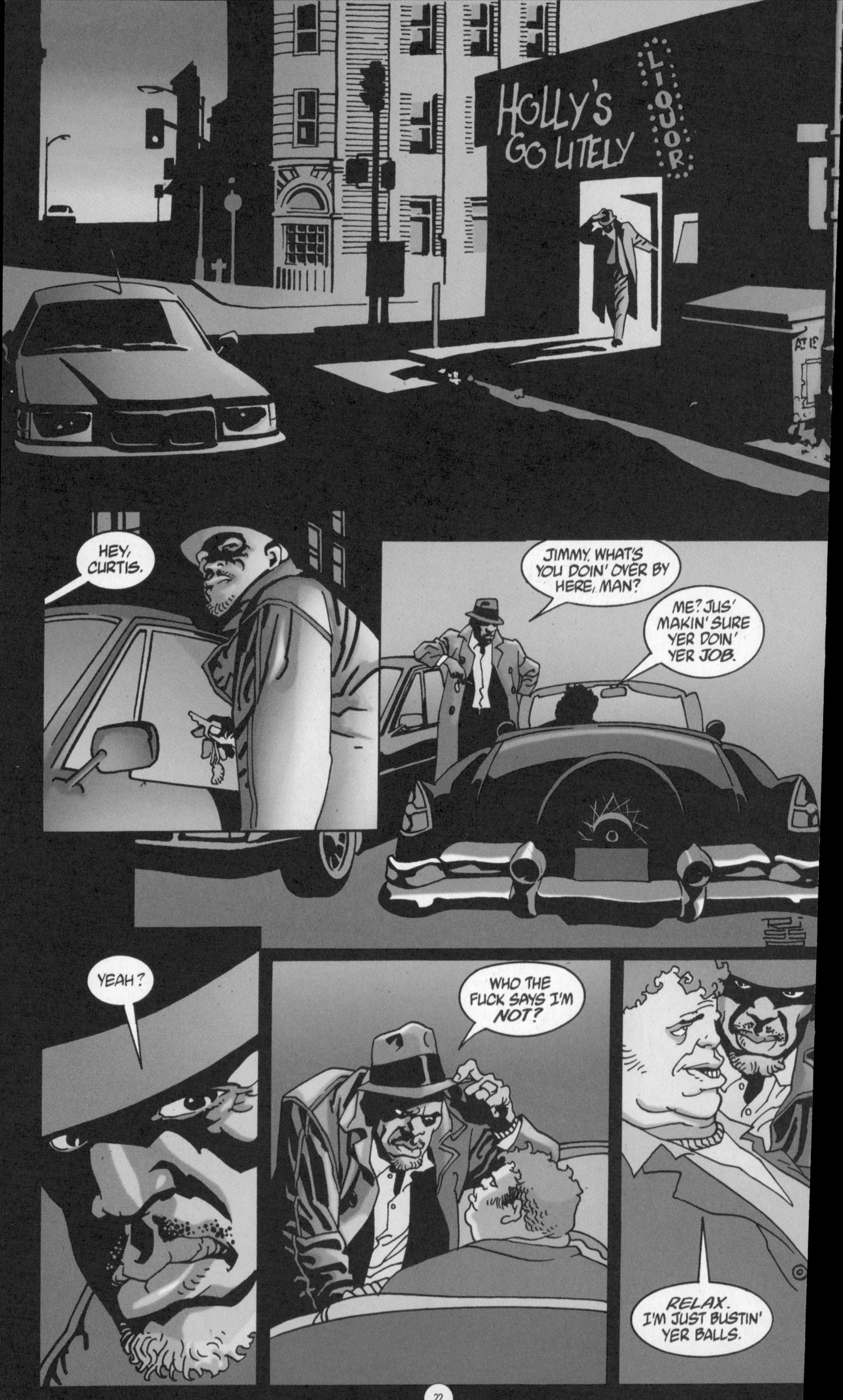
HOLLY'S GO LITELY
LIQUOR
HEY, CURTIS.
JIMMY, WHAT'S YOU DOIN' OVER BY HERE, MAN?
ME? JUS' MAKIN' SURE YER DOIN' YER JOB.
YEAH?
WHO THE FUCK SAYS I'M NOT?
RELAX. I'M JUST BUSTIN' YER BALLS.

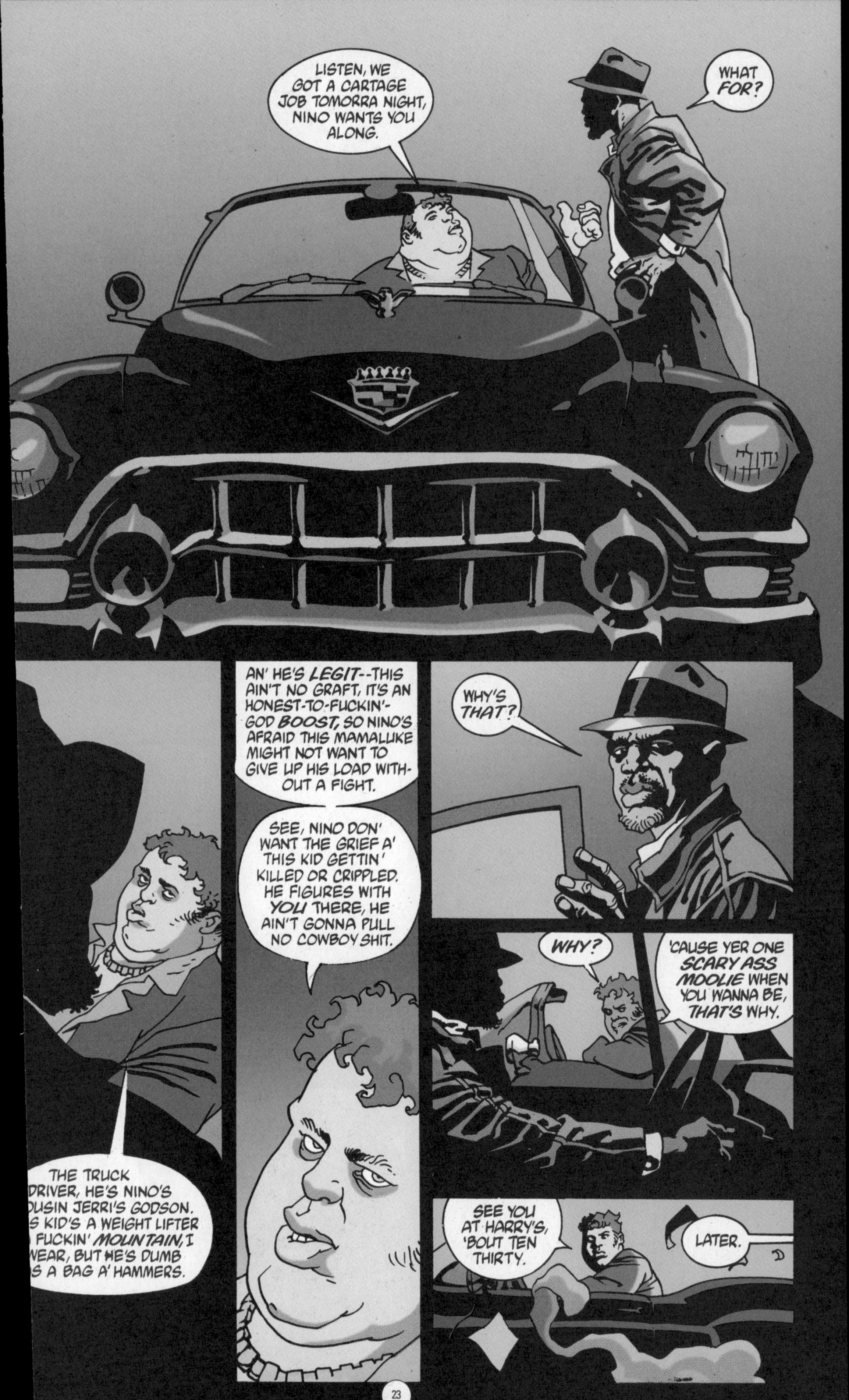

LISTEN, WE GOT A CARTAGE JOB TOMORRA NIGHT, NINO WANTS YOU ALONG.
WHAT FOR?
THE TRUCK DRIVER, HE'S NINO'S COUSIN JERRI'S GODSON. KID'S A WEIGHT LIFTER FUCKIN' MOUNTAIN, I SWEAR, BUT HE'S DUMB AS A BAG A' HAMMERS.
AN' HE'S LEGIT--THIS AIN'T NO GRAFT, IT'S AN HONEST-TO-FUCKIN'-GOD BOOST, SO NINO'S AFRAID THIS MAMALUKE MIGHT NOT WANT TO GIVE UP HIS LOAD WITH-OUT A FIGHT.
SEE, NINO DON' WANT THE GRIEF A' THIS KID GETTIN' KILLED OR CRIPPLED. HE FIGURES WITH YOU THERE, HE AIN'T GONNA PULL NO COWBOY SHIT.
WHY'S THAT?
WHY?
'CAUSE YER ONE SCARY ASS MOOLIE WHEN YOU WANNA BE, THAT'S WHY.
SEE YOU AT HARRY'S, 'BOUT TEN THIRTY.
LATER.

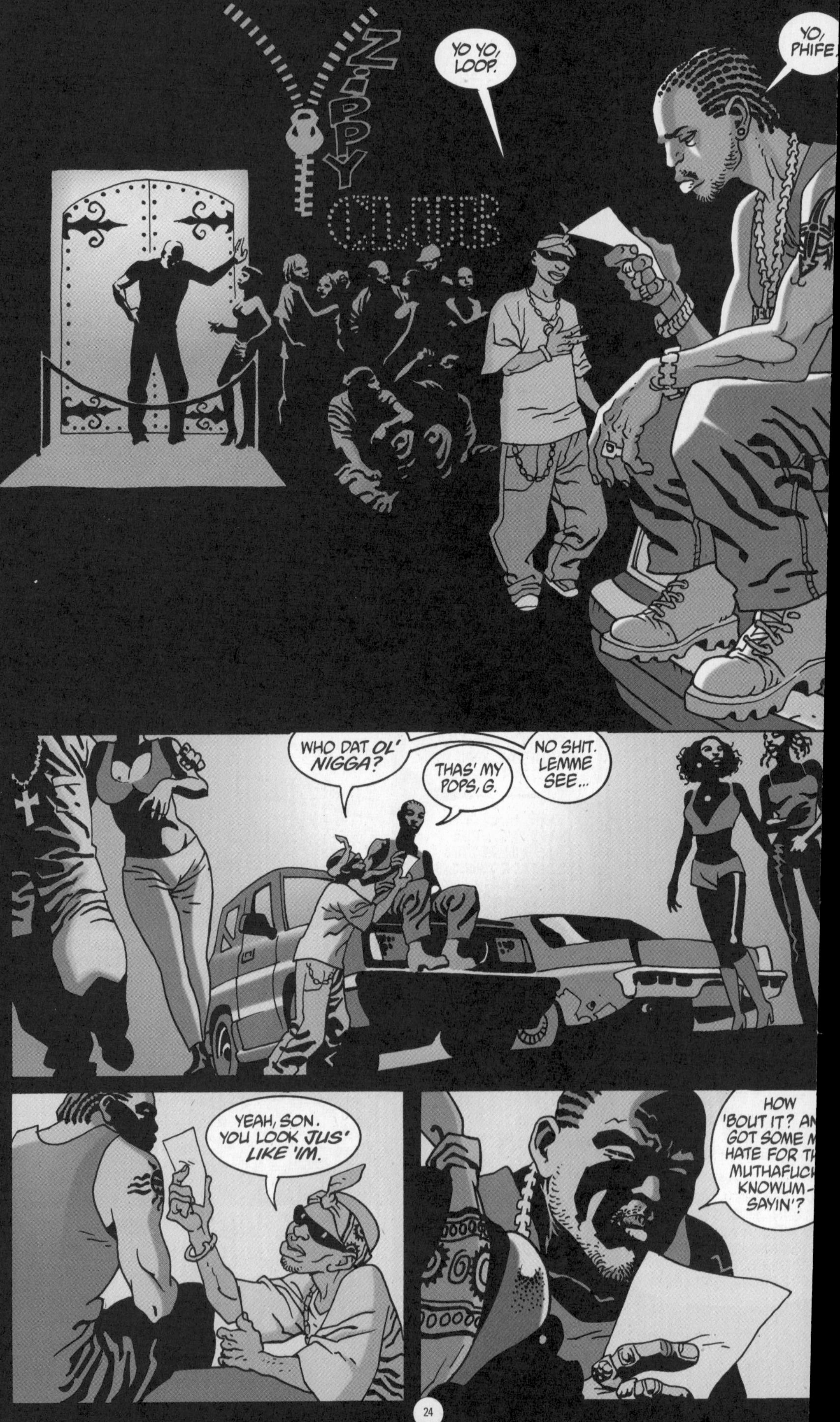
ZIPPY CLUB
YO YO, LOOP.
YO, PHIFE.
WHO DAT OL' NIGGA?
THAS' MY POPS, G.
NO SHIT. LEMME SEE...
YEAH, SON. YOU LOOK JUS' LIKE 'IM.
HOW 'BOUT IT? AN GOT SOME M HATE FOR TH MUTHAFUCK KNOWUM-SAYIN'?

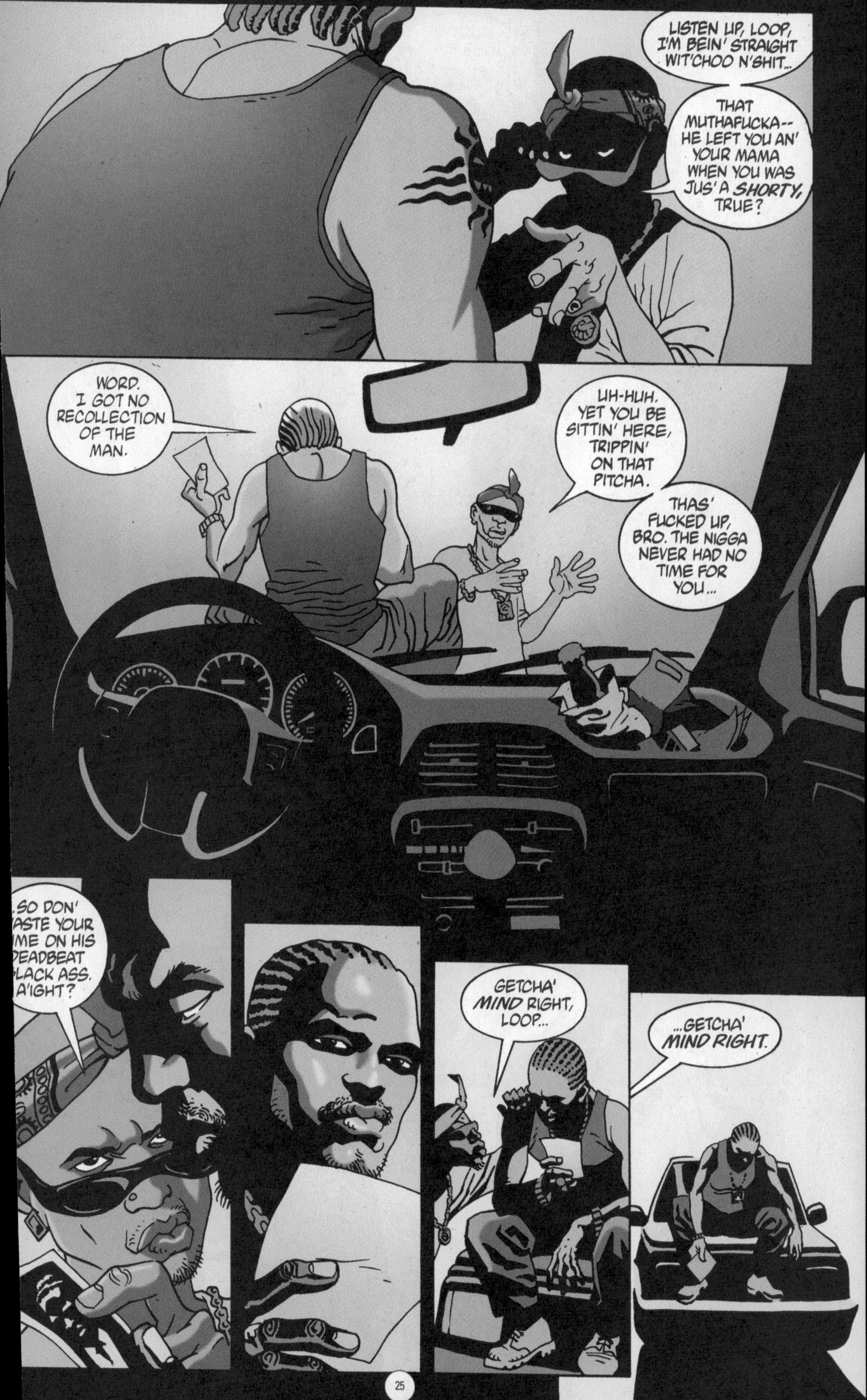
LISTEN UP, LOOP, I'M BEIN' STRAIGHT WIT'CHOO N'SHIT...
THAT MUTHAFUCKA-- HE LEFT YOU AN' YOUR MAMA WHEN YOU WAS JUS' A SHORTY, TRUE?
WORD. I GOT NO RECOLLECTION OF THE MAN.
UH-HUH. YET YOU BE SITTIN' HERE, TRIPPIN' ON THAT PITCHA.
THAS' FUCKED UP, BRO. THE NIGGA NEVER HAD NO TIME FOR YOU...
...SO DON' WASTE YOUR TIME ON HIS DEADBEAT BLACK ASS. A'IGHT?
GETCHA' MIND RIGHT, LOOP...
...GETCHA' MIND RIGHT.

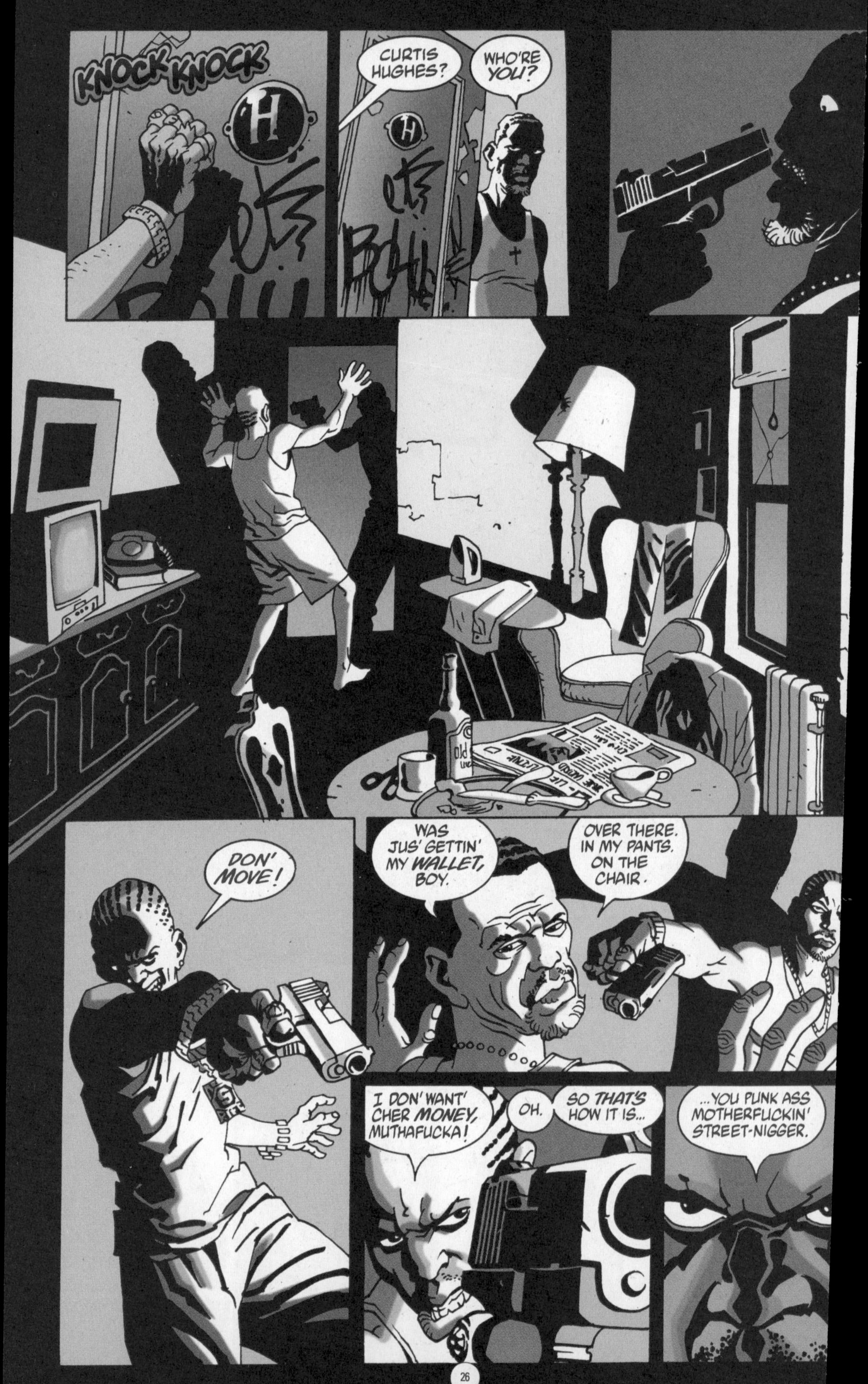
KNOCK KNOCK
CURTIS HUGHES?
WHO'RE YOU?
DON' MOVE!
WAS JUS' GETTIN' MY WALLET, BOY.
OVER THERE. IN MY PANTS. ON THE CHAIR.
I DON' WANT' CHER MONEY, MUTHAFUCKA!
OH.
SO THAT'S HOW IT IS...
...YOU PUNK ASS MOTHERFUCKIN' STREET-NIGGER.

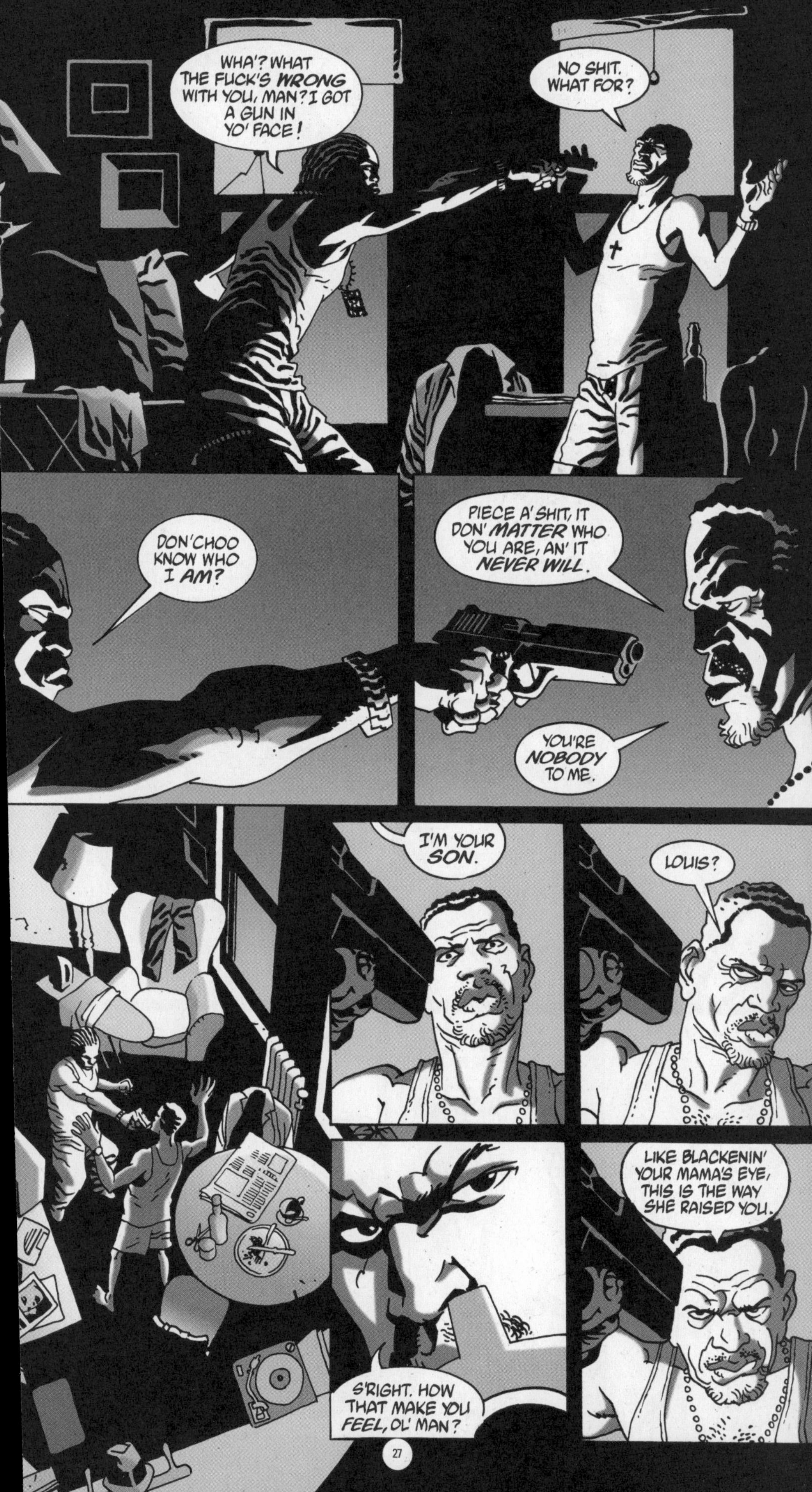
WHA'? WHAT THE FUCK'S WRONG WITH YOU, MAN? I GOT A GUN IN YO' FACE!
NO SHIT. WHAT FOR?
DON'CHOO KNOW WHO I AM?
PIECE A' SHIT, IT DON' MATTER WHO YOU ARE, AN' IT NEVER WILL.
YOU'RE NOBODY TO ME.
I'M YOUR SON.
LOUIS?
S'RIGHT. HOW THAT MAKE YOU FEEL, OL' MAN?
LIKE BLACKENIN' YOUR MAMA'S EYE, THIS IS THE WAY SHE RAISED YOU.

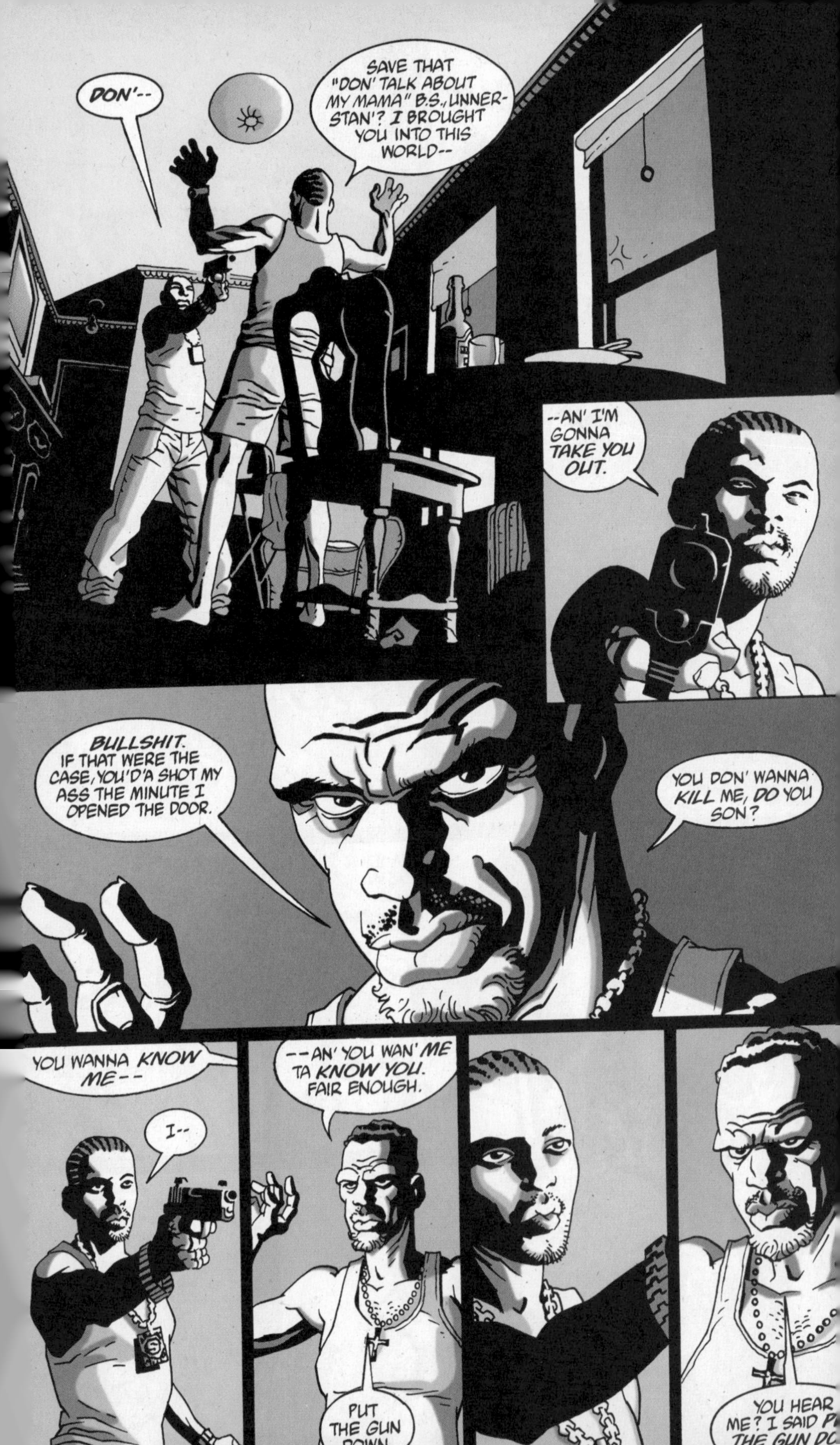
DON'--
SAVE THAT "DON' TALK ABOUT MY MAMA" B.S., UNNER-STAN'? I BROUGHT YOU INTO THIS WORLD--
--AN' I'M GONNA TAKE YOU OUT.
BULLSHIT. IF THAT WERE THE CASE, YOU'D'A SHOT MY ASS THE MINUTE I OPENED THE DOOR.
YOU DON' WANNA KILL ME, DO YOU SON?
YOU WANNA KNOW ME--
I--
--AN' YOU WAN' ME TA KNOW YOU. FAIR ENOUGH.
PUT THE GUN DOWN.
YOU HEAR ME? I SAID PU
THE GUN DO

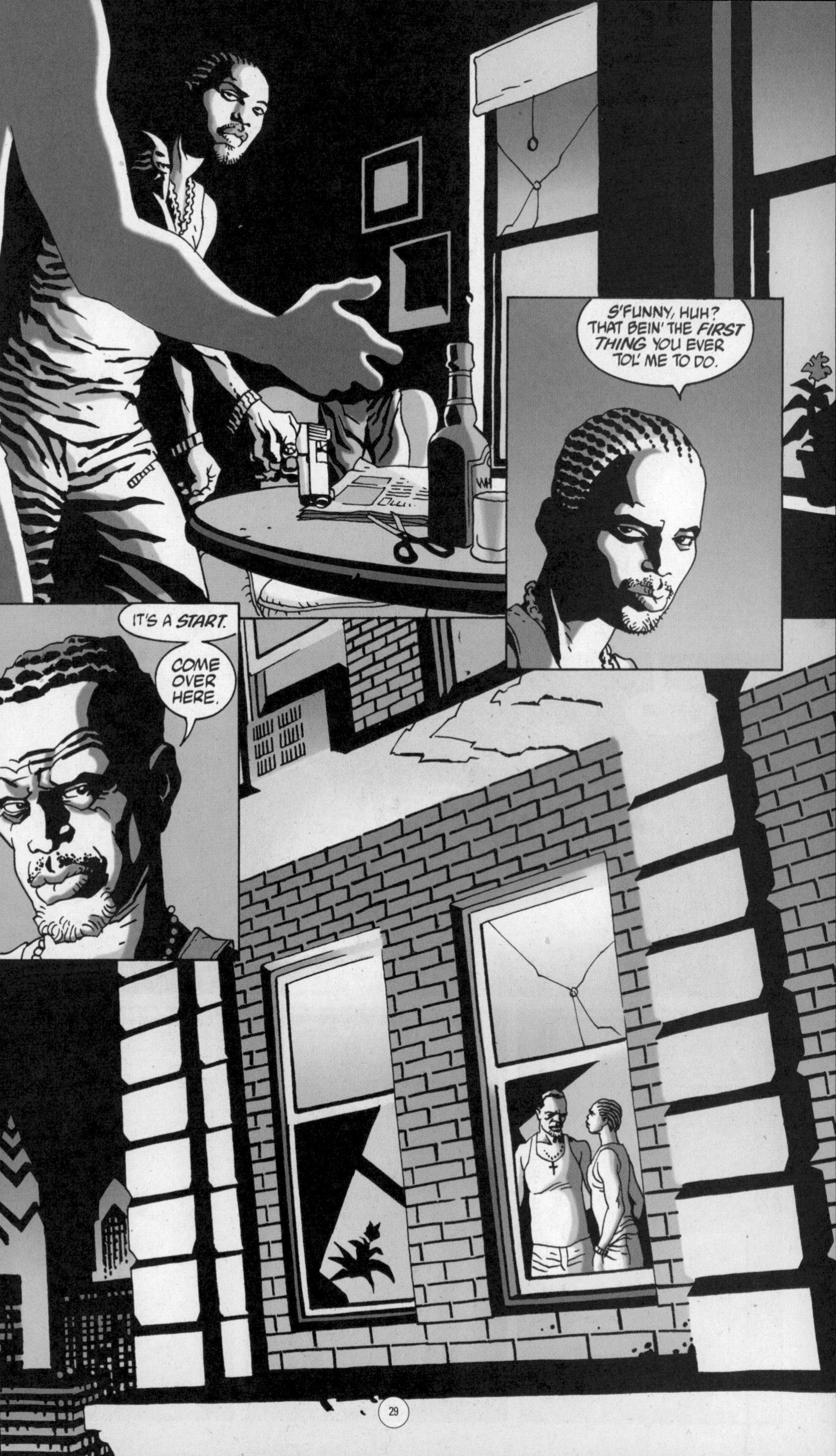

S'FUNNY, HUH? THAT BEIN' THE FIRST THING YOU EVER TOL' ME TO DO.
IT'S A START.
COME OVER HERE.

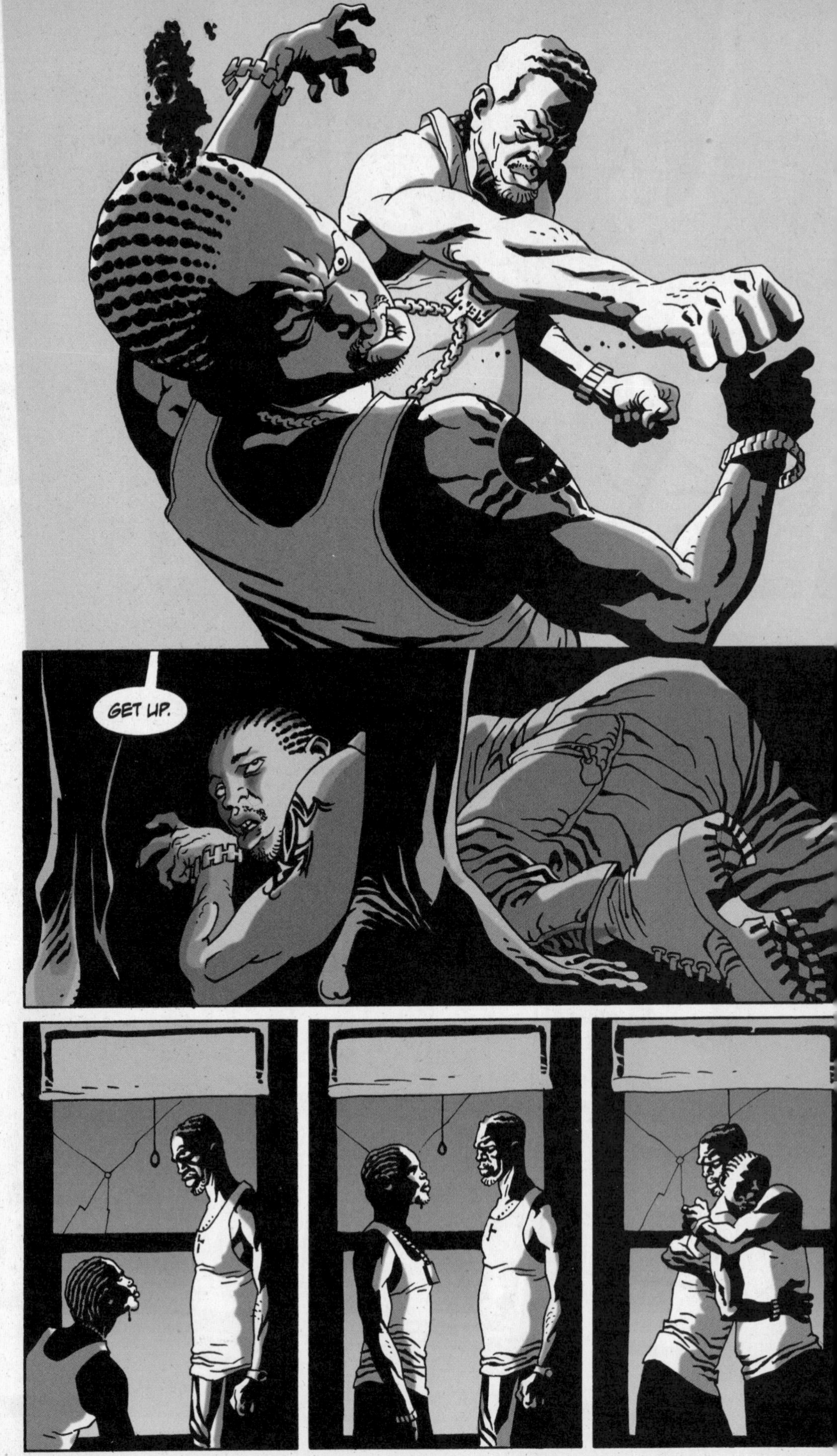
GET UP.

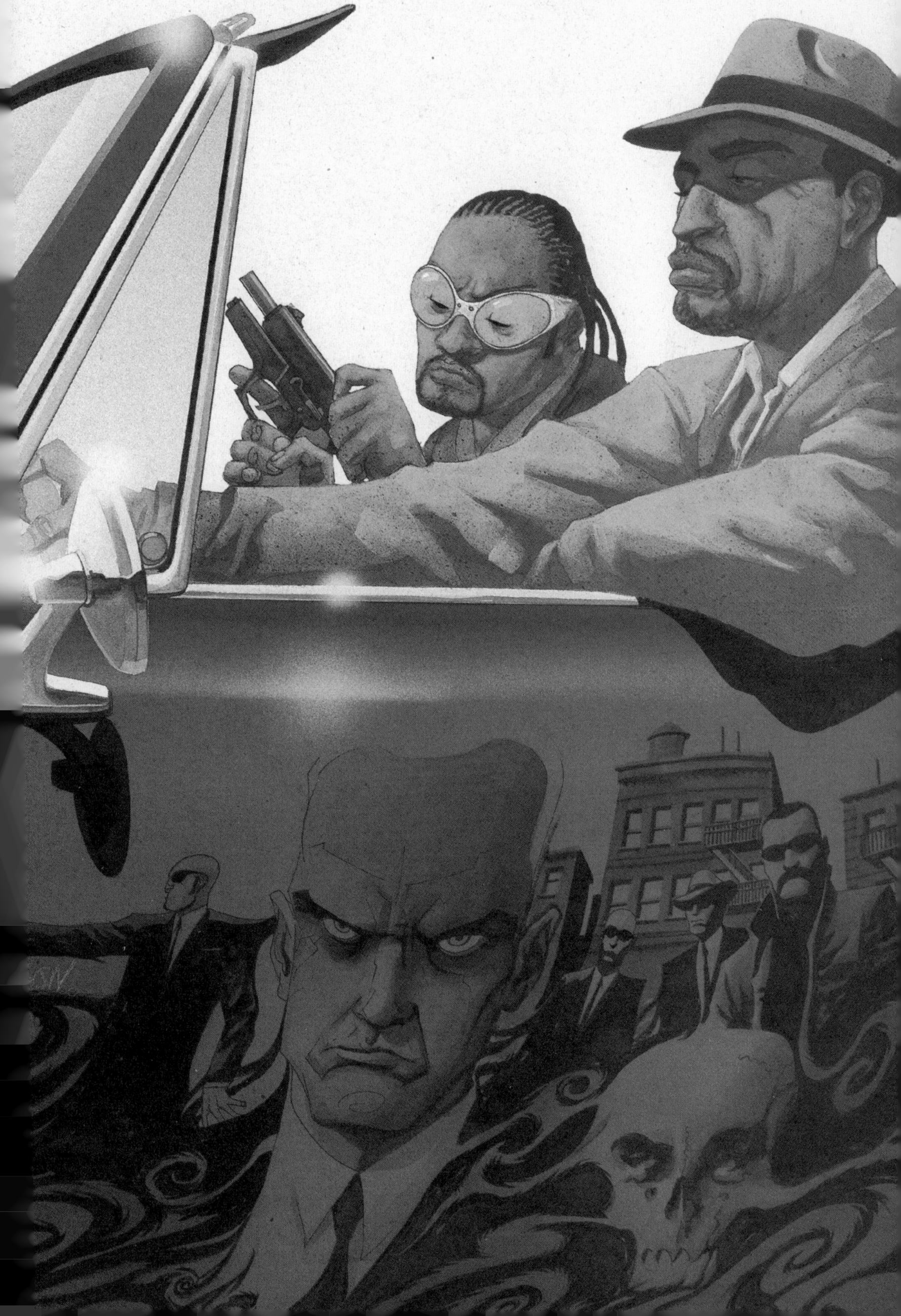

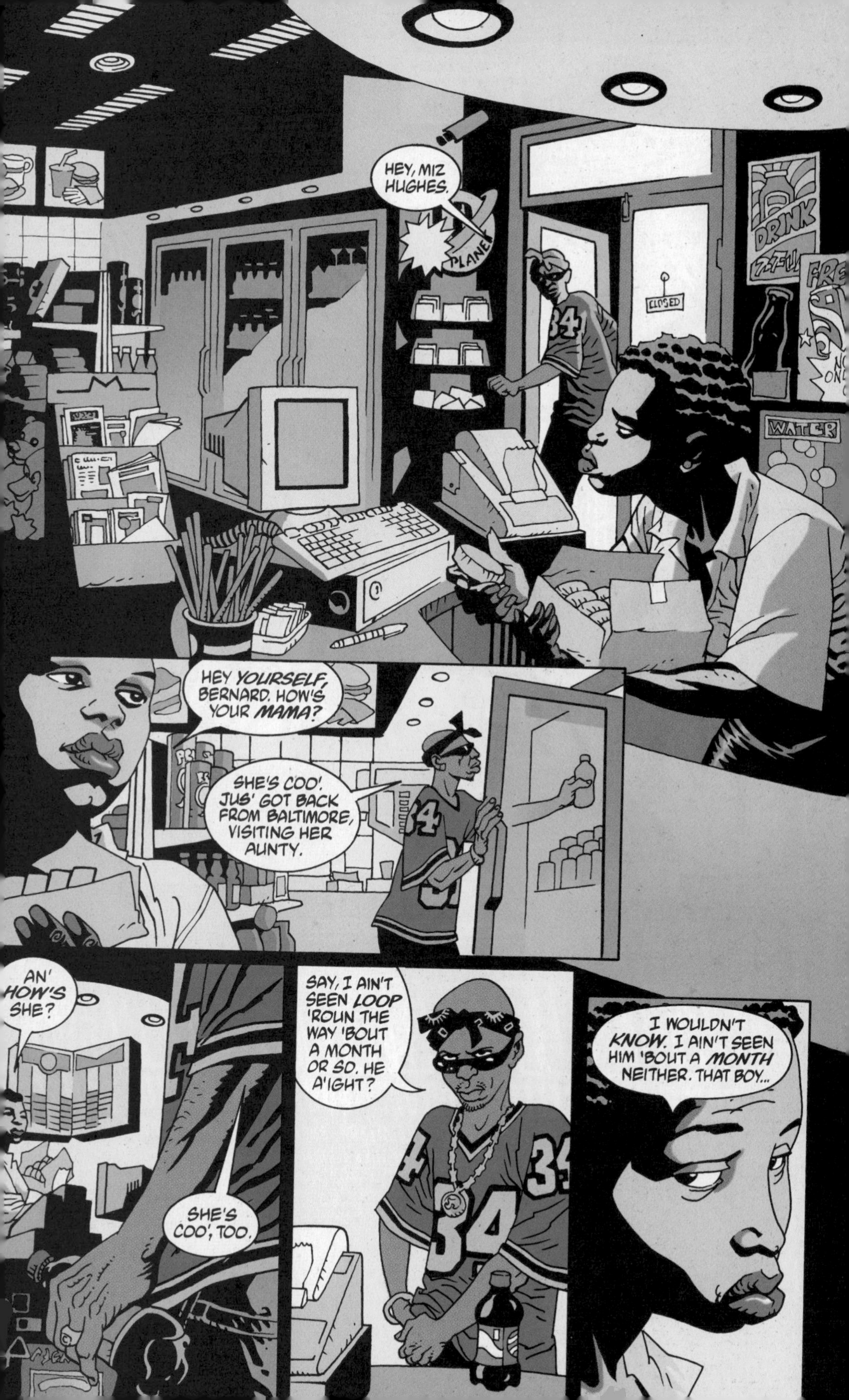
HEY, MIZ HUGHES.
PLANET
CLOSED
DRINK
WATER
HEY YOURSELF, BERNARD. HOW'S YOUR MAMA?
SHE'S COO'. JUS' GOT BACK FROM BALTIMORE, VISITING HER AUNTY.
AN' HOW'S SHE?
SHE'S COO', TOO.
SAY, I AIN'T SEEN LOOP 'ROUN THE WAY 'BOUT A MONTH OR SO. HE A'IGHT?
I WOULDN'T KNOW. I AIN'T SEEN HIM 'BOUT A MONTH NEITHER. THAT BOY...

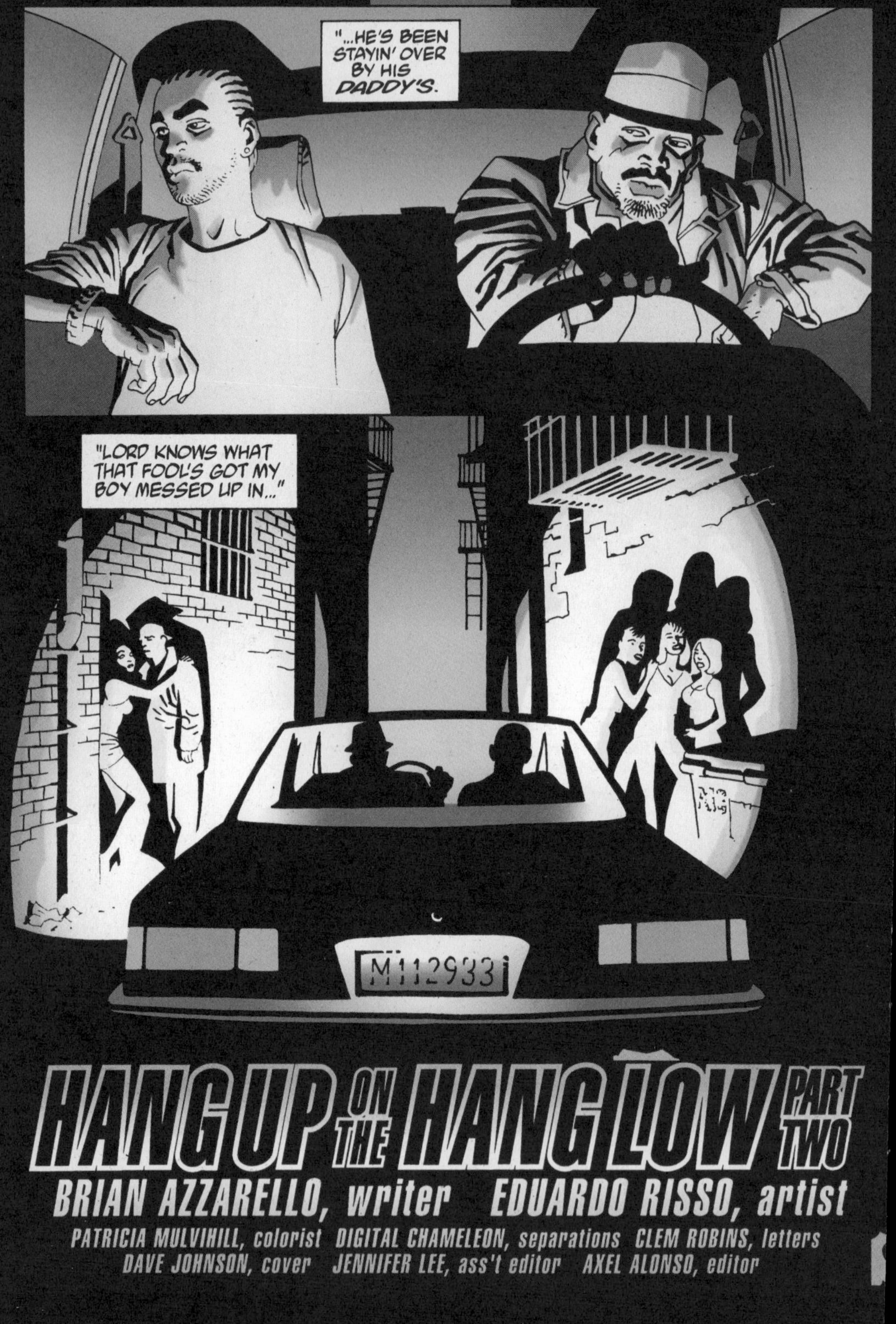
"...HE'S BEEN STAYIN' OVER BY HIS DADDY'S.
"LORD KNOWS WHAT THAT FOOL'S GOT MY BOY MESSED UP IN..."
M112933

HANG UP ON THE HANG LOW PART TWO

BRIAN AZZARELLO, writer EDUARDO RISSO, artist

PATRICIA MULVIHILL, colorist DIGITAL CHAMELEON, separations CLEM ROBINS, letters
DAVE JOHNSON, cover JENNIFER LEE, ass't editor AXEL ALONSO, editor

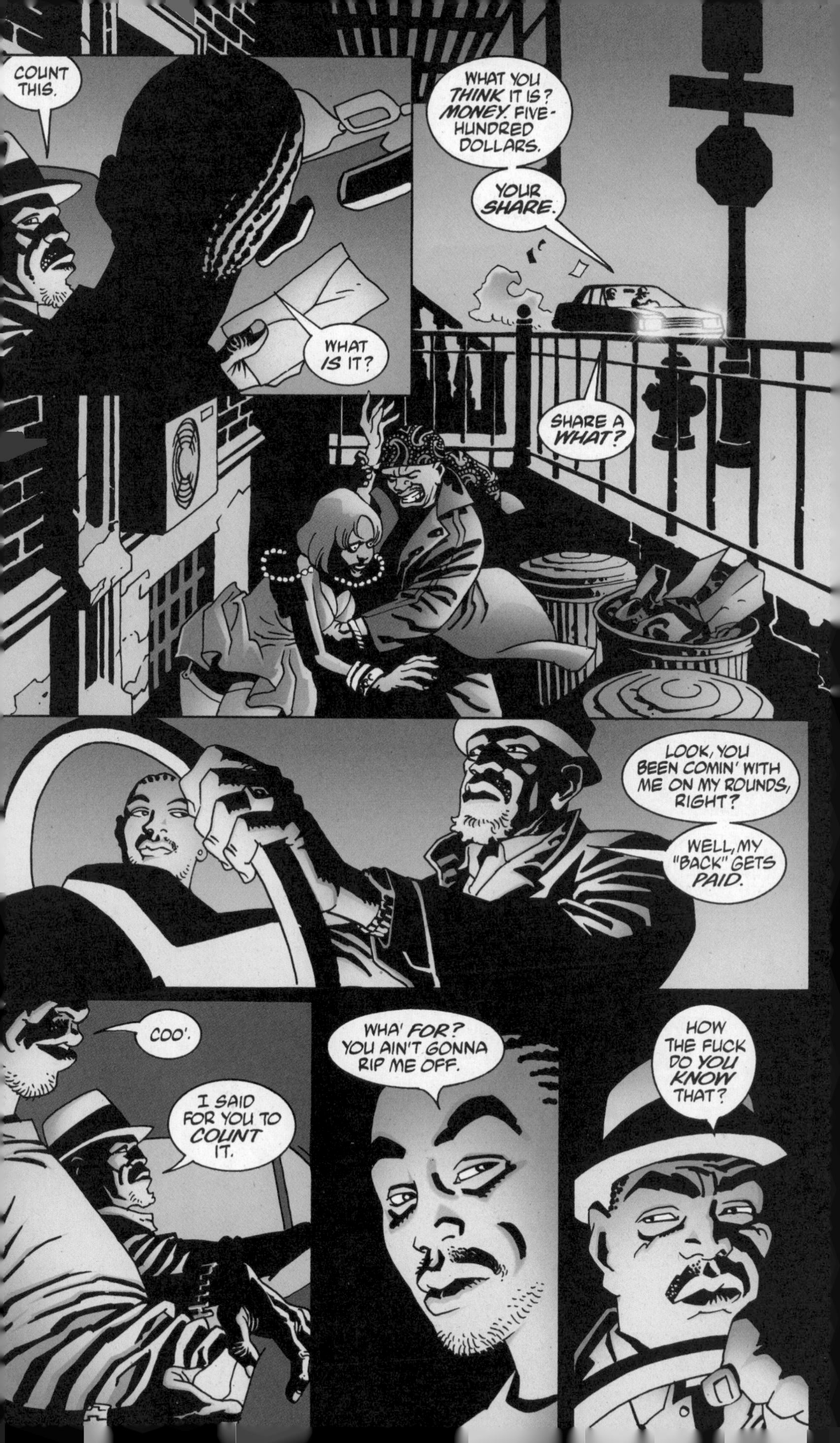
COUNT THIS.
WHAT IS IT?
WHAT YOU THINK IT IS? MONEY. FIVE-HUNDRED DOLLARS.
YOUR SHARE.
SHARE A WHAT?
LOOK, YOU BEEN COMIN' WITH ME ON MY ROUNDS, RIGHT?
WELL, MY "BACK" GETS PAID.
COO'.
I SAID FOR YOU TO COUNT IT.
WHA' FOR? YOU AIN'T GONNA RIP ME OFF.
HOW THE FUCK DO YOU KNOW THAT?

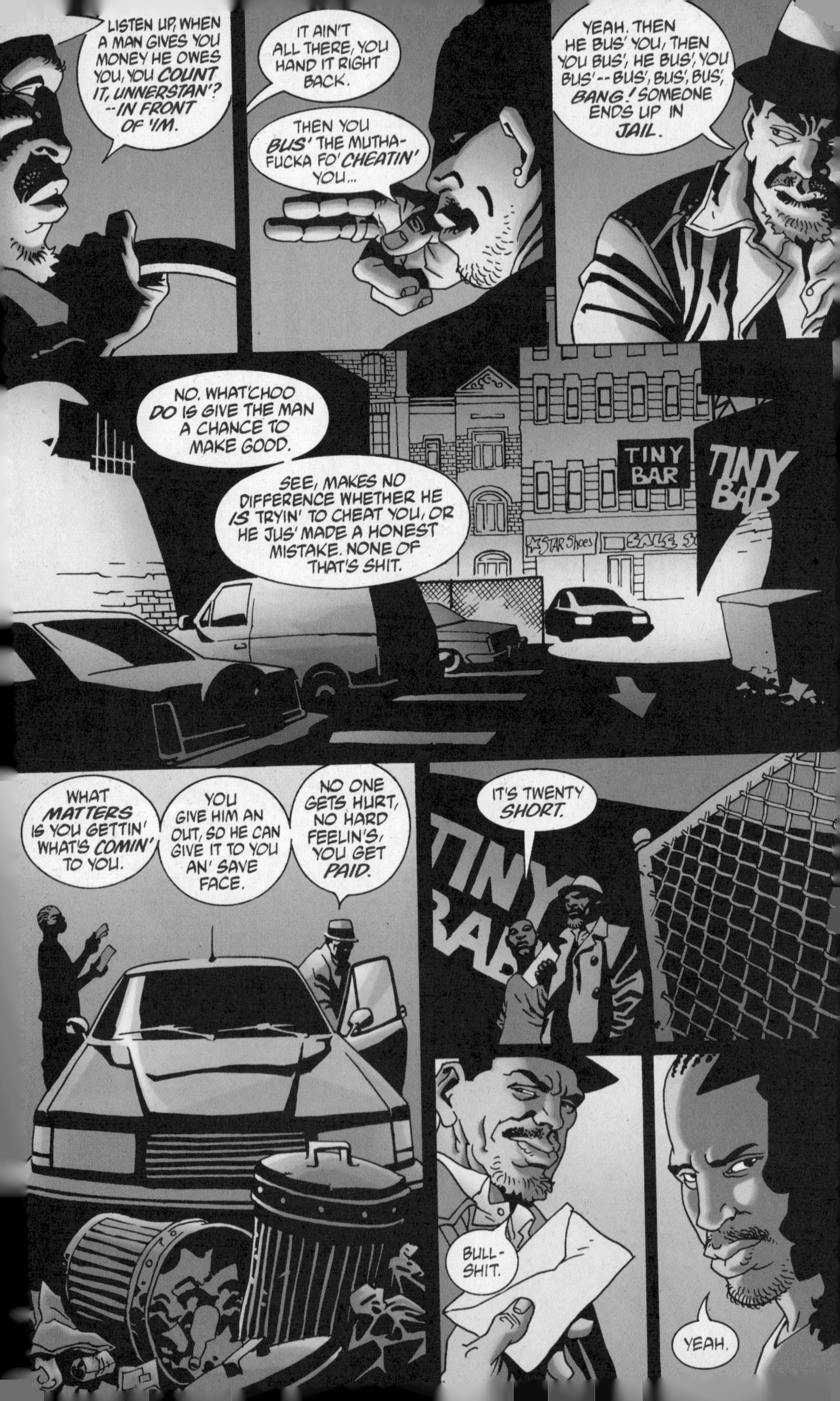
LISTEN UP, WHEN A MAN GIVES YOU MONEY HE OWES YOU, YOU COUNT IT, UNNERSTAN'? --IN FRONT OF 'IM.
IT AIN'T ALL THERE, YOU HAND IT RIGHT BACK.
THEN YOU BUS' THE MUTHA-FUCKA FO' CHEATIN' YOU...
YEAH. THEN HE BUS' YOU, THEN YOU BUS', HE BUS', YOU BUS'--BUS', BUS', BUS', BANG! SOMEONE ENDS UP IN JAIL.
NO. WHAT'CHOO DO IS GIVE THE MAN A CHANCE TO MAKE GOOD.
TINY BAR
TINY BAR
SEE, MAKES NO DIFFERENCE WHETHER HE IS TRYIN' TO CHEAT YOU, OR HE JUS' MADE A HONEST MISTAKE. NONE OF THAT'S SHIT.
STAR Shoes
SALE
WHAT MATTERS IS YOU GETTIN' WHAT'S COMIN' TO YOU.
YOU GIVE HIM AN OUT, SO HE CAN GIVE IT TO YOU AN' SAVE FACE.
NO ONE GETS HURT, NO HARD FEELIN'S, YOU GET PAID.
IT'S TWENTY SHORT.
BULL-SHIT.
YEAH.

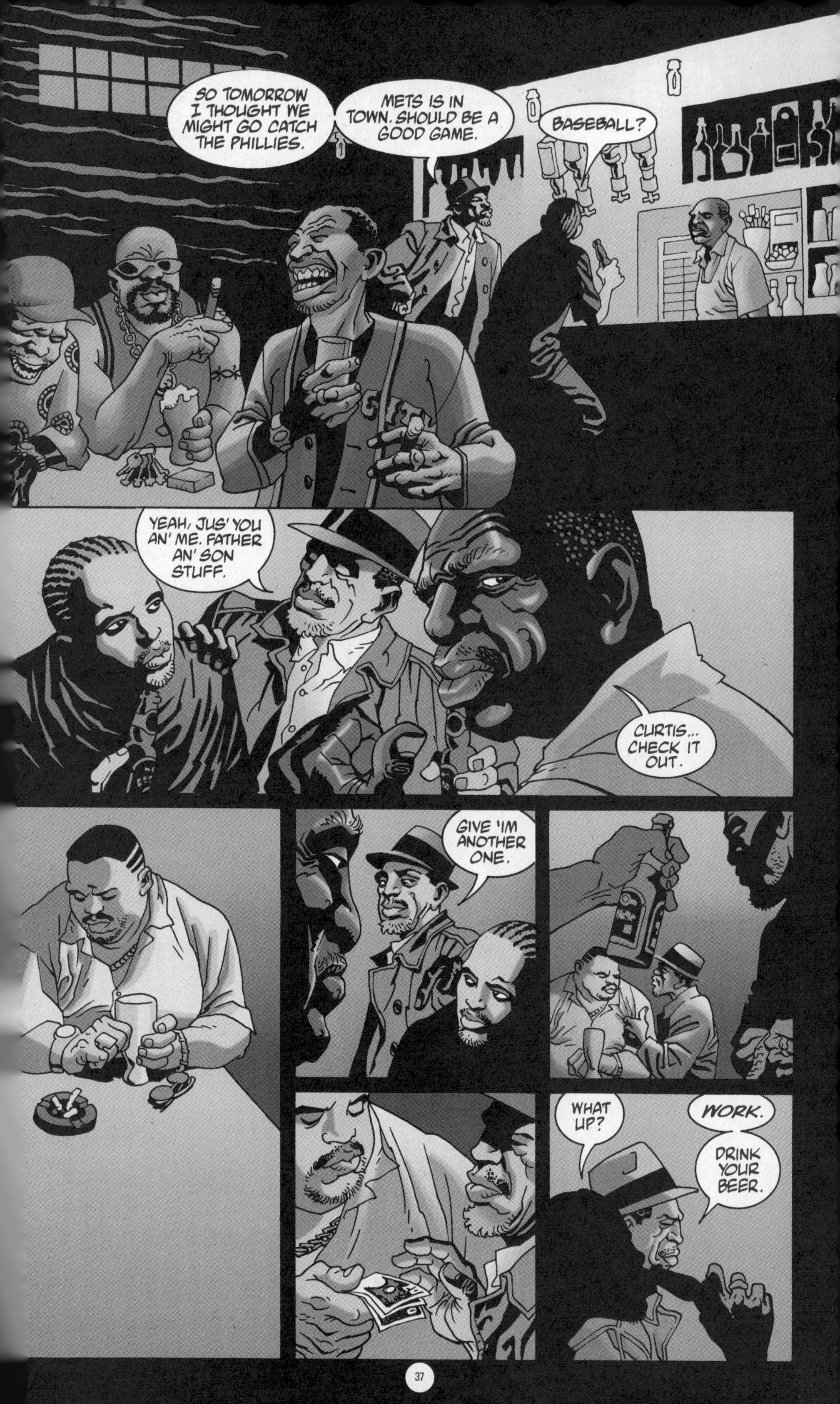
SO TOMORROW I THOUGHT WE MIGHT GO CATCH THE PHILLIES.
METS IS IN TOWN. SHOULD BE A GOOD GAME.
BASEBALL?
YEAH, JUS' YOU AN' ME. FATHER AN' SON STUFF.
CURTIS... CHECK IT OUT.
GIVE 'IM ANOTHER ONE.
WHAT UP?
WORK.
DRINK YOUR BEER.

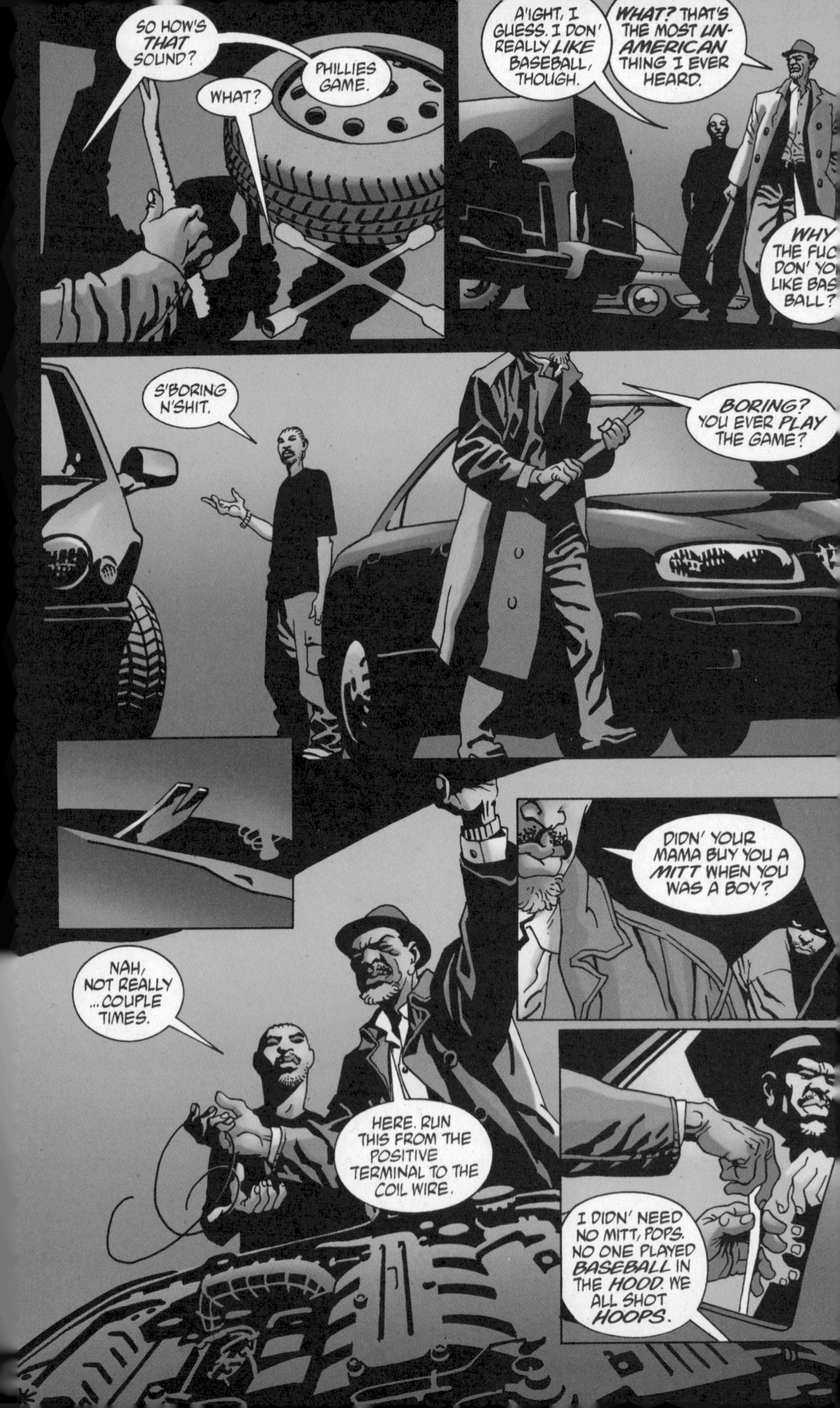
SO HOW'S *THAT* SOUND?
WHAT?
PHILLIES GAME.
A'IGHT, I GUESS. I DON' REALLY *LIKE* BASEBALL, THOUGH.
WHAT? THAT'S THE MOST *UN-AMERICAN* THING I EVER HEARD.
WHY THE FUC DON' YO LIKE BAS BALL?
S'BORING N'SHIT.
BORING? YOU EVER *PLAY* THE GAME?
DIDN' YOUR MAMA BUY YOU A *MITT* WHEN YOU WAS A BOY?
NAH, NOT REALLY ...COUPLE TIMES.
HERE. RUN THIS FROM THE POSITIVE TERMINAL TO THE COIL WIRE.
I DIDN' NEED NO MITT, POPS. NO ONE PLAYED *BASEBALL* IN THE *HOOD*. WE ALL SHOT *HOOPS*.

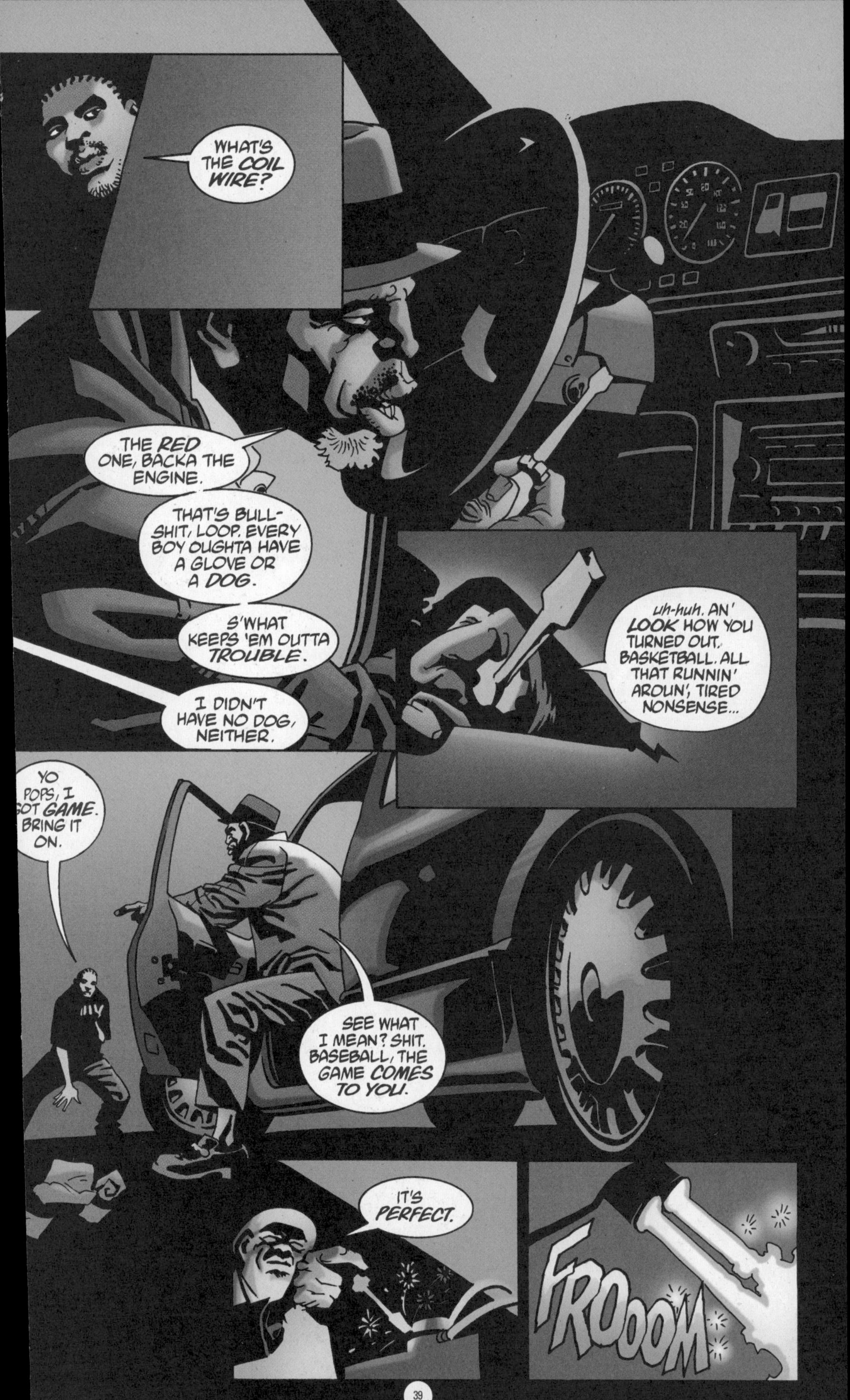
WHAT'S THE COIL WIRE?
THE RED ONE, BACKA THE ENGINE.
THAT'S BULL-SHIT, LOOP. EVERY BOY OUGHTA HAVE A GLOVE OR A DOG.
S'WHAT KEEPS 'EM OUTTA TROUBLE.
I DIDN'T HAVE NO DOG, NEITHER.
uh-huh. AN' LOOK HOW YOU TURNED OUT. BASKETBALL. ALL THAT RUNNIN' AROUN', TIRED NONSENSE...
YO POPS, I GOT GAME. BRING IT ON.
SEE WHAT I MEAN? SHIT. BASEBALL, THE GAME COMES TO YOU.
IT'S PERFECT.
FROOOM

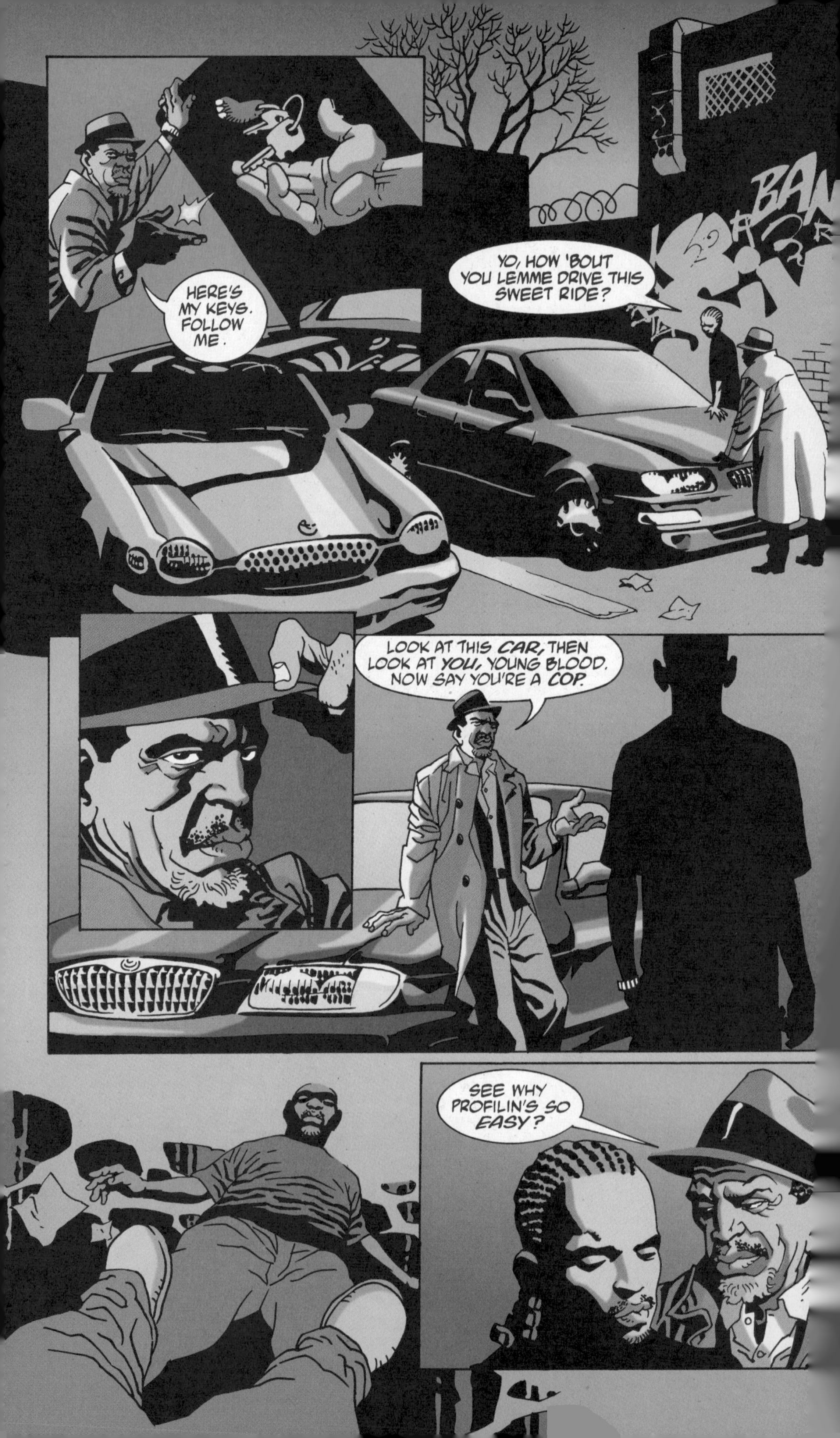
HERE'S MY KEYS. FOLLOW ME.
YO, HOW 'BOUT YOU LEMME DRIVE THIS SWEET RIDE?
LOOK AT THIS CAR, THEN LOOK AT YOU, YOUNG BLOOD. NOW SAY YOU'RE A COP.
SEE WHY PROFILIN'S SO EASY?

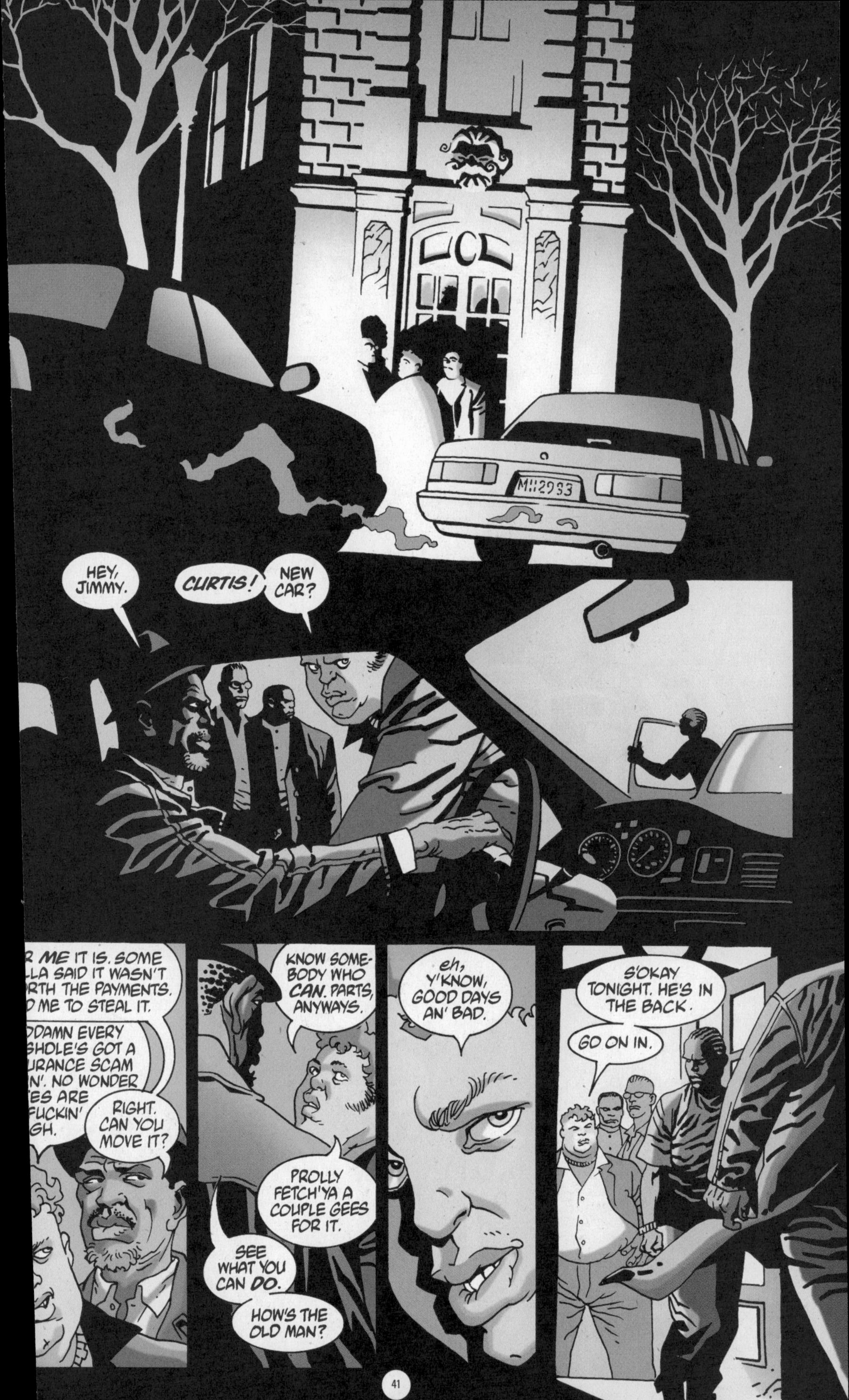

HEY, JIMMY.
CURTIS!
NEW CAR?
R ME IT IS. SOME
LLA SAID IT WASN'T
RTH THE PAYMENTS.
D ME TO STEAL IT.
DDAMN EVERY
SHOLE'S GOT A
URANCE SCAM
N'. NO WONDER
ES ARE
FUCKIN'
GH.
RIGHT. CAN YOU MOVE IT?
KNOW SOMEBODY WHO CAN. PARTS, ANYWAYS.
PROLLY FETCH'YA A COUPLE GEES FOR IT.
SEE WHAT YOU CAN DO.
HOW'S THE OLD MAN?
eh, Y'KNOW, GOOD DAYS AN' BAD.
S'OKAY TONIGHT. HE'S IN THE BACK.
GO ON IN.

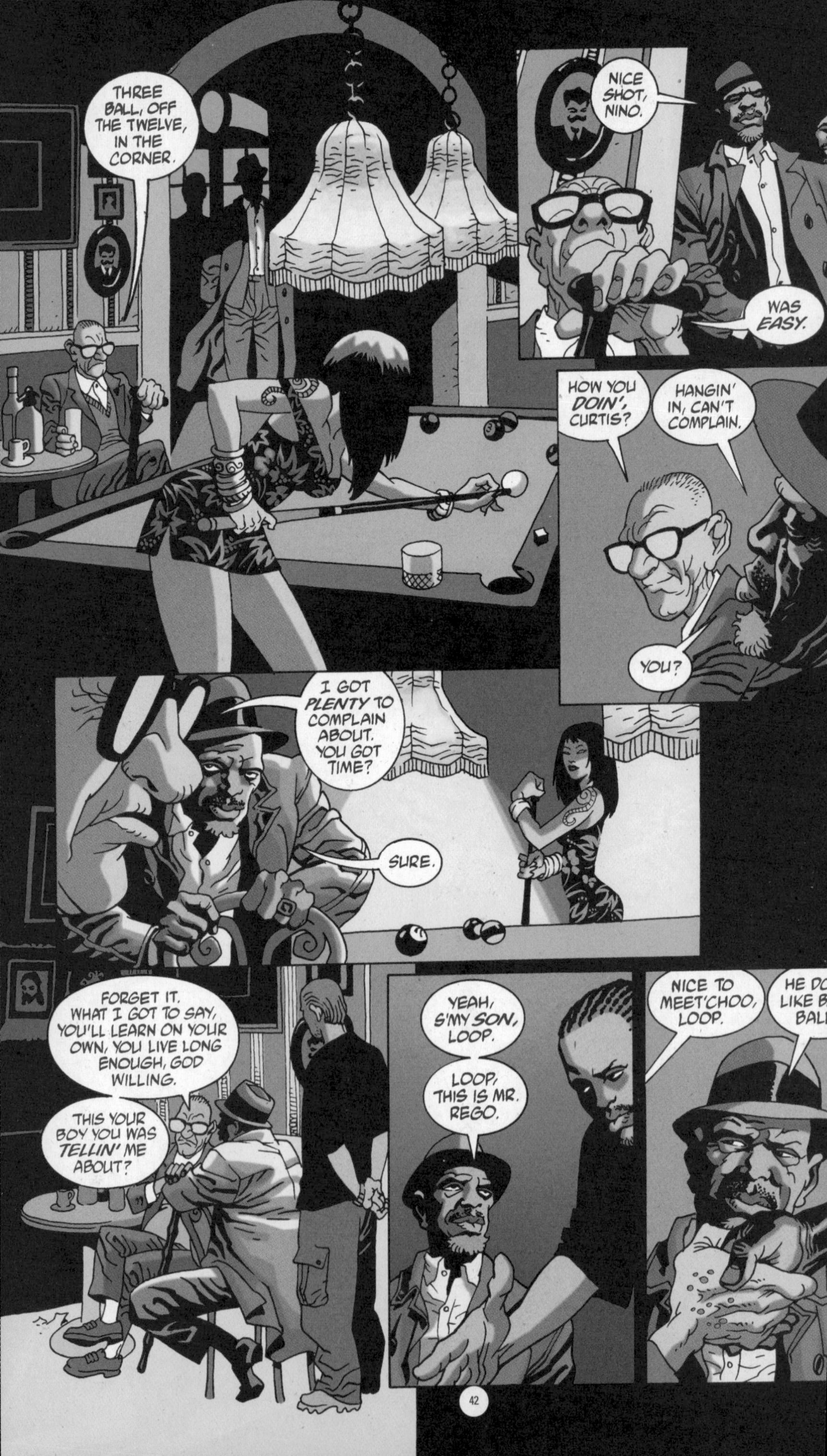
THREE BALL, OFF THE TWELVE, IN THE CORNER.
NICE SHOT, NINO.
WAS EASY.
HOW YOU DOIN', CURTIS?
HANGIN' IN, CAN'T COMPLAIN.
YOU?
I GOT PLENTY TO COMPLAIN ABOUT. YOU GOT TIME?
SURE.
FORGET IT. WHAT I GOT TO SAY, YOU'LL LEARN ON YOUR OWN, YOU LIVE LONG ENOUGH, GOD WILLING.
THIS YOUR BOY YOU WAS TELLIN' ME ABOUT?
YEAH, S'MY SON, LOOP.
LOOP, THIS IS MR. REGO.
NICE TO MEET'CHOO, LOOP.

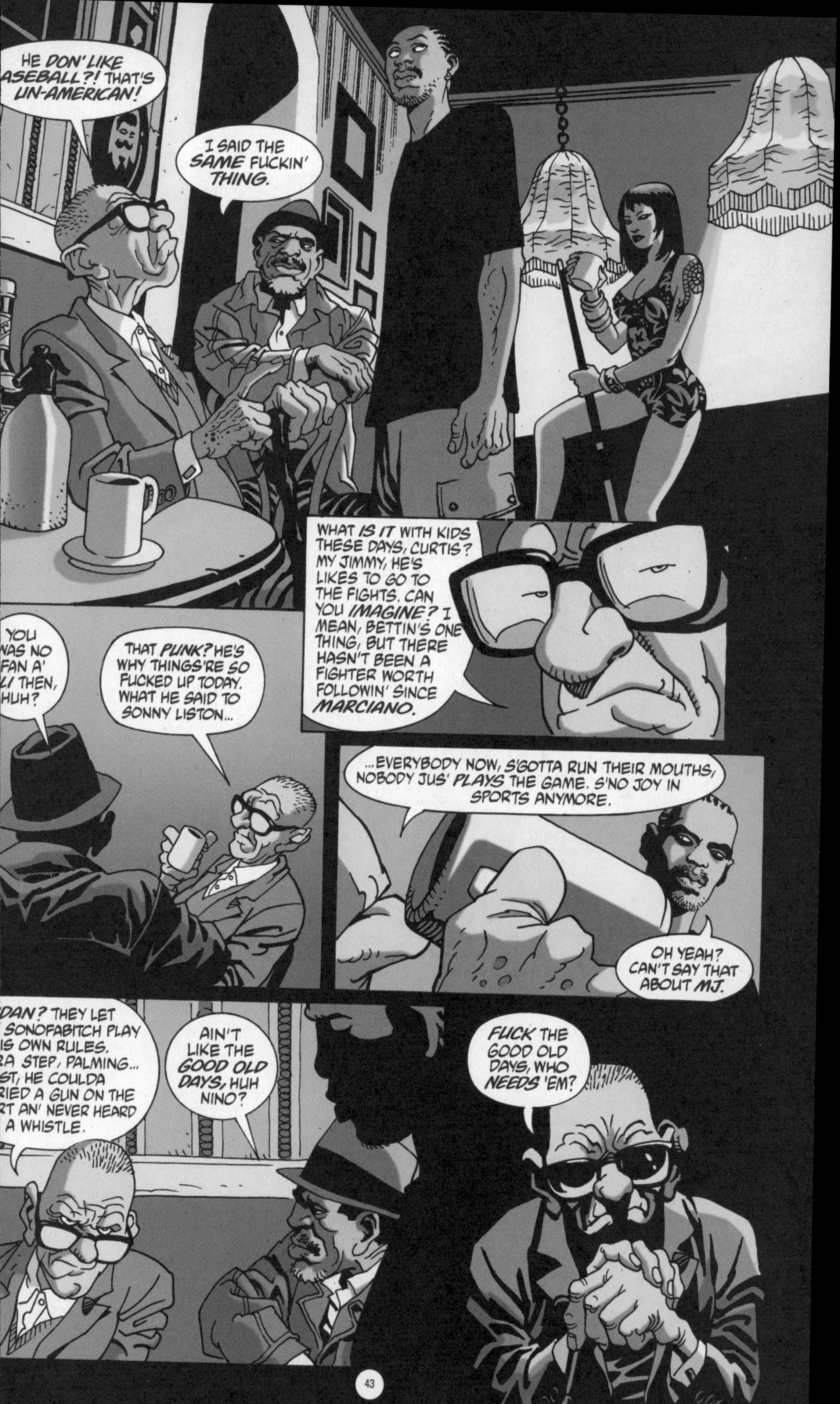
HE DON' LIKE ASEBALL?! THAT'S UN-AMERICAN!
I SAID THE SAME FUCKIN' THING.
WHAT IS IT WITH KIDS THESE DAYS, CURTIS? MY JIMMY, HE'S LIKES TO GO TO THE FIGHTS. CAN YOU IMAGINE? I MEAN, BETTIN'S ONE THING, BUT THERE HASN'T BEEN A FIGHTER WORTH FOLLOWIN' SINCE MARCIANO.
YOU WAS NO FAN A' LI THEN, HUH?
THAT PUNK? HE'S WHY THINGS'RE SO FUCKED UP TODAY. WHAT HE SAID TO SONNY LISTON...
...EVERYBODY NOW, S'GOTTA RUN THEIR MOUTHS, NOBODY JUS' PLAYS THE GAME. S'NO JOY IN SPORTS ANYMORE.
OH YEAH? CAN'T SAY THAT ABOUT MJ.
DAN? THEY LET SONOFABITCH PLAY IS OWN RULES. RA STEP, PALMING... ST, HE COULDA RIED A GUN ON THE RT AN' NEVER HEARD A WHISTLE.
AIN'T LIKE THE GOOD OLD DAYS, HUH NINO?
FUCK THE GOOD OLD DAYS, WHO NEEDS 'EM?

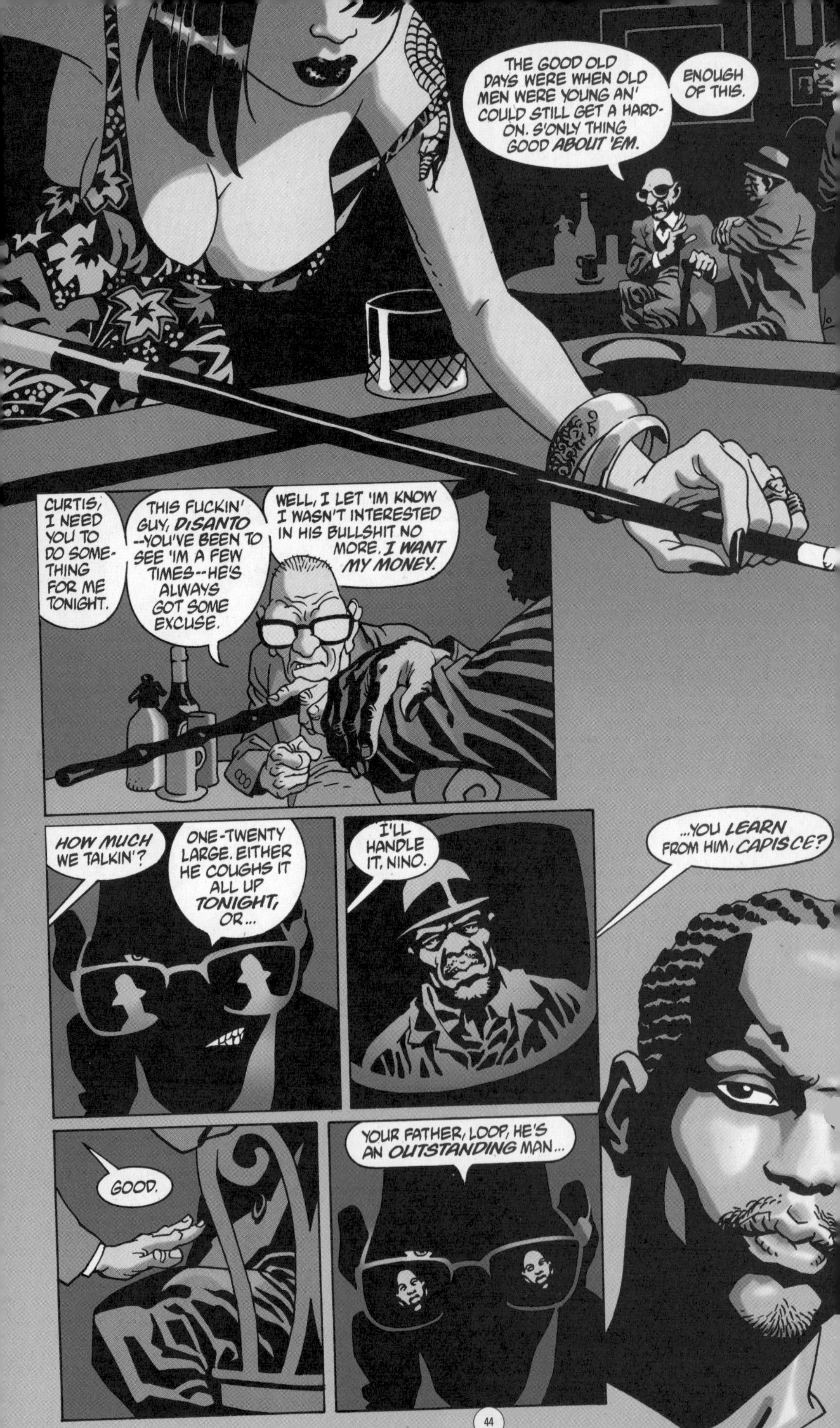

THE GOOD OLD DAYS WERE WHEN OLD MEN WERE YOUNG AN' COULD STILL GET A HARD-ON. S'ONLY THING GOOD ABOUT 'EM.
ENOUGH OF THIS.
CURTIS, I NEED YOU TO DO SOME-THING FOR ME TONIGHT.
THIS FUCKIN' GUY, DISANTO --YOU'VE BEEN TO SEE 'IM A FEW TIMES--HE'S ALWAYS GOT SOME EXCUSE.
WELL, I LET 'IM KNOW I WASN'T INTERESTED IN HIS BULLSHIT NO MORE. I WANT MY MONEY.
HOW MUCH WE TALKIN'?
ONE-TWENTY LARGE. EITHER HE COUGHS IT ALL UP TONIGHT, OR...
I'LL HANDLE IT, NINO.
GOOD.
YOUR FATHER, LOOP, HE'S AN OUTSTANDING MAN...
...YOU LEARN FROM HIM, CAPISCE?

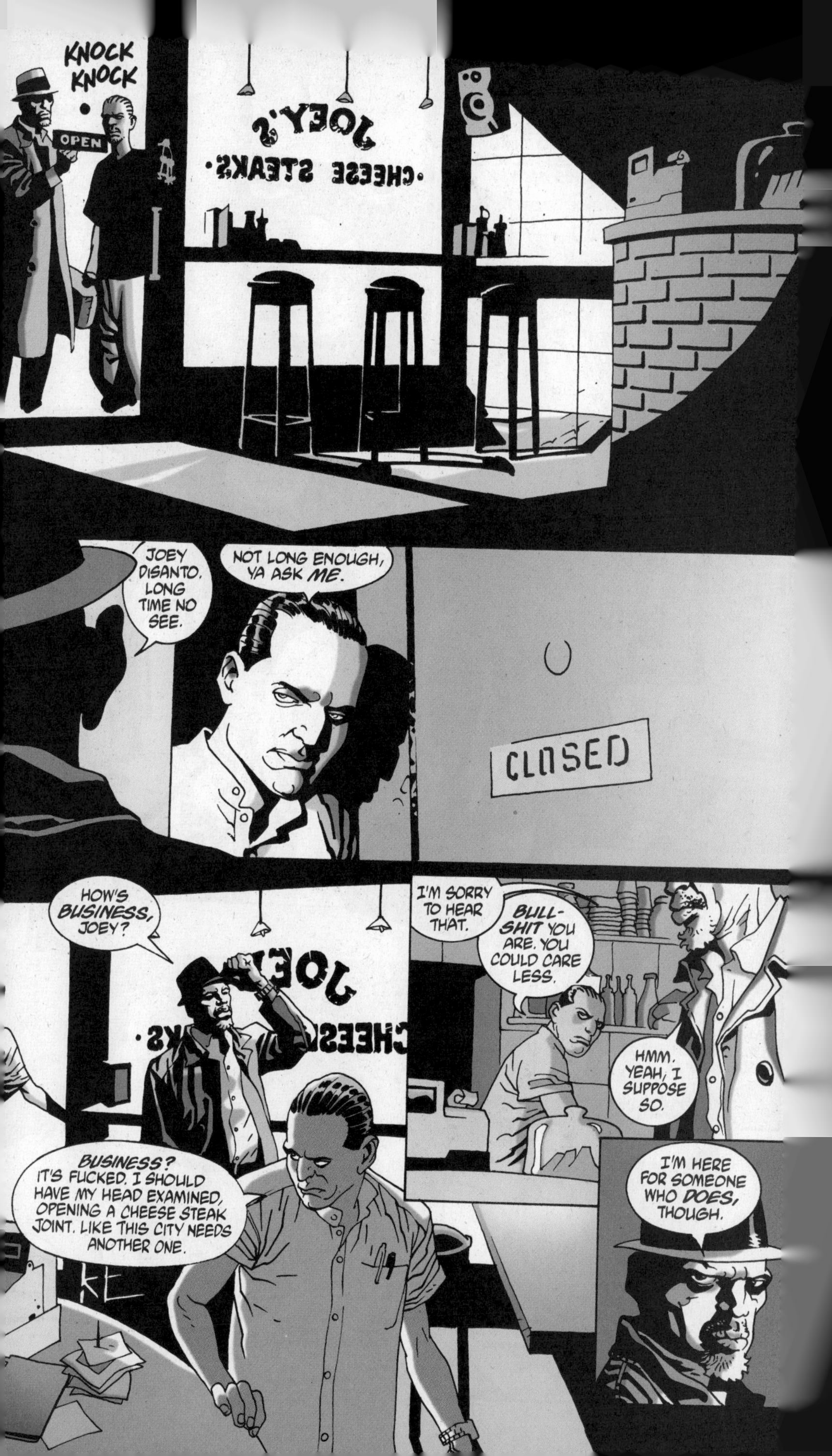
KNOCK KNOCK
OPEN
JOEY'S
·CHEESE STEAKS·
JOEY DISANTO. LONG TIME NO SEE.
NOT LONG ENOUGH, YA ASK *ME*.
CLOSED
HOW'S *BUSINESS*, JOEY?
BUSINESS? IT'S FUCKED. I SHOULD HAVE MY HEAD EXAMINED, OPENING A CHEESE STEAK JOINT. LIKE THIS CITY NEEDS ANOTHER ONE.
I'M SORRY TO HEAR THAT.
BULL-SHIT YOU ARE. YOU COULD CARE LESS.
HMM. YEAH, I SUPPOSE SO.
I'M HERE FOR SOMEONE WHO *DOES*, THOUGH.

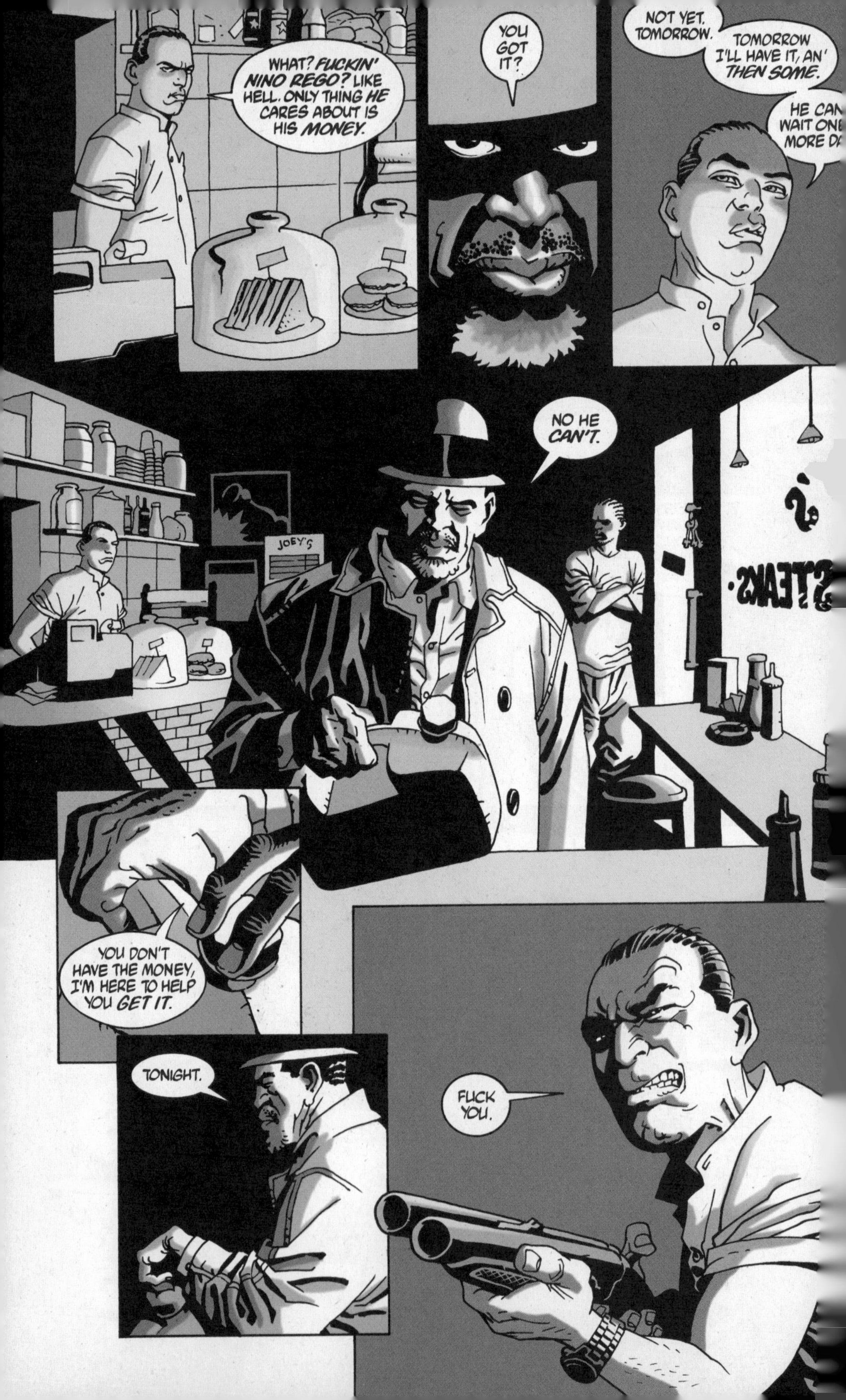
WHAT? FUCKIN' NINO REGO? LIKE HELL. ONLY THING HE CARES ABOUT IS HIS MONEY.
YOU GOT IT?
NOT YET. TOMORROW.
TOMORROW I'LL HAVE IT, AN' THEN SOME.
NO HE CAN'T.
JOEY'S
STEAKS
YOU DON'T HAVE THE MONEY, I'M HERE TO HELP YOU GET IT.
TONIGHT.
FUCK YOU.

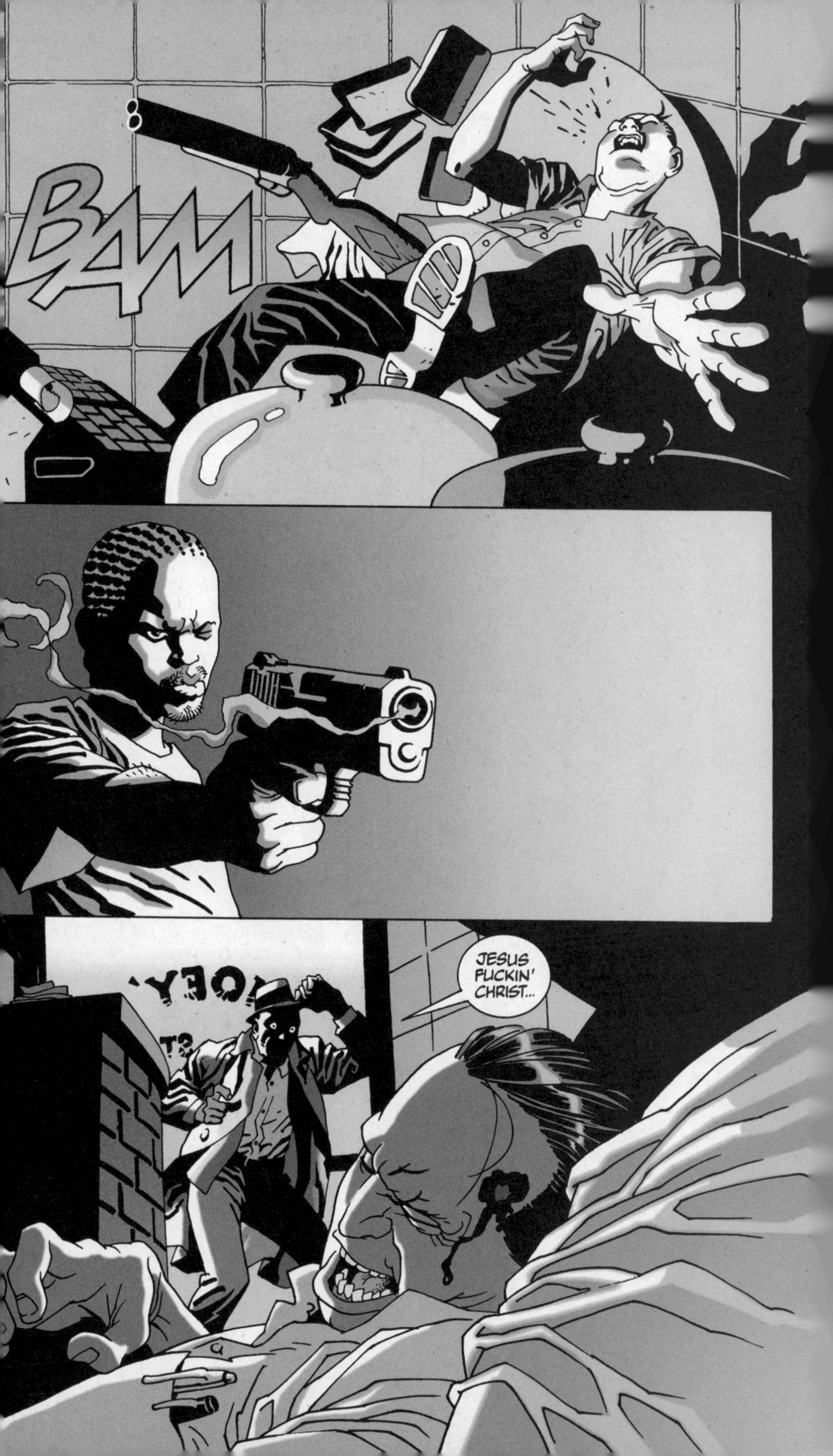
BAM
JESUS FUCKIN' CHRIST...

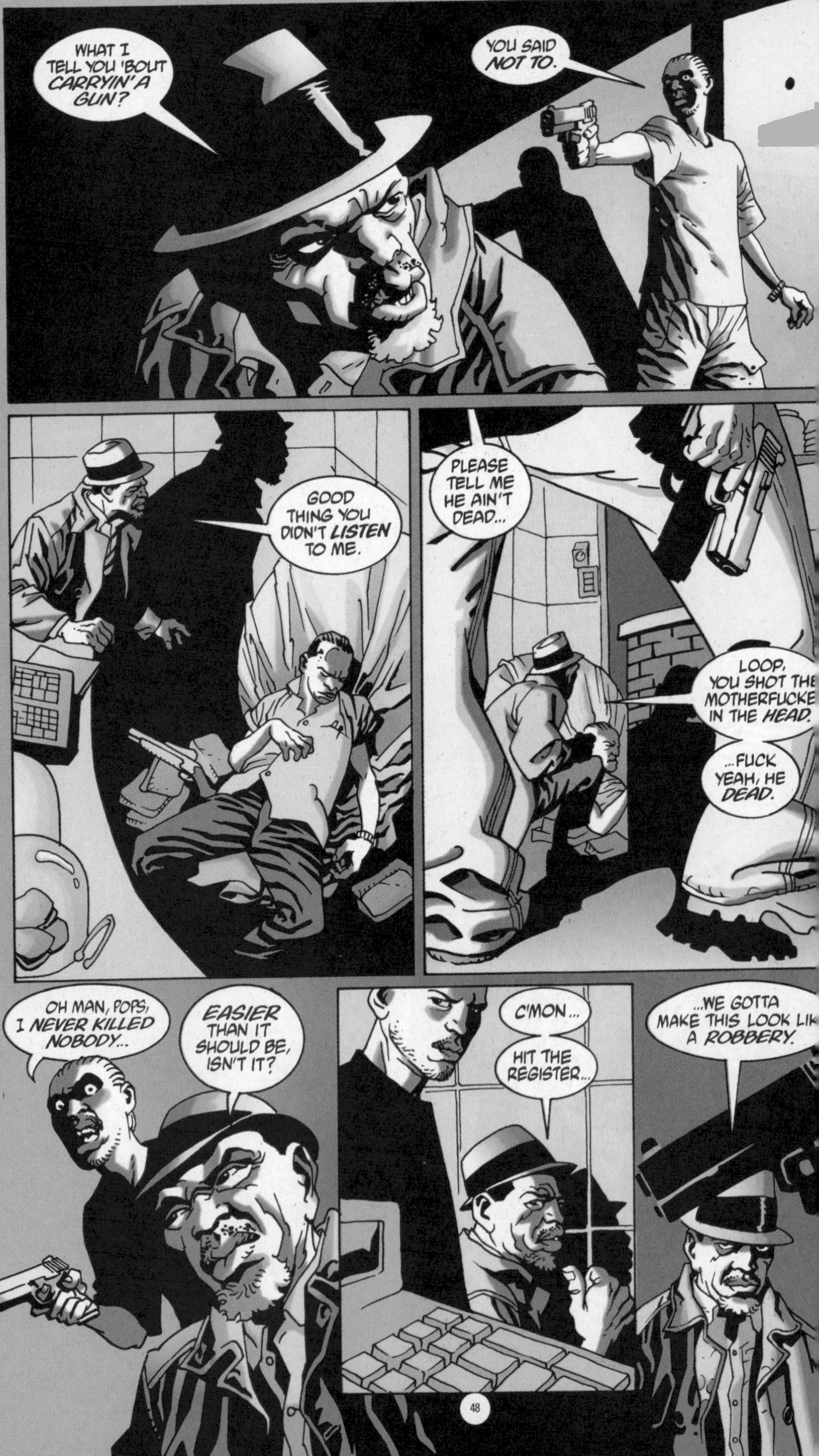
WHAT I TELL YOU 'BOUT CARRYIN' A GUN?
YOU SAID NOT TO.
GOOD THING YOU DIDN'T LISTEN TO ME.
PLEASE TELL ME HE AIN'T DEAD...
LOOP, YOU SHOT THE MOTHERFUCKE IN THE HEAD.
...FUCK YEAH, HE DEAD.
OH MAN, POPS, I NEVER KILLED NOBODY...
EASIER THAN IT SHOULD BE, ISN'T IT?
C'MON...
HIT THE REGISTER...
...WE GOTTA MAKE THIS LOOK LIK A ROBBERY.

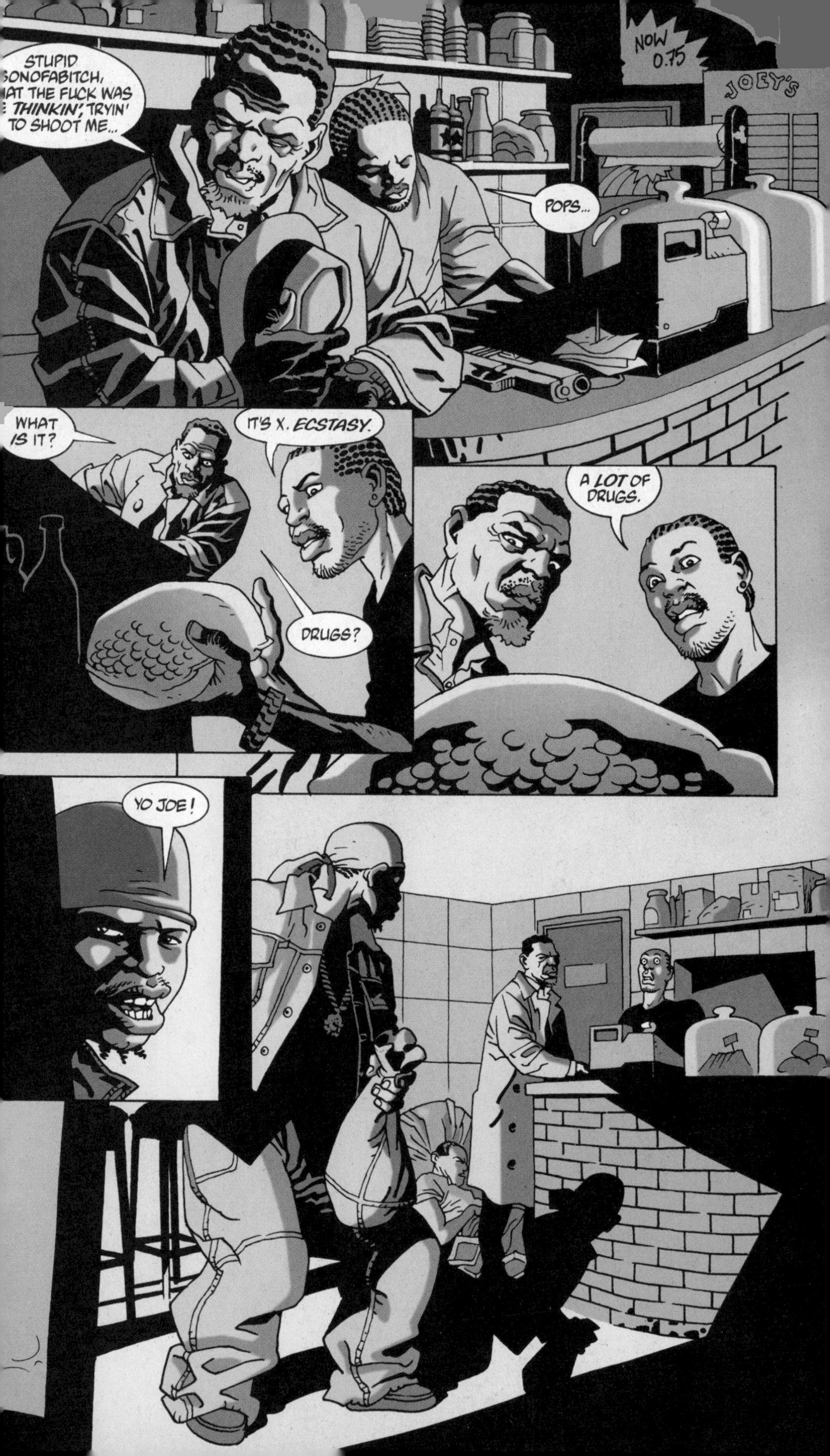
NOW 0.75
JOEY'S
STUPID SONOFABITCH, WHAT THE FUCK WAS HE *THINKIN';* TRYIN' TO SHOOT ME...
POPS...
WHAT IS IT?
IT'S X. *ECSTASY.*
DRUGS?
A *LOT* OF DRUGS.
YO JOE!

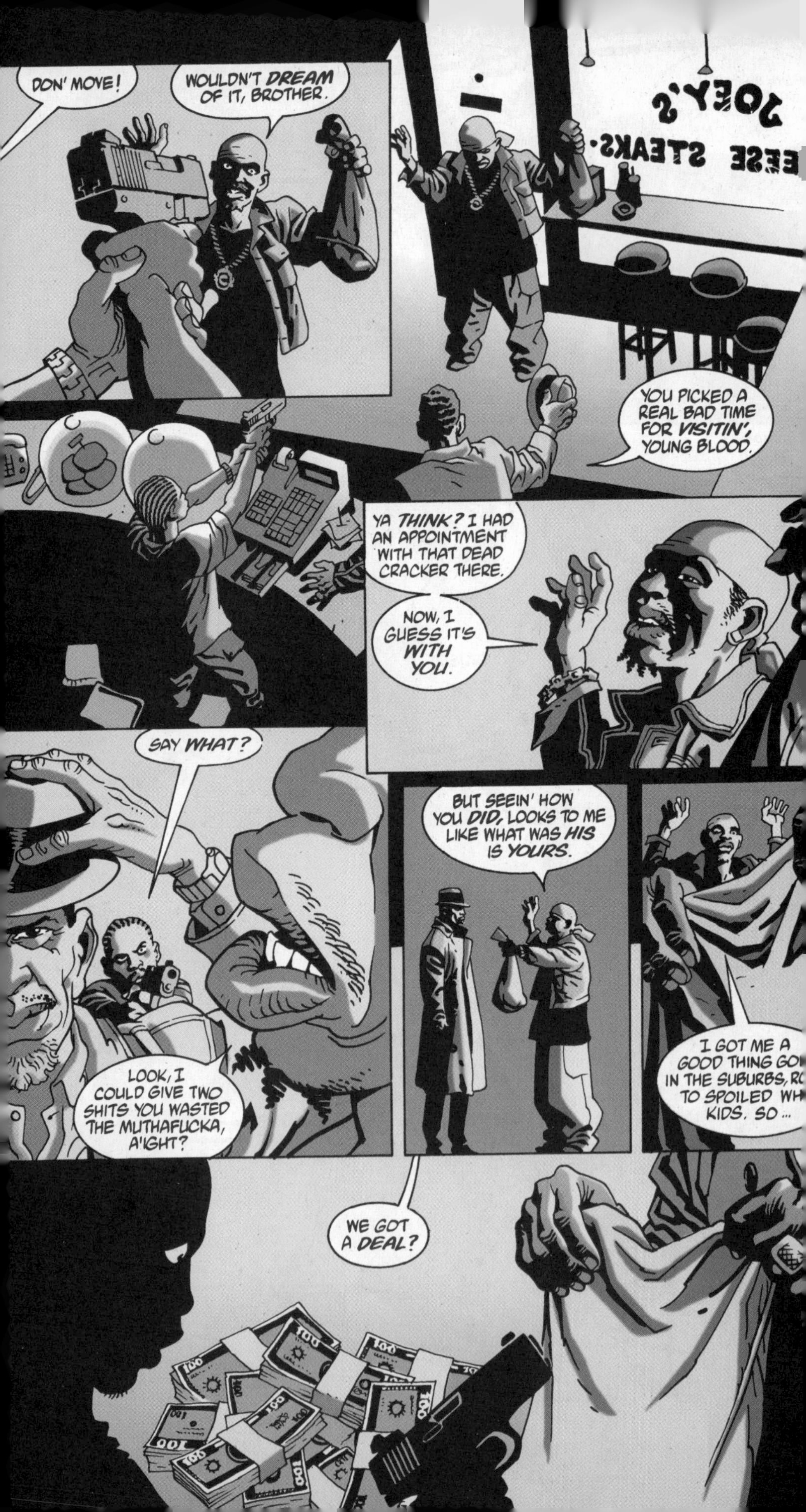

DON' MOVE!
WOULDN'T DREAM OF IT, BROTHER.
JOEY'S
EESE STEAKS.
YOU PICKED A REAL BAD TIME FOR VISITIN', YOUNG BLOOD.
YA THINK? I HAD AN APPOINTMENT WITH THAT DEAD CRACKER THERE.
NOW, I GUESS IT'S WITH YOU.
SAY WHAT?
LOOK, I COULD GIVE TWO SHITS YOU WASTED THE MUTHAFUCKA, A'IGHT?
BUT SEEIN' HOW YOU DID, LOOKS TO ME LIKE WHAT WAS HIS IS YOURS.
I GOT ME A GOOD THING GO
IN THE SUBURBS, R
TO SPOILED WH
KIDS. SO...
WE GOT A DEAL?

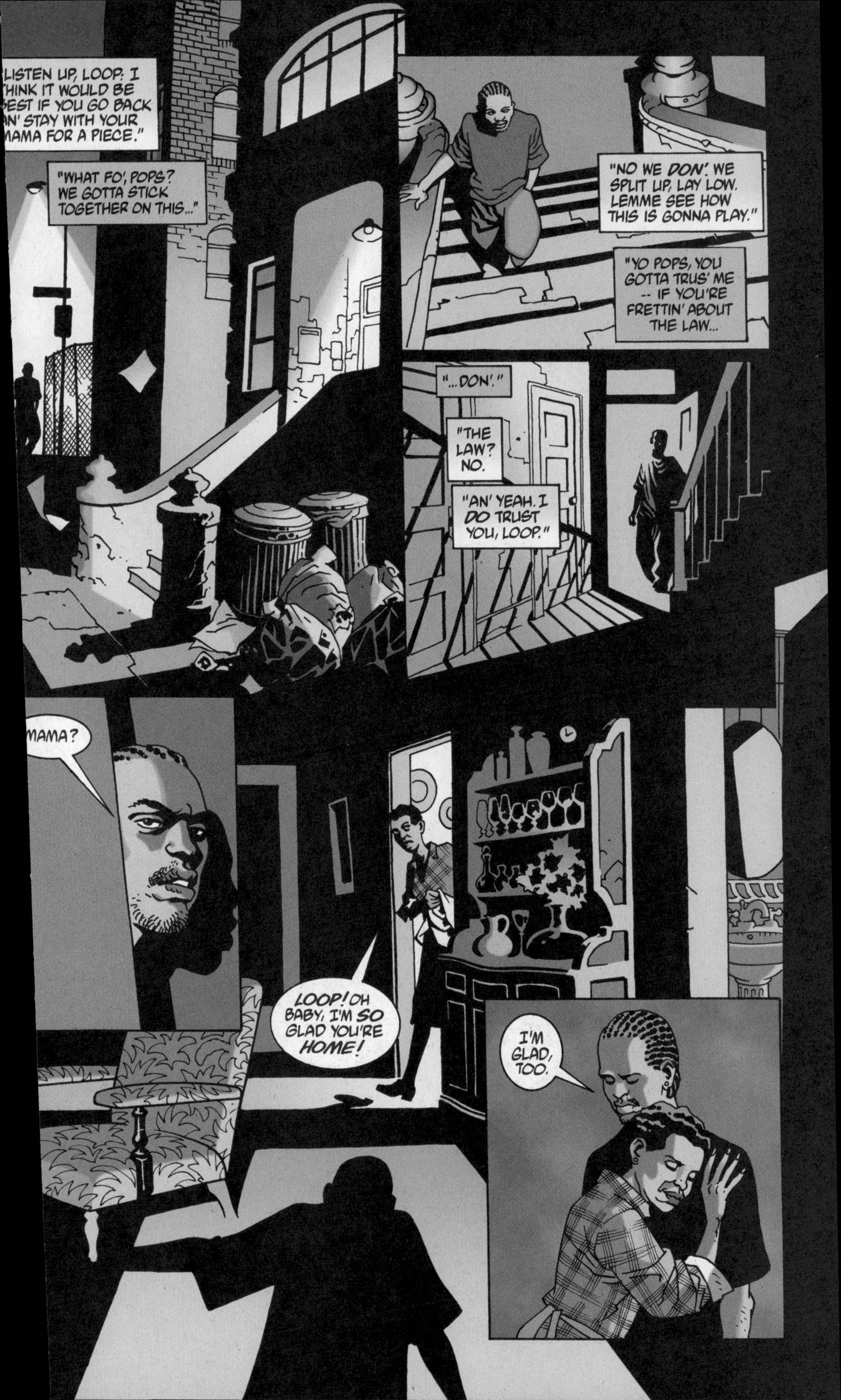
"LISTEN UP, LOOP: I THINK IT WOULD BE BEST IF YOU GO BACK AN' STAY WITH YOUR MAMA FOR A PIECE."
"WHAT FO', POPS? WE GOTTA STICK TOGETHER ON THIS..."
"NO WE DON'. WE SPLIT UP, LAY LOW. LEMME SEE HOW THIS IS GONNA PLAY."
"YO POPS, YOU GOTTA TRUS' ME -- IF YOU'RE FRETTIN' ABOUT THE LAW...
"...DON'."
"THE LAW? NO.
"AN' YEAH. I DO TRUST YOU, LOOP."
MAMA?
LOOP! OH BABY, I'M SO GLAD YOU'RE HOME!
I'M GLAD, TOO.

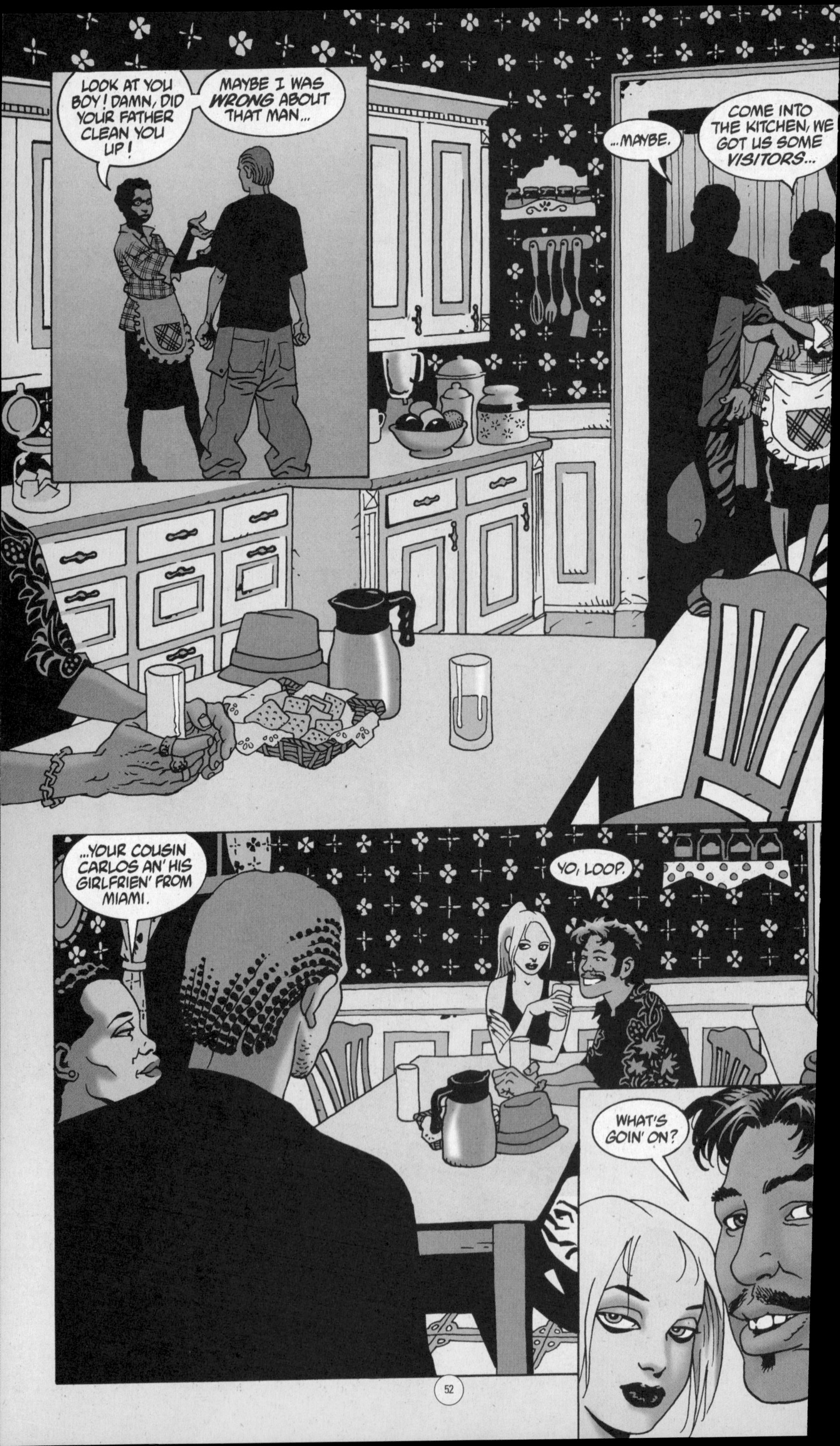
LOOK AT YOU BOY! DAMN, DID YOUR FATHER CLEAN YOU UP!
MAYBE I WAS WRONG ABOUT THAT MAN...
...MAYBE.
COME INTO THE KITCHEN, WE GOT US SOME VISITORS...
...YOUR COUSIN CARLOS AN' HIS GIRLFRIEN' FROM MIAMI.
YO, LOOP.
WHAT'S GOIN' ON?

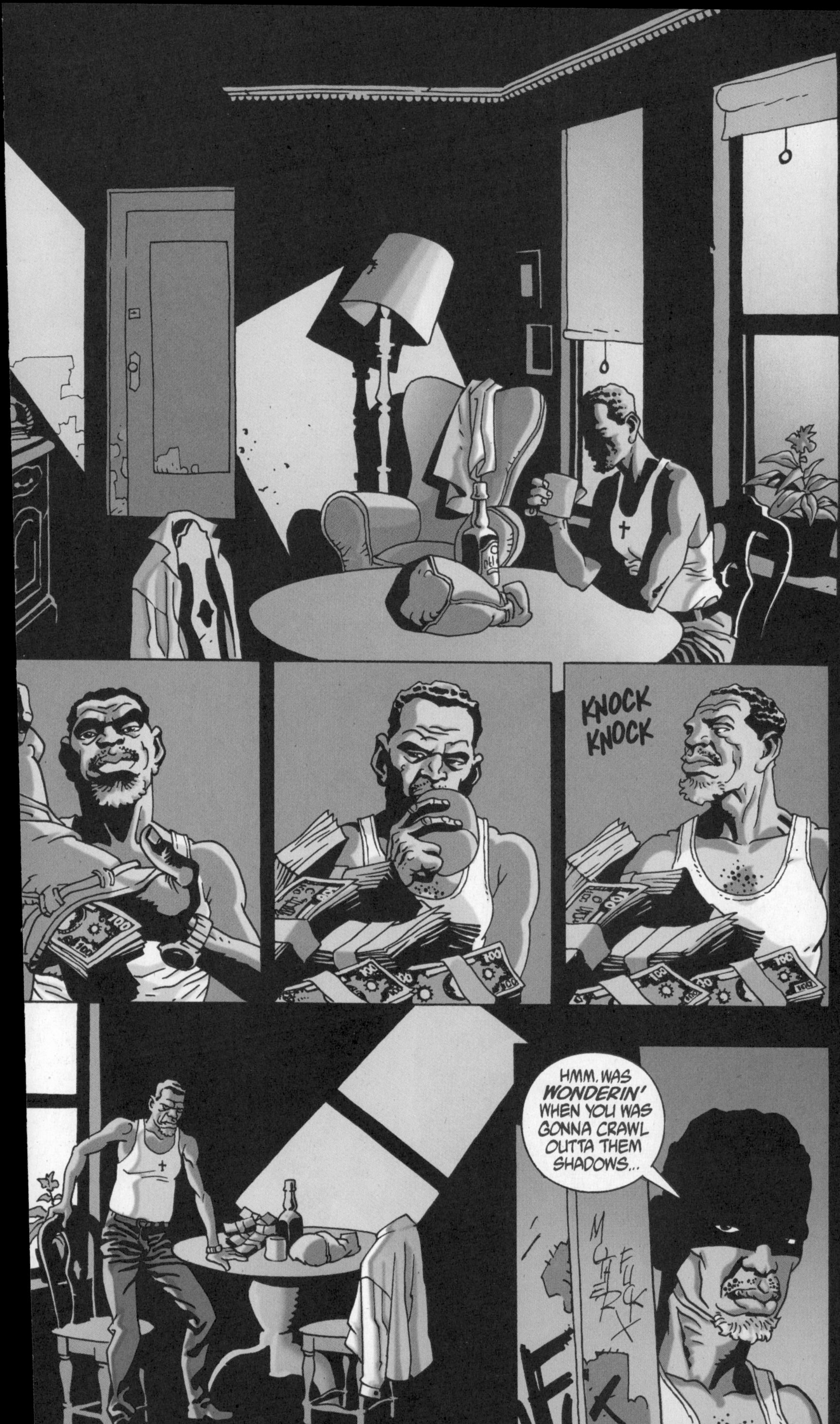
KNOCK KNOCK
HMM. WAS *WONDERIN'* WHEN YOU WAS GONNA CRAWL OUTTA THEM SHADOWS...

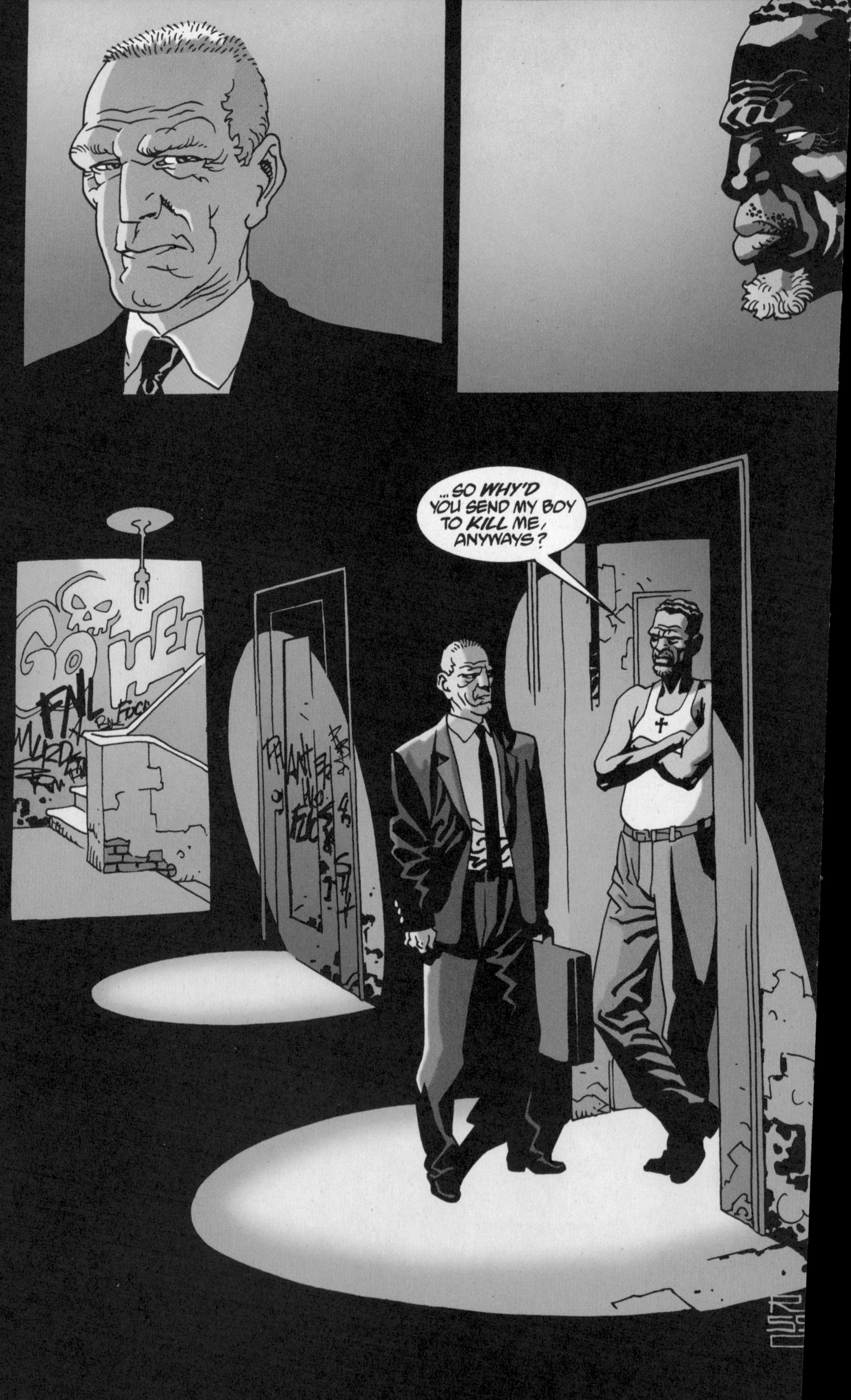
...SO WHY'D YOU SEND MY BOY TO KILL ME, ANYWAYS?

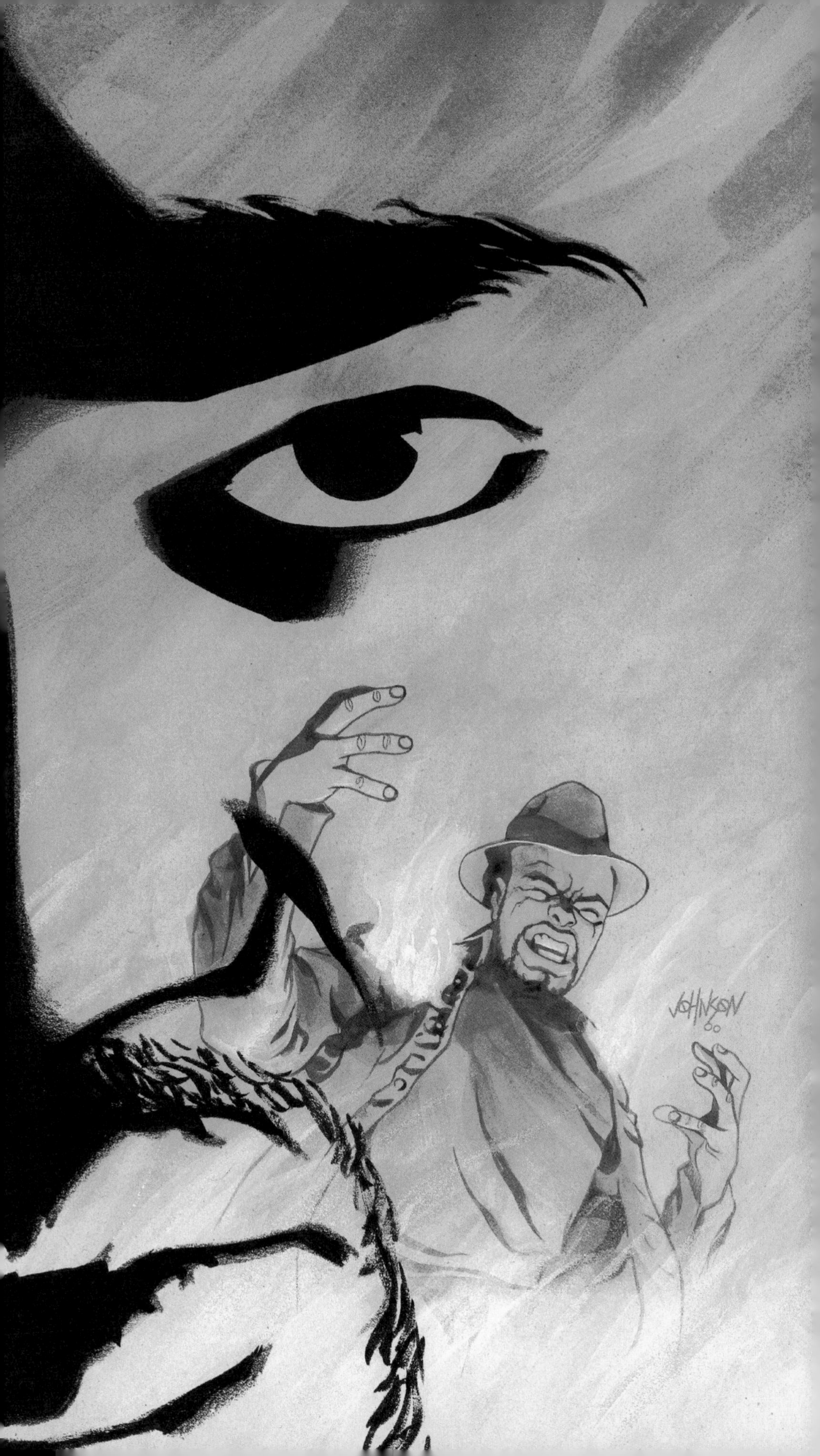
JOHNSON

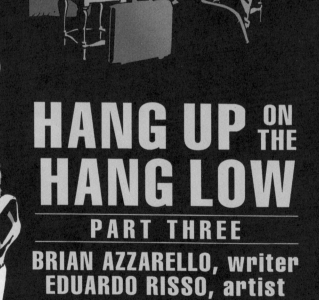

SO...

...HOW'S LIFE BEEN TREATING YOU, CURTIS?

WHY DON' YOU TELL ME, GRAVES?

NOT BAD, BUT THEN YOU DON'T ASK FOR MUCH OUT OF IT.

I WANTED SOMETHING ONCE.

YES, YOU DID BUT WHEN YOU DIDN'T GET IT...

...ALL YOU WANTED WAS TO BE LEFT ALONE.

HANG UP ON THE HANG LOW

PART THREE

BRIAN AZZARELLO, writer
EDUARDO RISSO, artist

PATRICIA MULVIHILL, colorist
DIGITAL CHAMELEON, separations
CLEM ROBINS, letters
DAVE JOHNSON, cover
JENNIFER LEE, ass't editor
AXEL ALONSO, editor

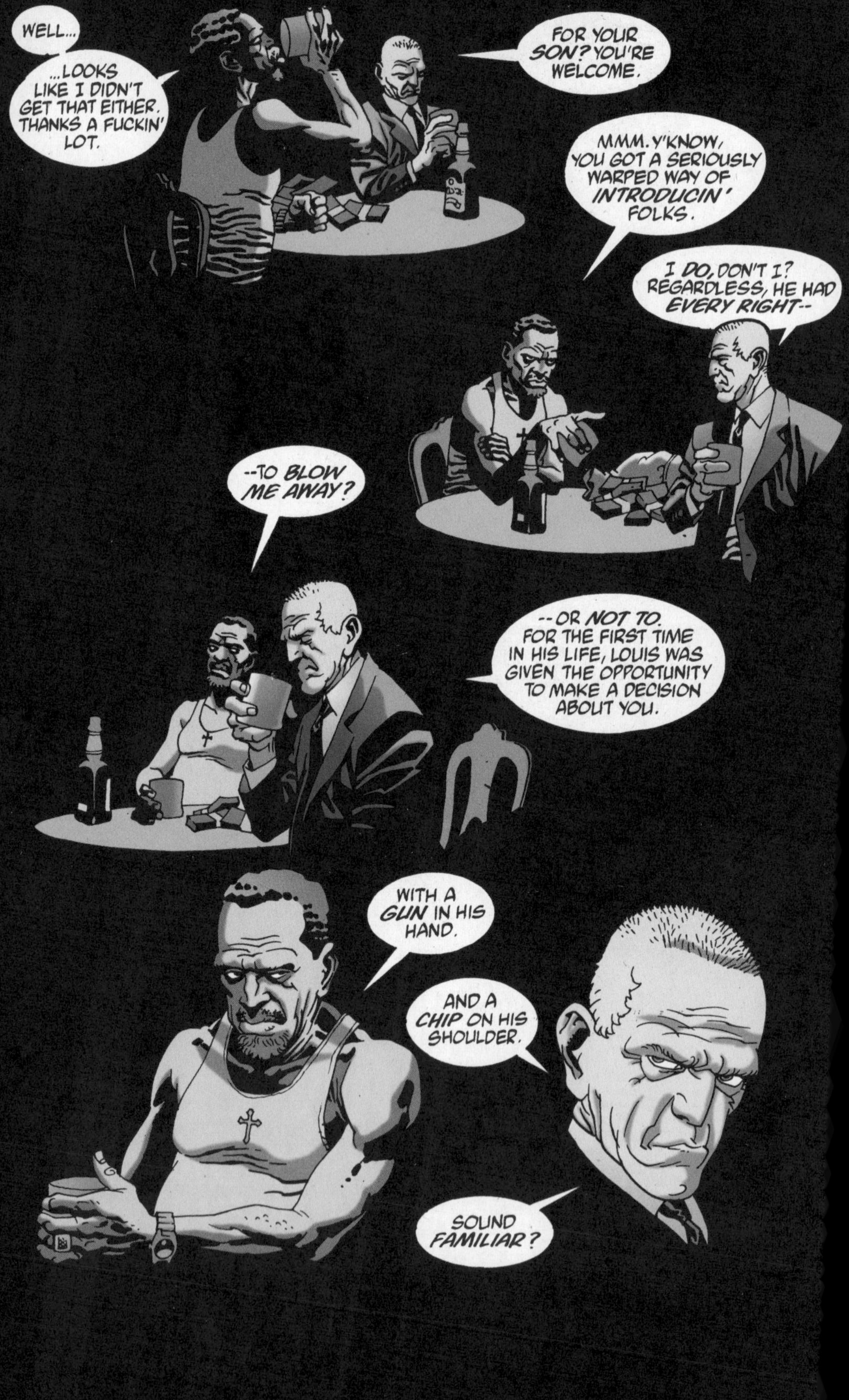

WELL...
...LOOKS LIKE I DIDN'T GET THAT EITHER. THANKS A FUCKIN' LOT.
FOR YOUR SON? YOU'RE WELCOME.
MMM. Y'KNOW, YOU GOT A SERIOUSLY WARPED WAY OF INTRODUCIN' FOLKS.
I DO, DON'T I? REGARDLESS, HE HAD EVERY RIGHT--
--TO BLOW ME AWAY?
--OR NOT TO. FOR THE FIRST TIME IN HIS LIFE, LOUIS WAS GIVEN THE OPPORTUNITY TO MAKE A DECISION ABOUT YOU.
WITH A GUN IN HIS HAND.
AND A CHIP ON HIS SHOULDER.
SOUND FAMILIAR?

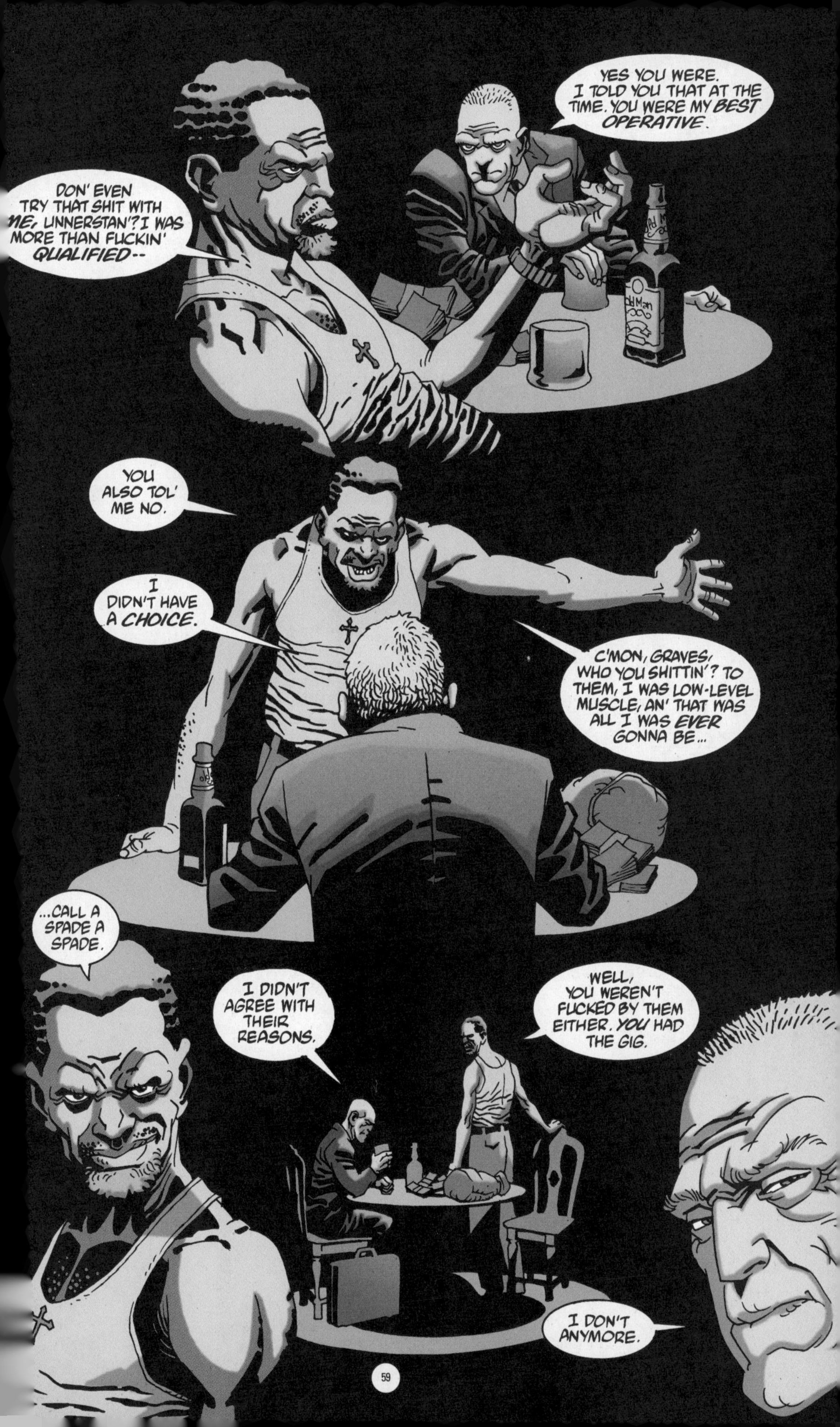
YES YOU WERE. I TOLD YOU THAT AT THE TIME. YOU WERE MY BEST OPERATIVE.
DON' EVEN TRY THAT SHIT WITH ME, UNNERSTAN'? I WAS MORE THAN FUCKIN' QUALIFIED--
YOU ALSO TOL' ME NO.
I DIDN'T HAVE A CHOICE.
C'MON, GRAVES, WHO YOU SHITTIN'? TO THEM, I WAS LOW-LEVEL MUSCLE, AN' THAT WAS ALL I WAS EVER GONNA BE...
...CALL A SPADE A SPADE.
I DIDN'T AGREE WITH THEIR REASONS.
WELL, YOU WEREN'T FUCKED BY THEM EITHER. YOU HAD THE GIG.
I DON'T ANYMORE.

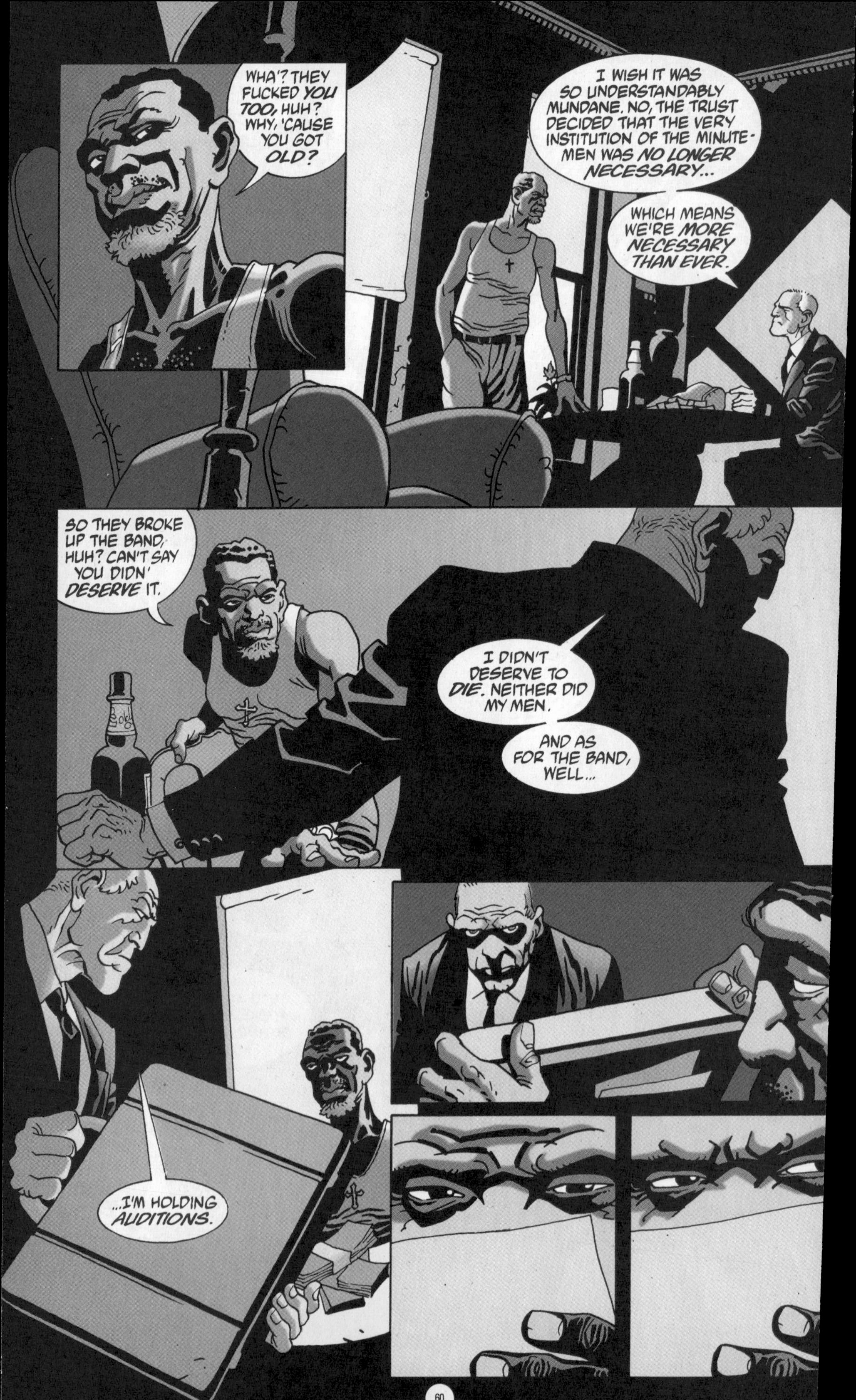
WHA'? THEY FUCKED YOU TOO, HUH? WHY, 'CAUSE YOU GOT OLD?
I WISH IT WAS SO UNDERSTANDABLY MUNDANE. NO, THE TRUST DECIDED THAT THE VERY INSTITUTION OF THE MINUTE-MEN WAS NO LONGER NECESSARY...
WHICH MEANS WE'RE MORE NECESSARY THAN EVER.
SO THEY BROKE UP THE BAND, HUH? CAN'T SAY YOU DIDN' DESERVE IT.
I DIDN'T DESERVE TO DIE. NEITHER DID MY MEN.
AND AS FOR THE BAND, WELL...
...I'M HOLDING AUDITIONS.

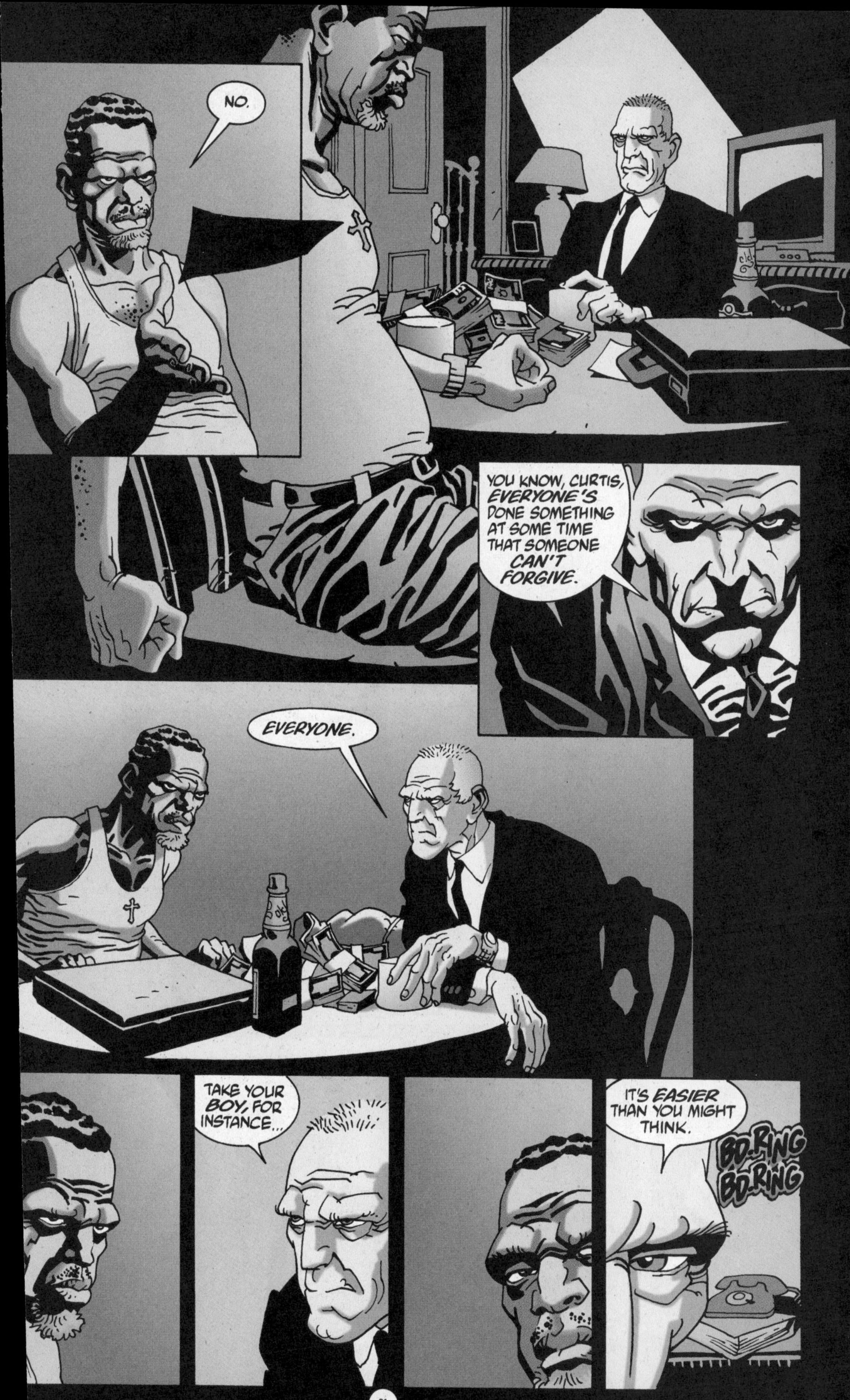

NO.
YOU KNOW, CURTIS, EVERYONE'S DONE SOMETHING AT SOME TIME THAT SOMEONE CAN'T FORGIVE.
EVERYONE.
TAKE YOUR BOY, FOR INSTANCE...
IT'S EASIER THAN YOU MIGHT THINK.
BD-RING
BD-RING

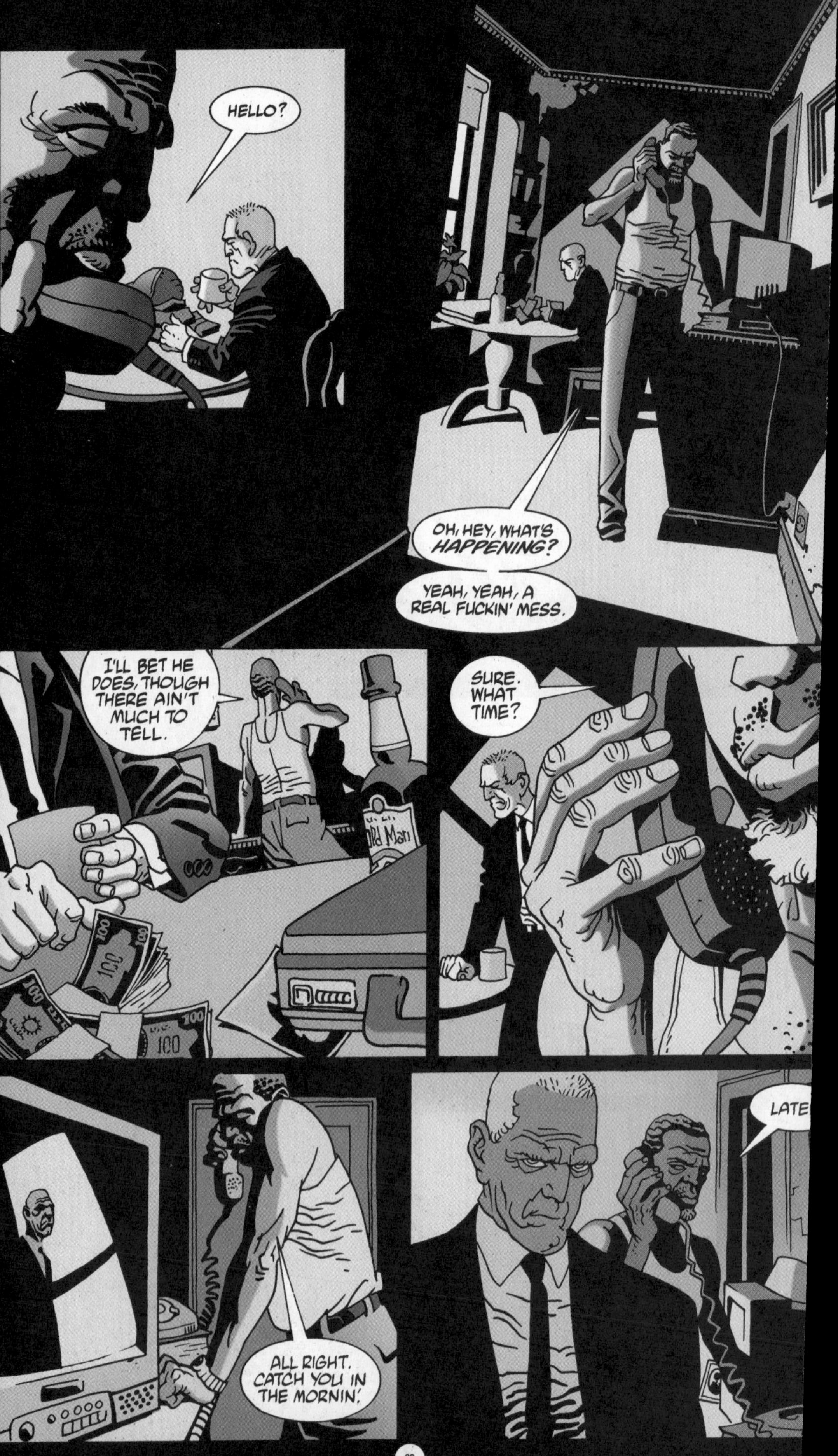
HELLO?
OH, HEY, WHAT'S HAPPENING?
YEAH, YEAH, A REAL FUCKIN' MESS.
I'LL BET HE DOES, THOUGH THERE AIN'T MUCH TO TELL.
SURE. WHAT TIME?
ALL RIGHT. CATCH YOU IN THE MORNIN'.
LATE

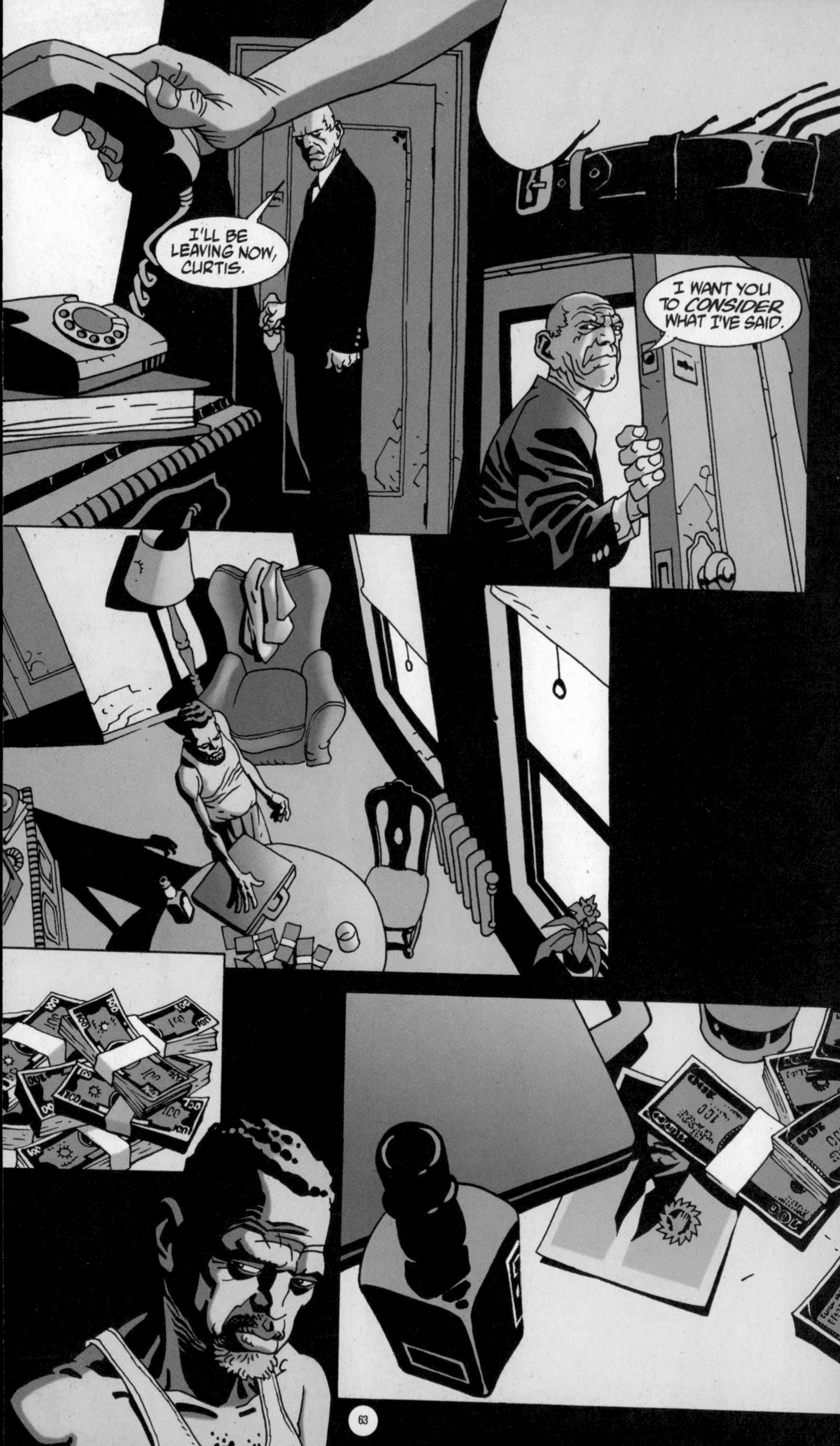
I'LL BE LEAVING NOW, CURTIS.
I WANT YOU TO CONSIDER WHAT I'VE SAID.

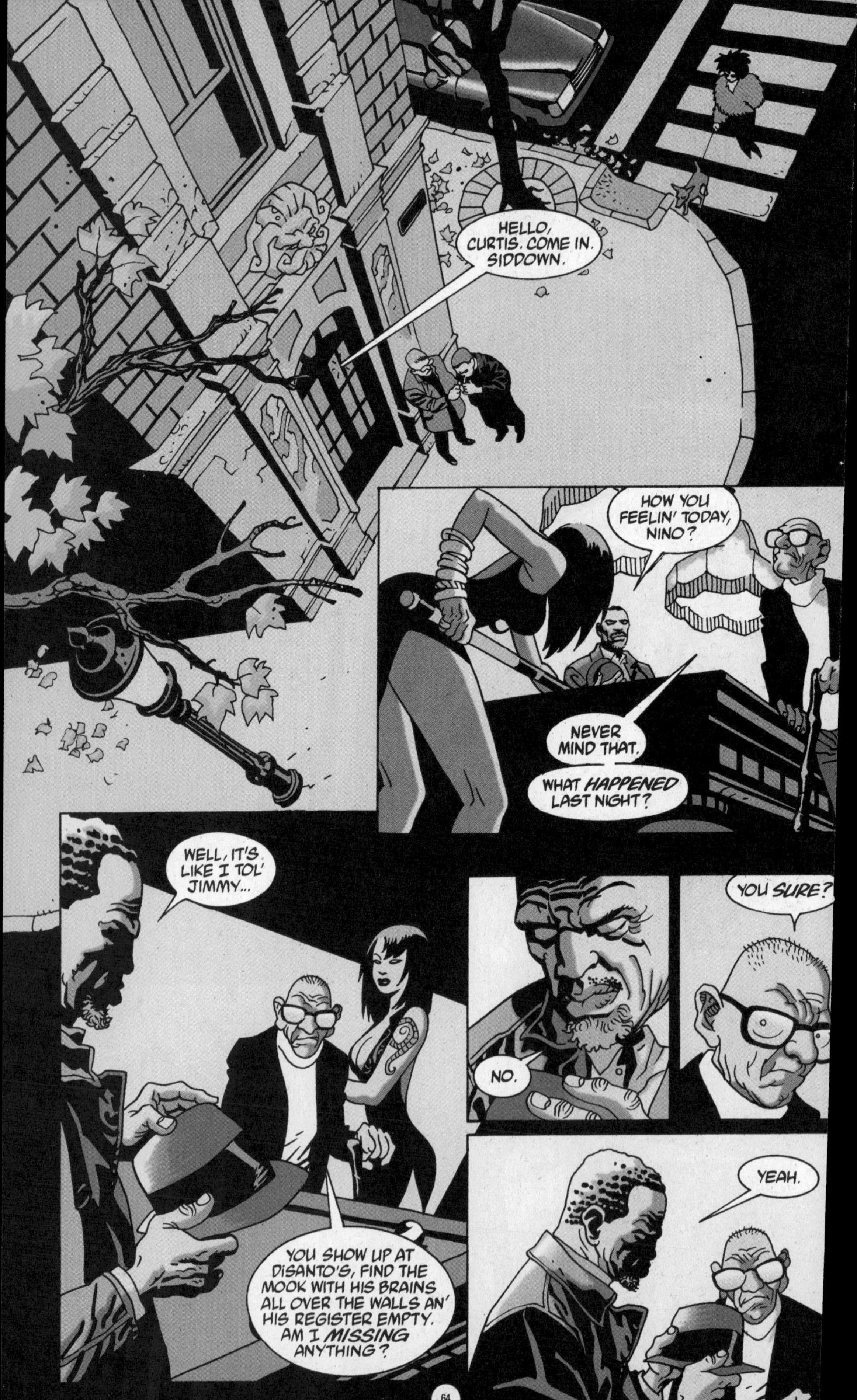
HELLO, CURTIS. COME IN. SIDDOWN.
HOW YOU FEELIN' TODAY, NINO?
NEVER MIND THAT.
WHAT HAPPENED LAST NIGHT?
WELL, IT'S LIKE I TOL' JIMMY...
YOU SHOW UP AT DiSANTO'S, FIND THE MOOK WITH HIS BRAINS ALL OVER THE WALLS AN' HIS REGISTER EMPTY. AM I MISSING ANYTHING?
NO.
YOU SURE?
YEAH.

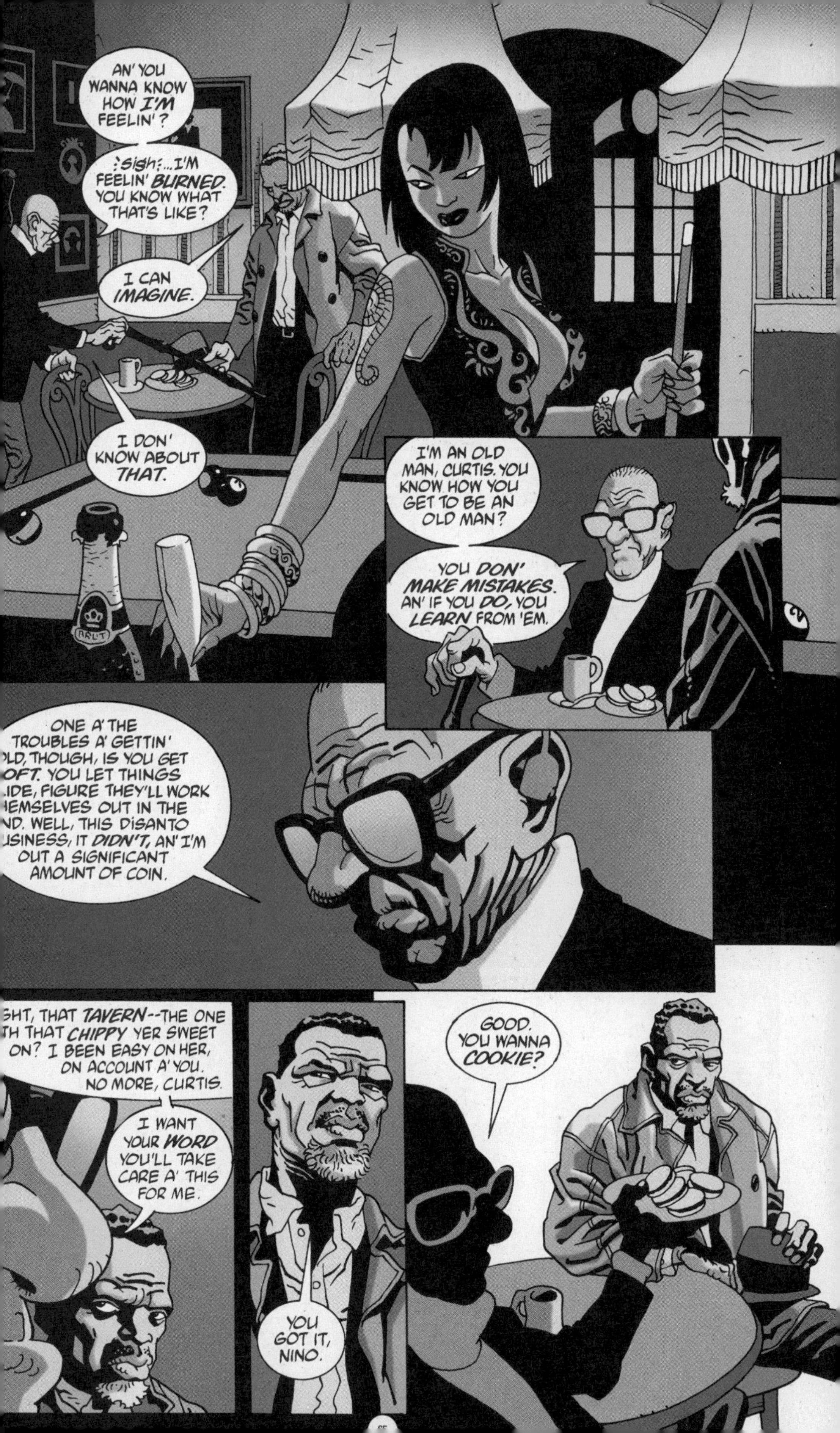
AN' YOU WANNA KNOW HOW I'M FEELIN'?
:sigh:...I'M FEELIN' BURNED. YOU KNOW WHAT THAT'S LIKE?
I CAN IMAGINE.
I DON' KNOW ABOUT THAT.
I'M AN OLD MAN, CURTIS. YOU KNOW HOW YOU GET TO BE AN OLD MAN?
YOU DON' MAKE MISTAKES. AN' IF YOU DO, YOU LEARN FROM 'EM.
ONE A' THE TROUBLES A' GETTIN' OLD, THOUGH, IS YOU GET SOFT. YOU LET THINGS SLIDE, FIGURE THEY'LL WORK THEMSELVES OUT IN THE END. WELL, THIS DISANTO BUSINESS, IT DIDN'T, AN' I'M OUT A SIGNIFICANT AMOUNT OF COIN.
GHT, THAT TAVERN--THE ONE TH THAT CHIPPY YER SWEET ON? I BEEN EASY ON HER, ON ACCOUNT A' YOU. NO MORE, CURTIS.
I WANT YOUR WORD YOU'LL TAKE CARE A' THIS FOR ME.
YOU GOT IT, NINO.
GOOD. YOU WANNA COOKIE?

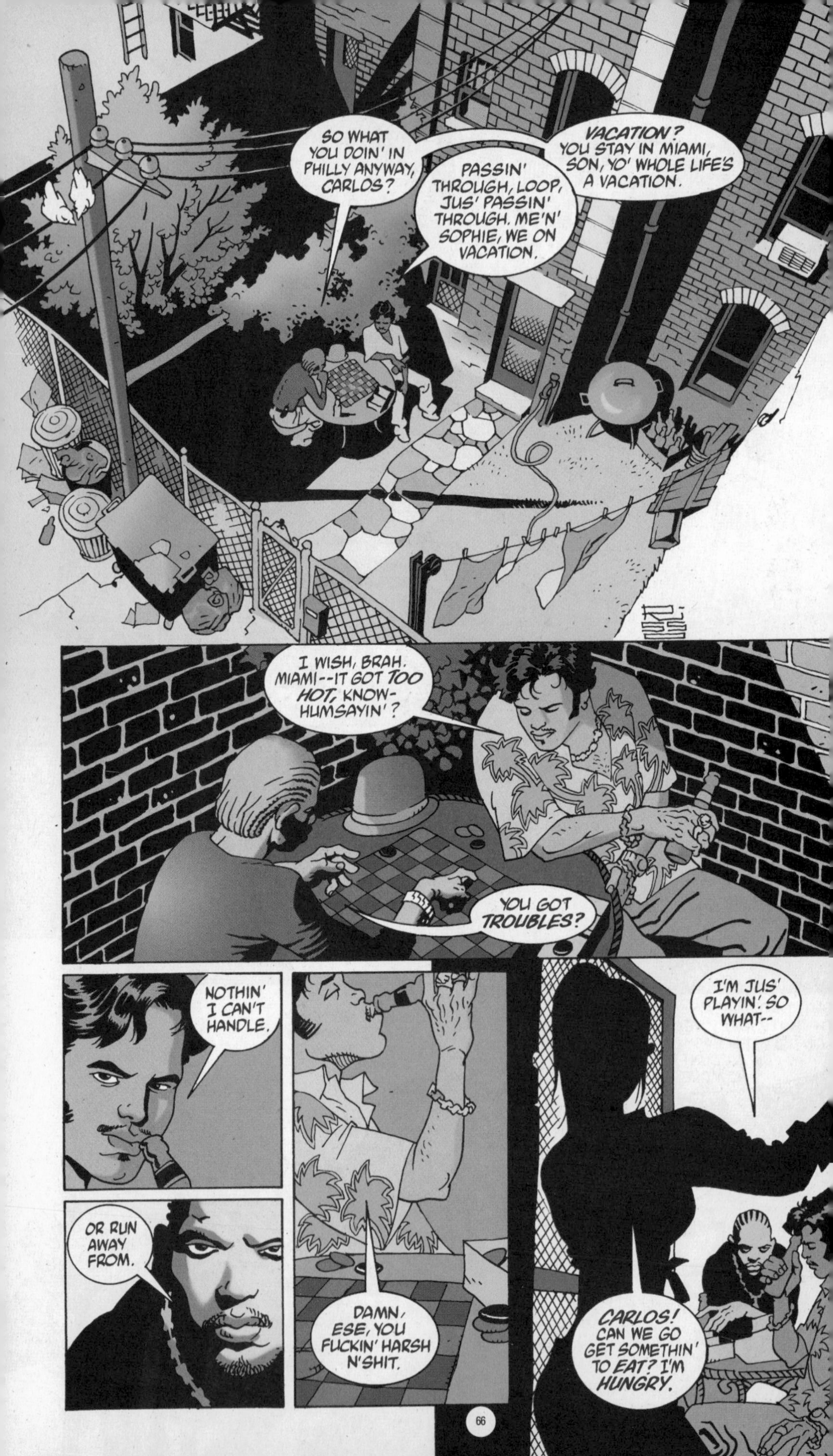
SO WHAT YOU DOIN' IN PHILLY ANYWAY, CARLOS?
PASSIN' THROUGH, LOOP, JUS' PASSIN' THROUGH. ME'N' SOPHIE, WE ON VACATION.
VACATION? YOU STAY IN MIAMI, SON, YO' WHOLE LIFE'S A VACATION.
I WISH, BRAH. MIAMI--IT GOT TOO HOT, KNOW-HUMSAYIN'?
YOU GOT TROUBLES?
NOTHIN' I CAN'T HANDLE.
OR RUN AWAY FROM.
DAMN, ESE, YOU FUCKIN' HARSH N'SHIT.
I'M JUS' PLAYIN'. SO WHAT--
CARLOS! CAN WE GO GET SOMETHIN' TO EAT? I'M HUNGRY.

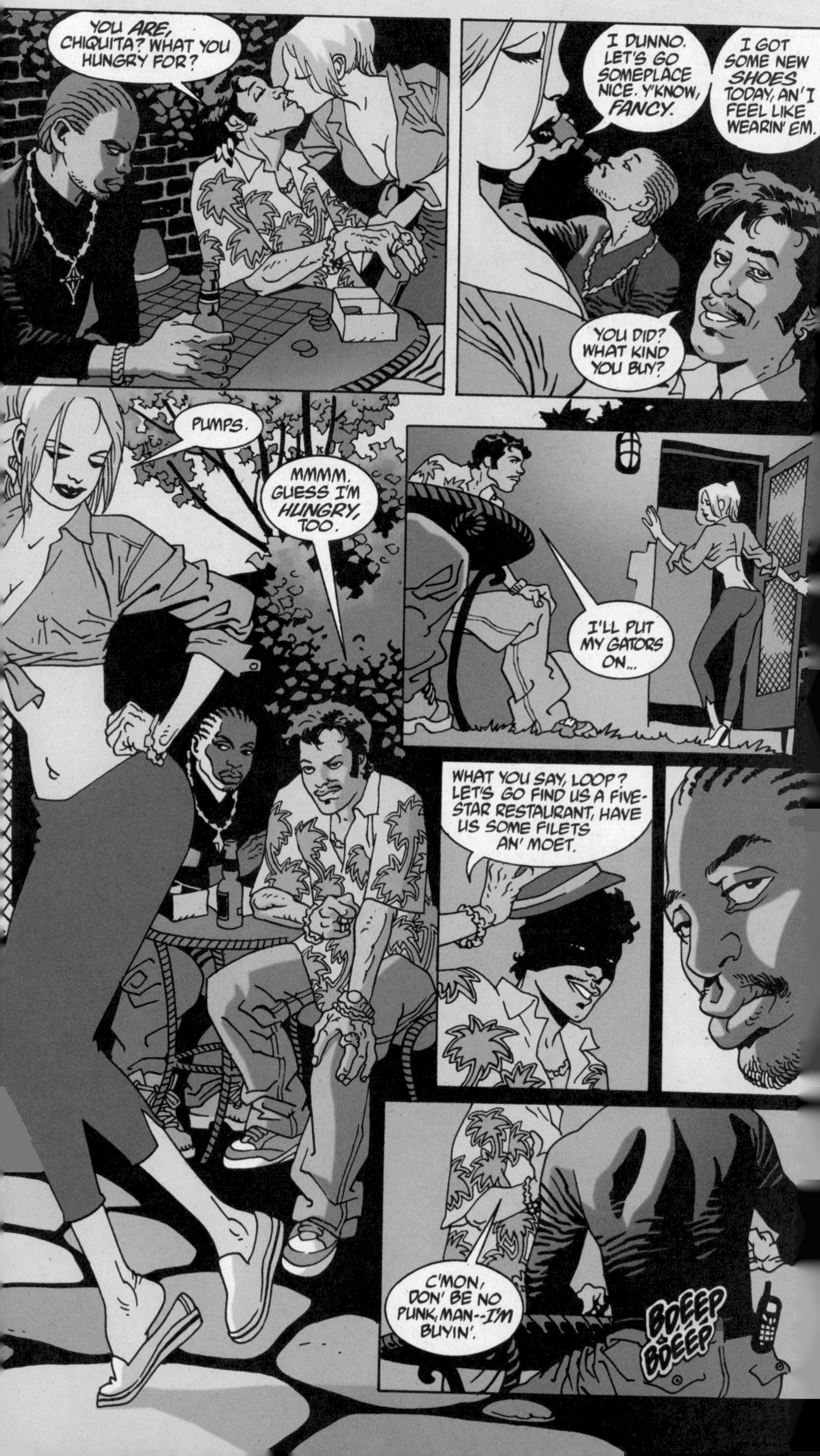
YOU ARE, CHIQUITA? WHAT YOU HUNGRY FOR?
I DUNNO. LET'S GO SOMEPLACE NICE. Y'KNOW, FANCY.
I GOT SOME NEW SHOES TODAY, AN' I FEEL LIKE WEARIN' EM.
YOU DID? WHAT KIND YOU BUY?
PUMPS.
MMMM. GUESS I'M HUNGRY, TOO.
I'LL PUT MY GATORS ON...
WHAT YOU SAY, LOOP? LET'S GO FIND US A FIVE-STAR RESTAURANT, HAVE US SOME FILETS AN' MOET.
C'MON, DON' BE NO PUNK, MAN--I'M BUYIN'.
BDEEP BDEEP

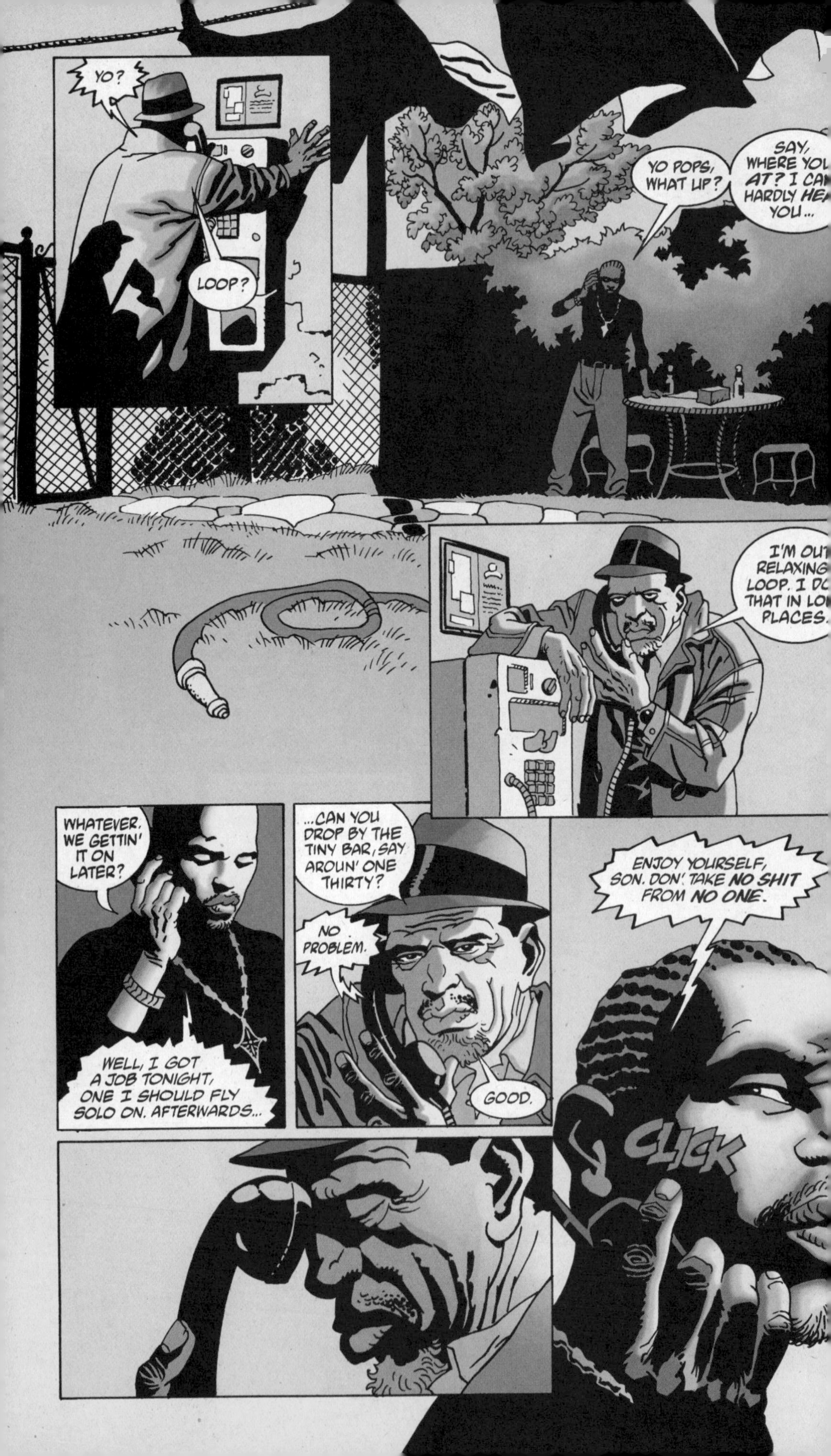
YO?
LOOP?
YO POPS, WHAT UP?
SAY, WHERE YOU AT? I CA HARDLY HEA YOU...
I'M OUT RELAXING LOOP. I DO THAT IN LO PLACES.
WHATEVER. WE GETTIN' IT ON LATER?
WELL, I GOT A JOB TONIGHT, ONE I SHOULD FLY SOLO ON. AFTERWARDS...
...CAN YOU DROP BY THE TINY BAR, SAY AROUN' ONE THIRTY?
NO PROBLEM.
GOOD.
ENJOY YOURSELF, SON. DON' TAKE NO SHIT FROM NO ONE.
CLICK

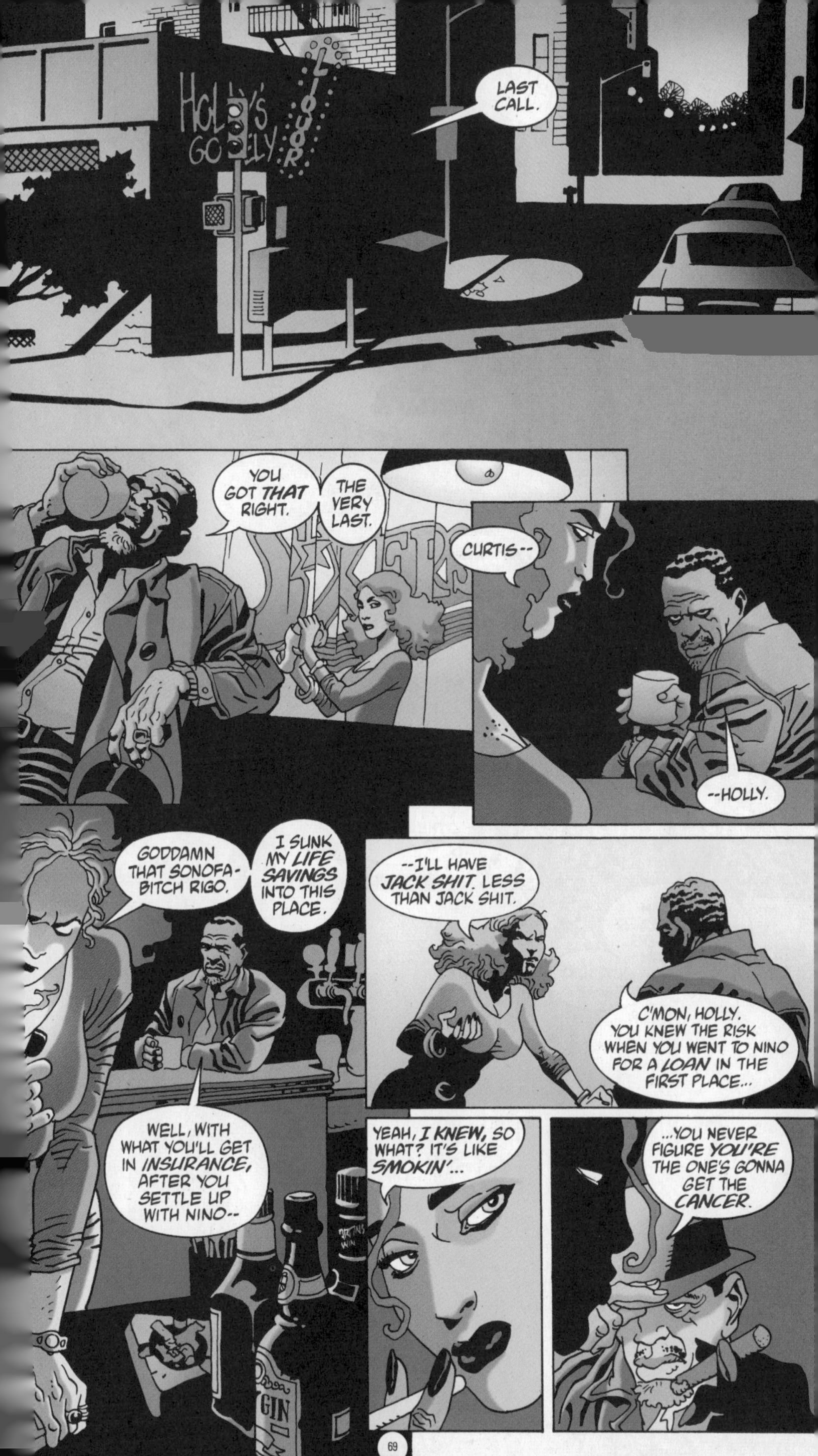
HOLLY'S
GO GOLY
LIQUOR
LAST CALL.
YOU GOT THAT RIGHT.
THE VERY LAST.
CURTIS--
--HOLLY.
GODDAMN THAT SONOFA-BITCH RIGO.
I SUNK MY LIFE SAVINGS INTO THIS PLACE.
WELL, WITH WHAT YOU'LL GET IN INSURANCE, AFTER YOU SETTLE UP WITH NINO--
--I'LL HAVE JACK SHIT. LESS THAN JACK SHIT.
C'MON, HOLLY. YOU KNEW THE RISK WHEN YOU WENT TO NINO FOR A LOAN IN THE FIRST PLACE...
YEAH, I KNEW, SO WHAT? IT'S LIKE SMOKIN'...
...YOU NEVER FIGURE YOU'RE THE ONE'S GONNA GET THE CANCER.
GIN

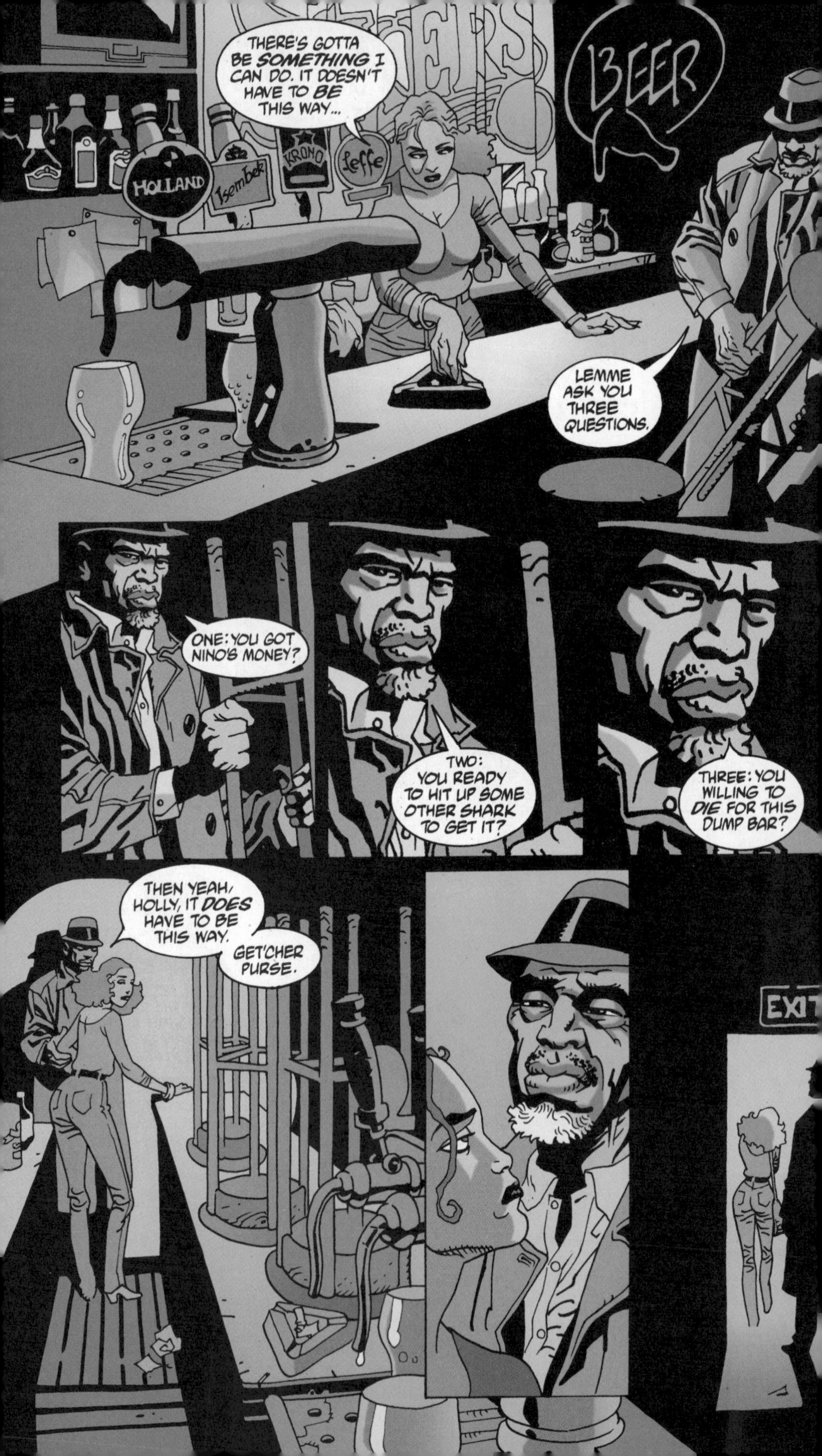
THERE'S GOTTA BE SOMETHING I CAN DO. IT DOESN'T HAVE TO BE THIS WAY...
BEER
HOLLAND
Isember
KRONO
Leffe
LEMME ASK YOU THREE QUESTIONS.
ONE: YOU GOT NINO'S MONEY?
TWO: YOU READY TO HIT UP SOME OTHER SHARK TO GET IT?
THREE: YOU WILLING TO DIE FOR THIS DUMP BAR?
THEN YEAH, HOLLY, IT DOES HAVE TO BE THIS WAY.
GET'CHER PURSE.
EXIT

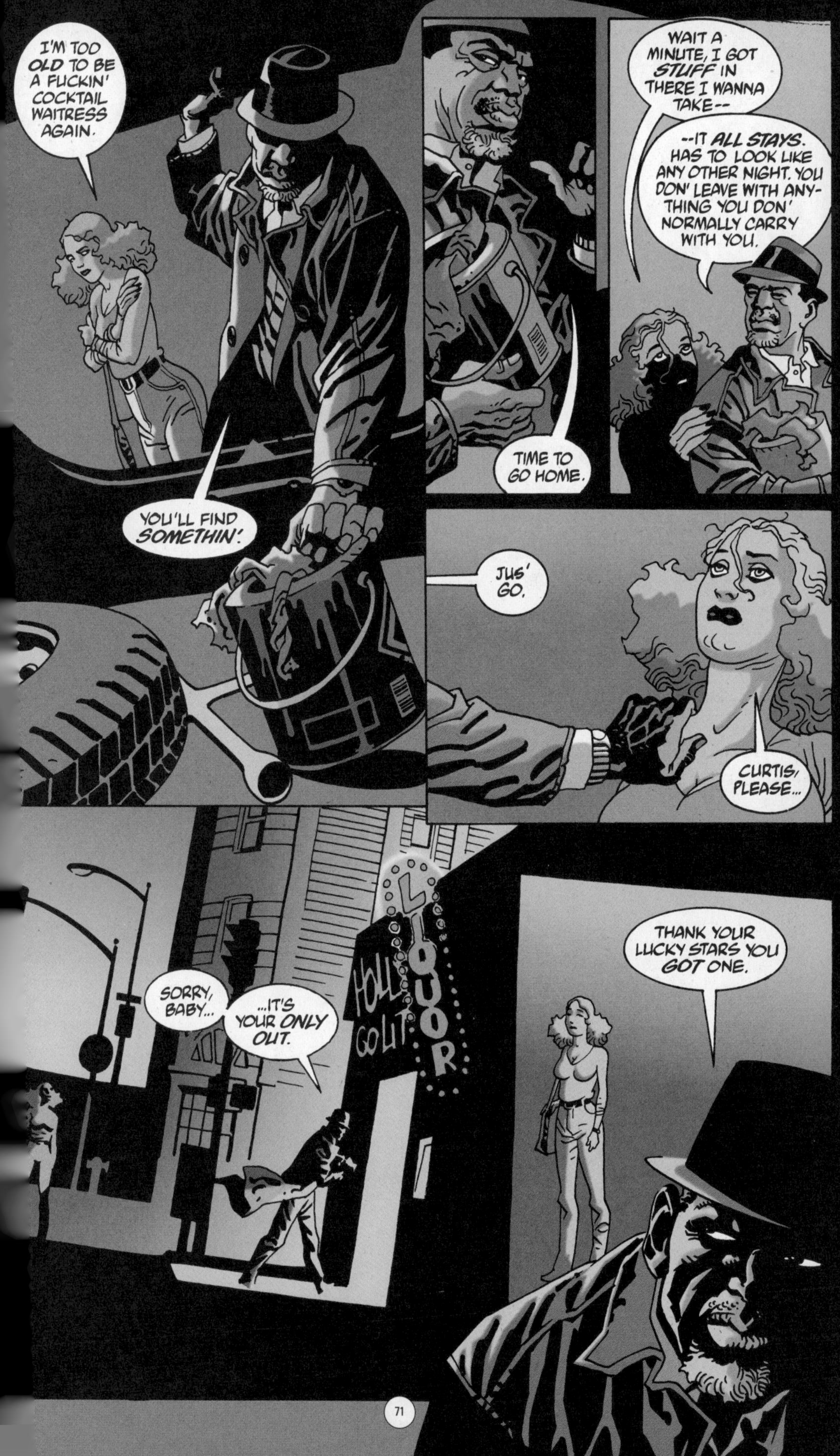

I'M TOO OLD TO BE A FUCKIN' COCKTAIL WAITRESS AGAIN.
YOU'LL FIND SOMETHIN'.
TIME TO GO HOME.
WAIT A MINUTE, I GOT STUFF IN THERE I WANNA TAKE--
--IT ALL STAYS. HAS TO LOOK LIKE ANY OTHER NIGHT. YOU DON' LEAVE WITH ANY-THING YOU DON' NORMALLY CARRY WITH YOU.
JUS' GO.
CURTIS, PLEASE...
SORRY, BABY...
...IT'S YOUR ONLY OUT.
THANK YOUR LUCKY STARS YOU GOT ONE.

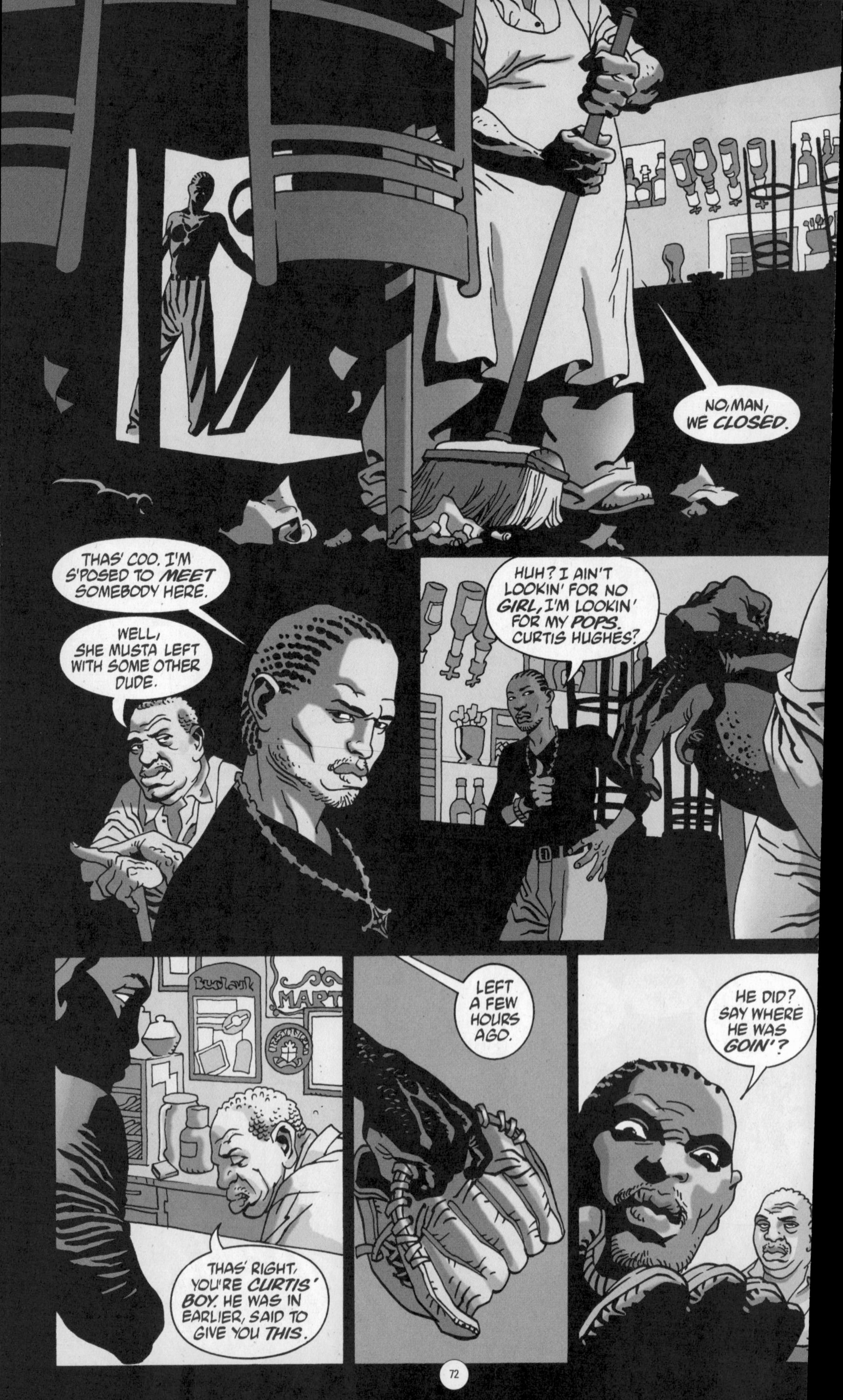
NO, MAN, WE CLOSED.
THAS' COO. I'M S'POSED TO MEET SOMEBODY HERE.
WELL, SHE MUSTA LEFT WITH SOME OTHER DUDE.
HUH? I AIN'T LOOKIN' FOR NO GIRL, I'M LOOKIN' FOR MY POPS. CURTIS HUGHES?
THAS' RIGHT, YOU'RE CURTIS' BOY. HE WAS IN EARLIER, SAID TO GIVE YOU THIS.
LEFT A FEW HOURS AGO.
HE DID? SAY WHERE HE WAS GOIN'?

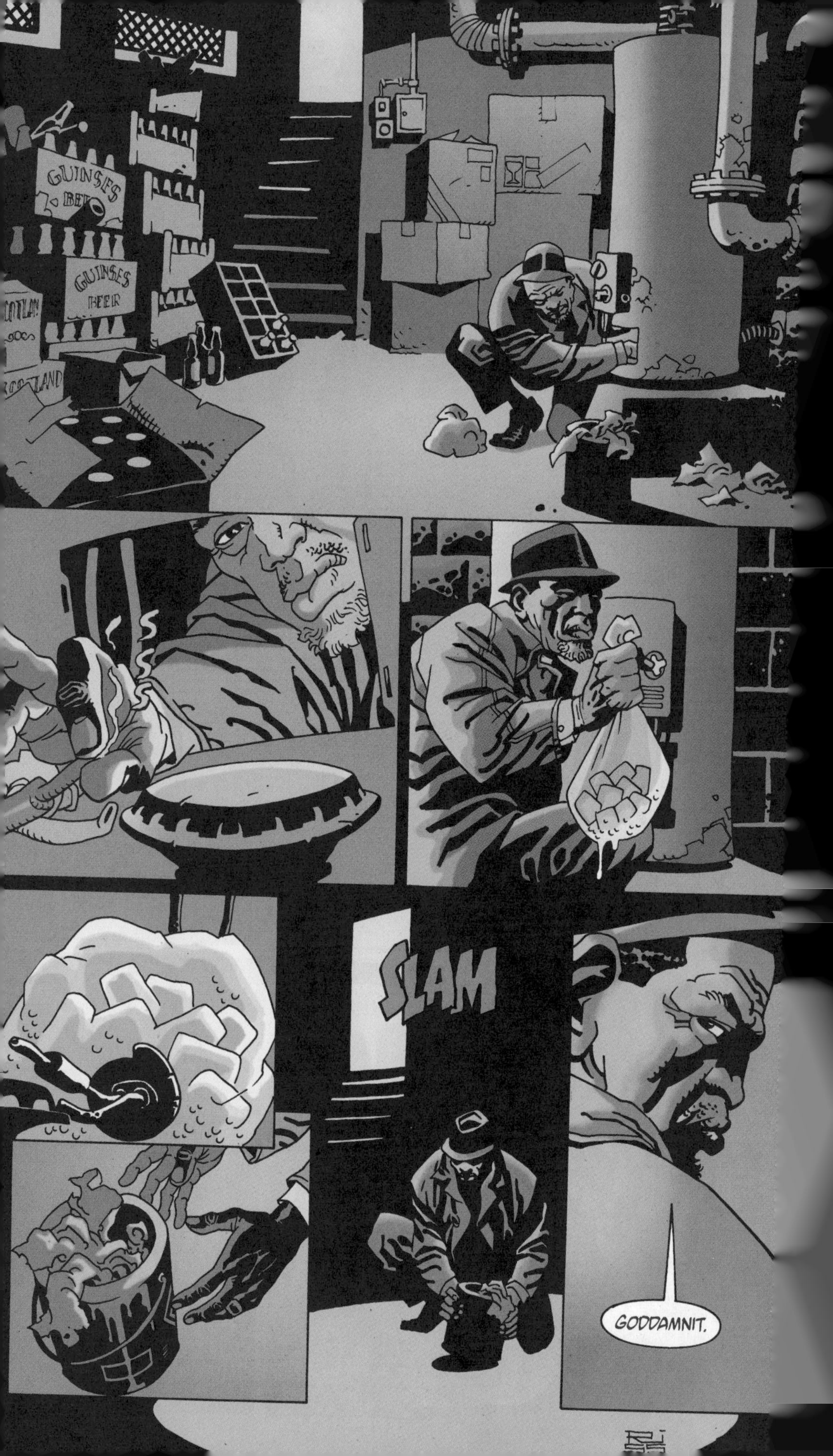
GUINSES BEER
GUINSES BEER
SLAM
GODDAMNIT.

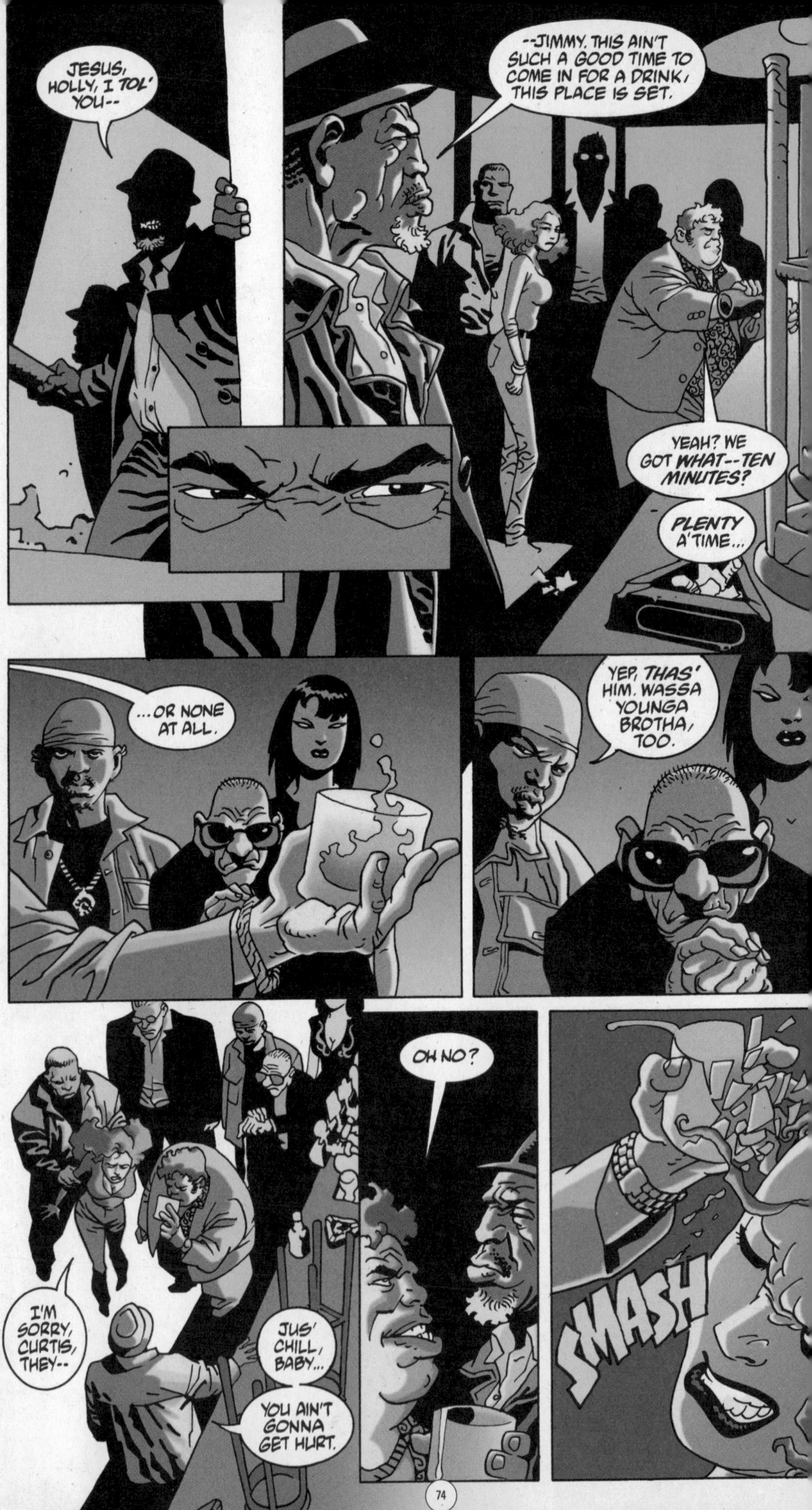

JESUS, HOLLY, I TOL' YOU--
--JIMMY. THIS AIN'T SUCH A GOOD TIME TO COME IN FOR A DRINK, THIS PLACE IS SET.
YEAH? WE GOT WHAT--TEN MINUTES?
PLENTY A'TIME...
...OR NONE AT ALL.
YEP, THAS' HIM. WASSA YOUNGA BROTHA, TOO.
I'M SORRY, CURTIS, THEY--
JUS' CHILL, BABY...
YOU AIN'T GONNA GET HURT.
OH NO?
SMASH

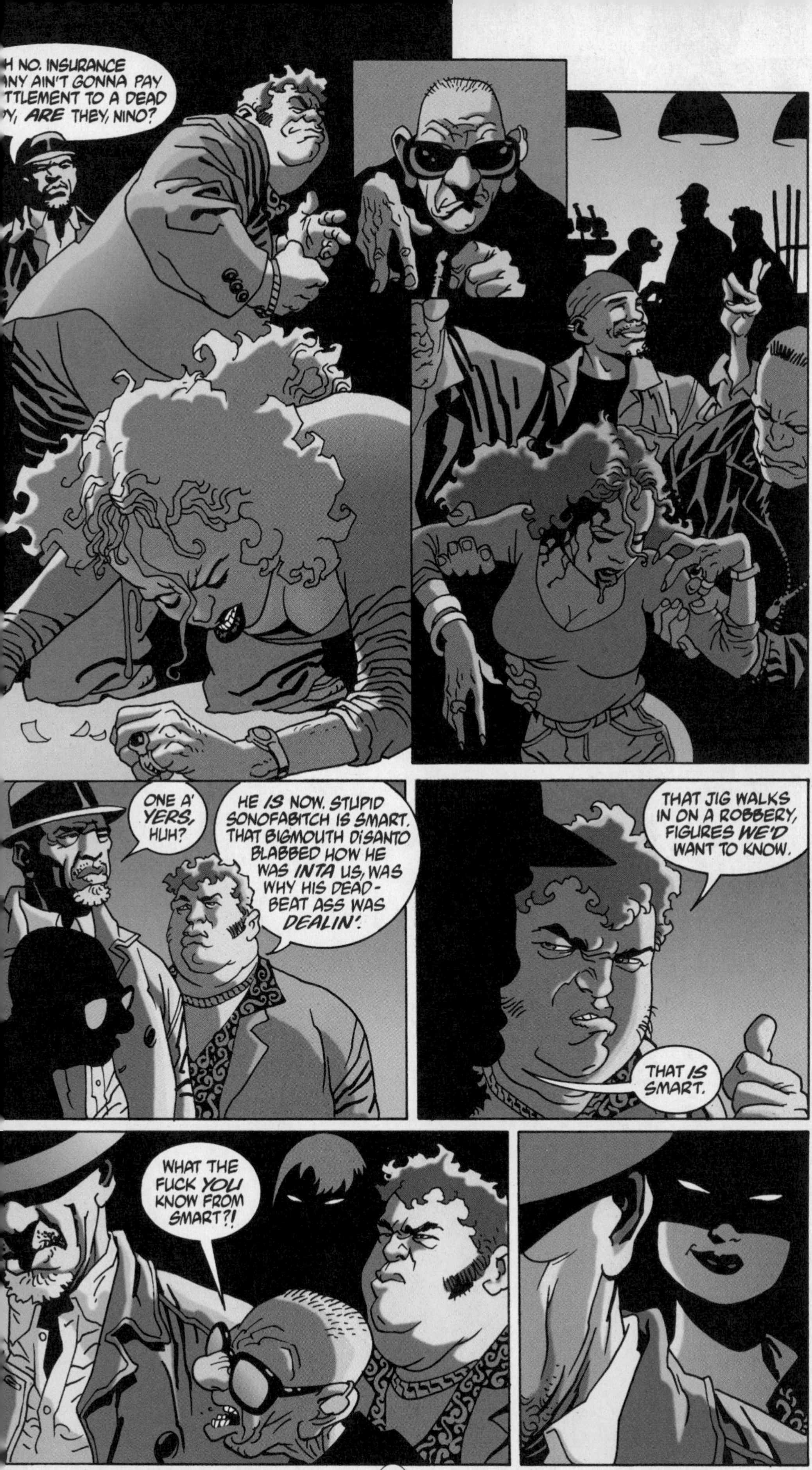
H NO. INSURANCE
NY AIN'T GONNA PAY
TTLEMENT TO A DEAD
Y, ARE THEY, NINO?
ONE A' YERS, HUH?
HE IS NOW. STUPID SONOFABITCH IS SMART. THAT BIGMOUTH DiSANTO BLABBED HOW HE WAS INTA US, WAS WHY HIS DEAD-BEAT ASS WAS DEALIN'.
THAT JIG WALKS IN ON A ROBBERY, FIGURES WE'D WANT TO KNOW.
THAT IS SMART.
WHAT THE FUCK YOU KNOW FROM SMART?!

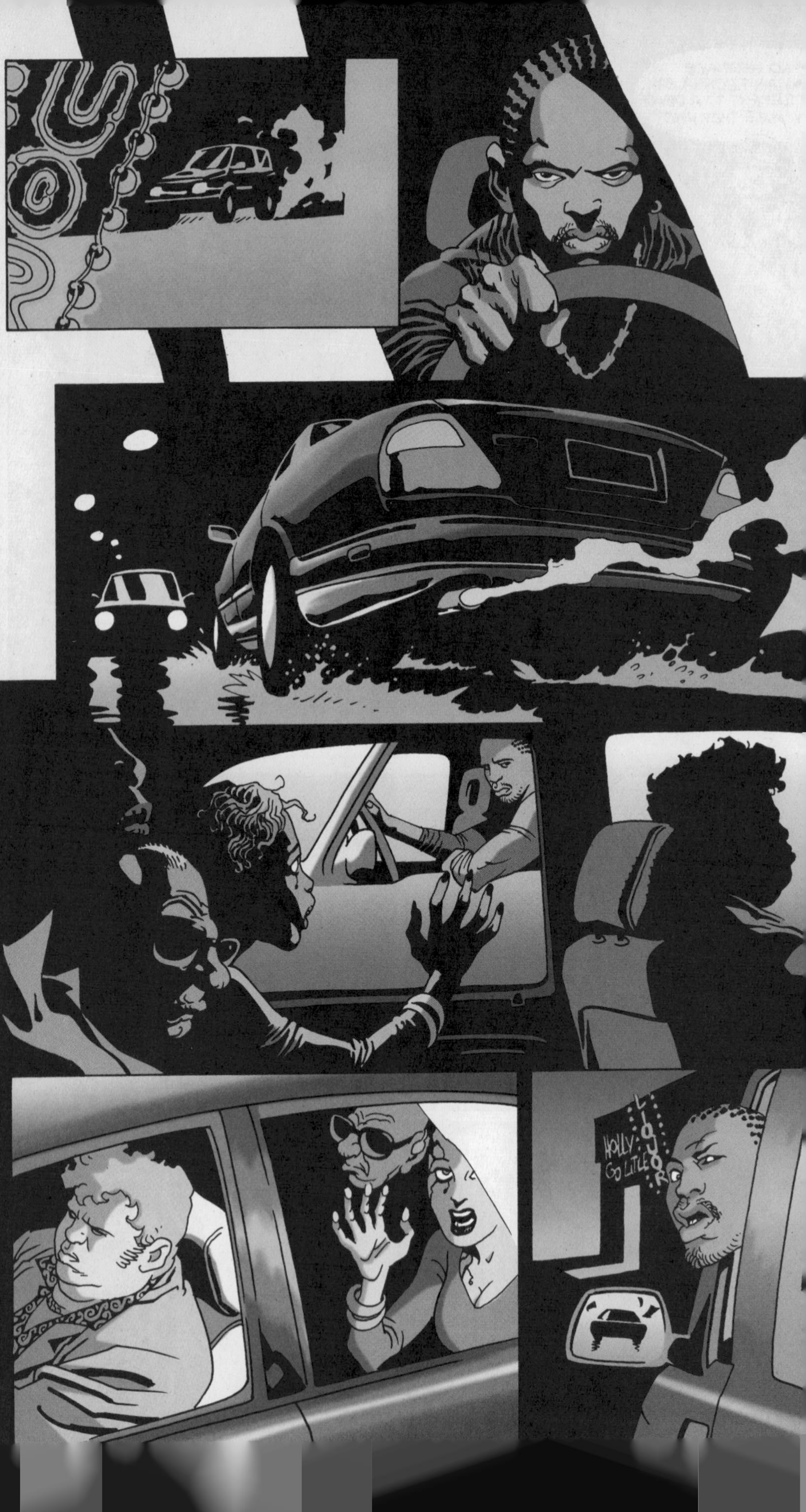
HOLLY GO LITLE
LIQUOR

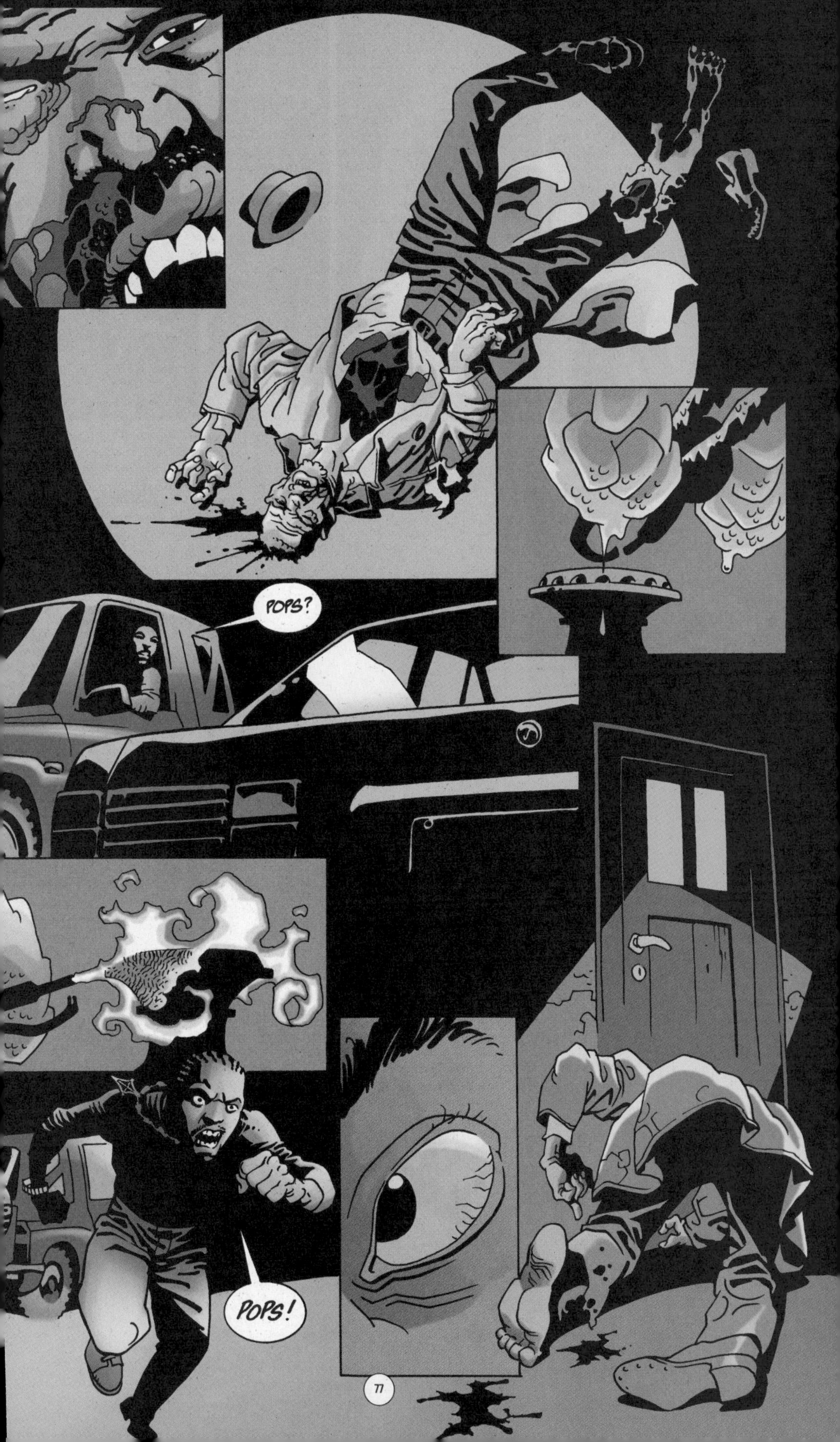
POPS?
POPS!

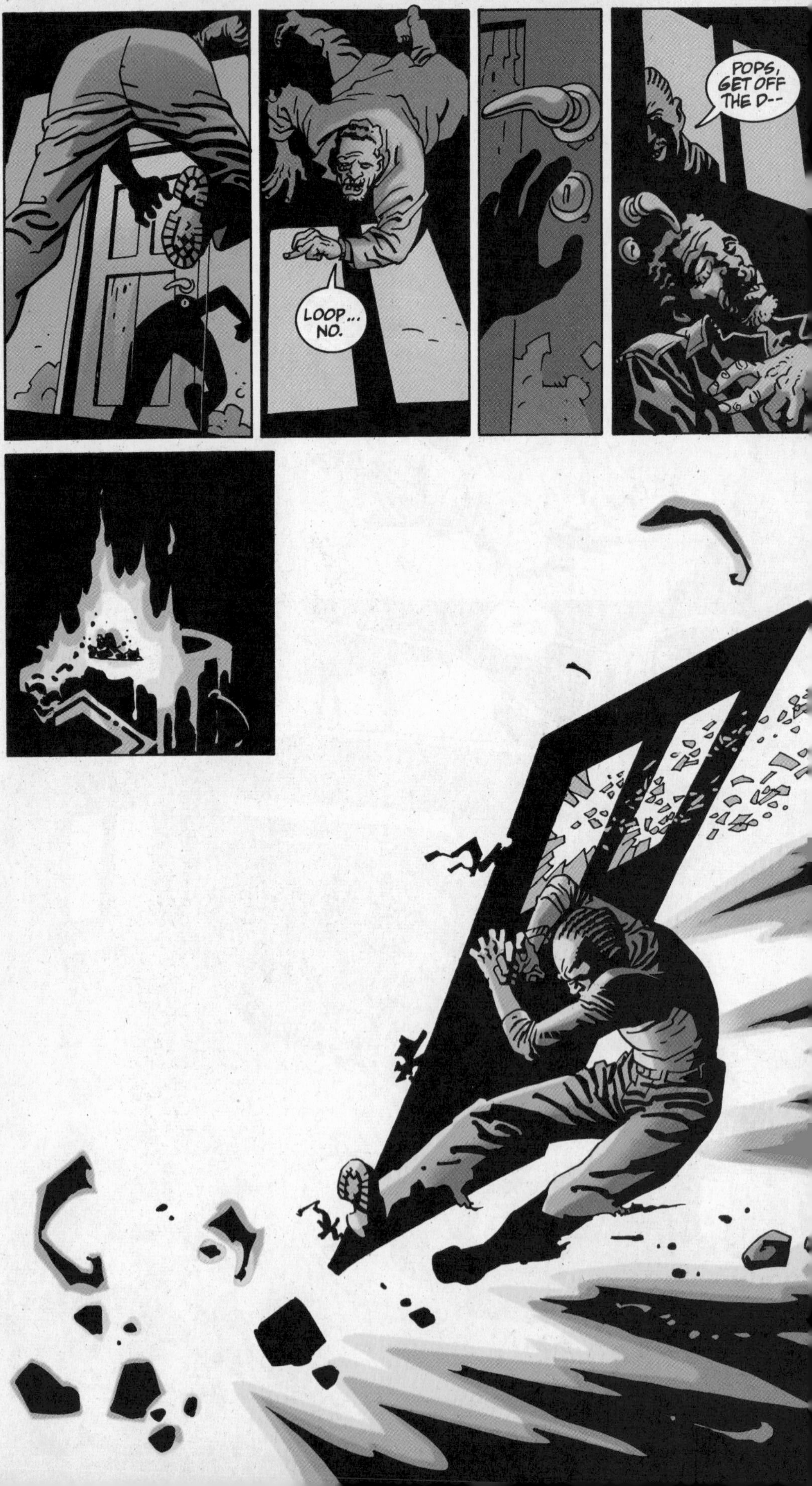
LOOP... NO.
POPS, GET OFF THE D--

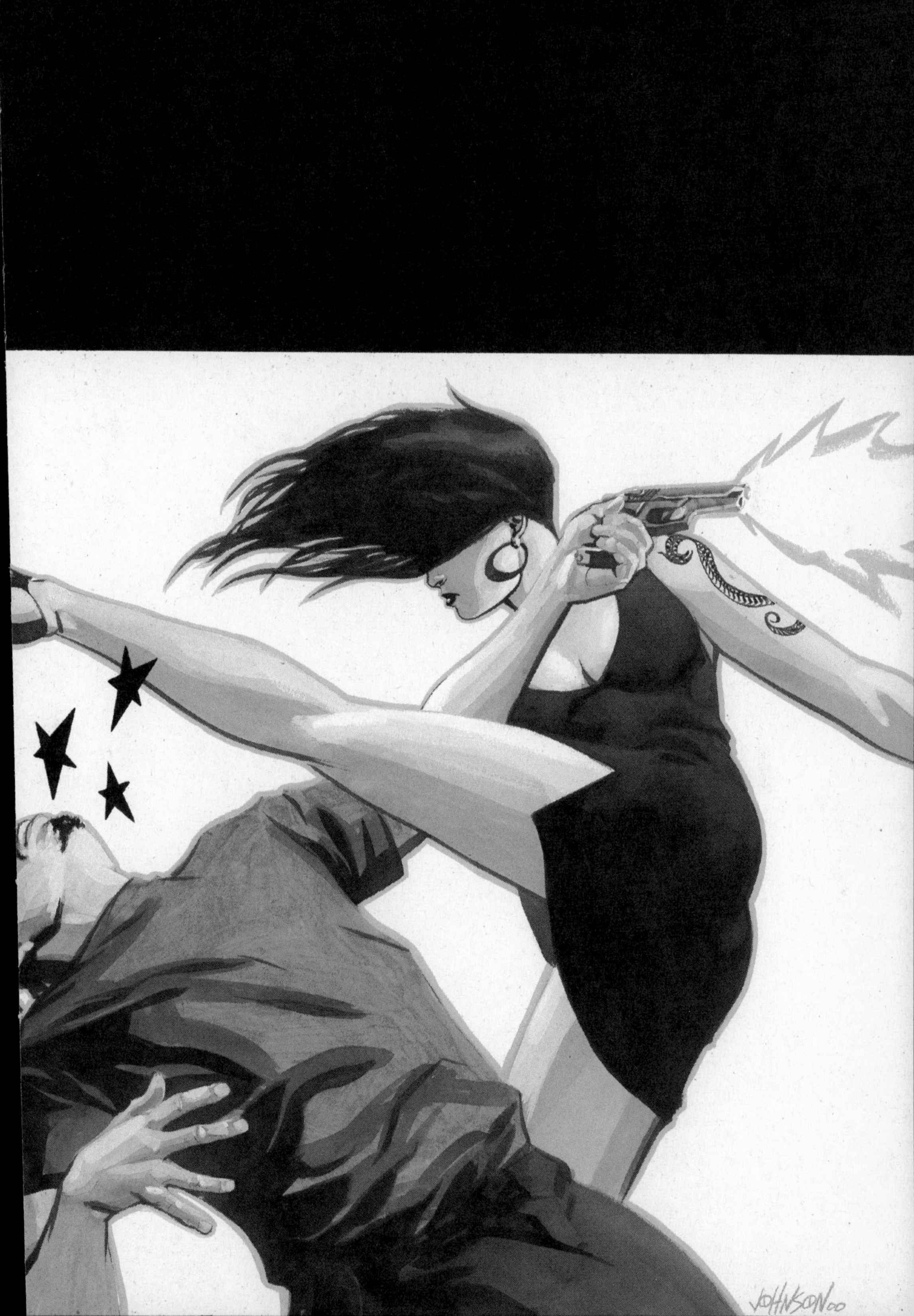
JOHNSON 00

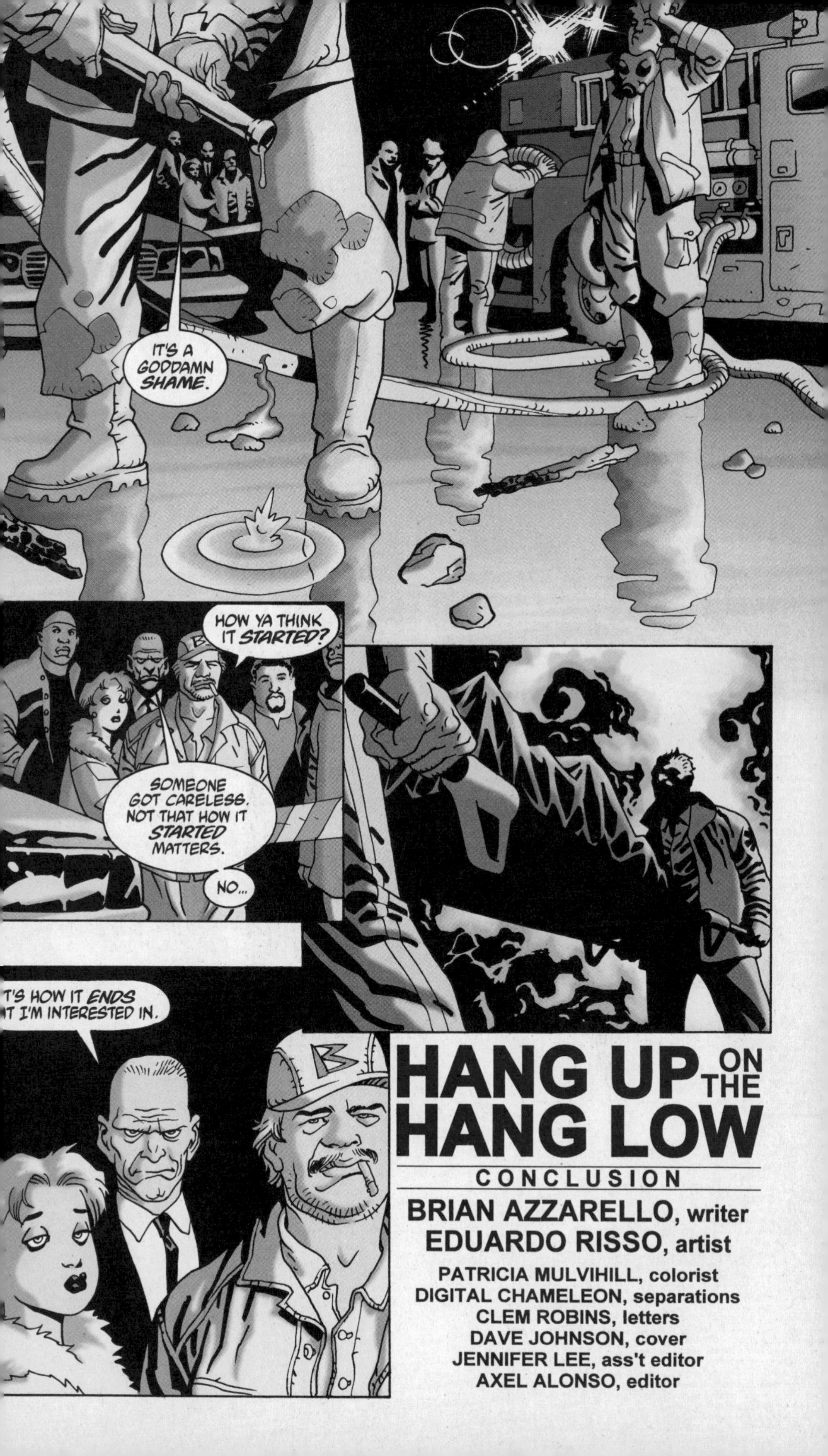
IT'S A GODDAMN SHAME.
HOW YA THINK IT STARTED?
SOMEONE GOT CARELESS. NOT THAT HOW IT STARTED MATTERS.
NO...
T'S HOW IT ENDS
T I'M INTERESTED IN.
HANG UP ON THE HANG LOW
CONCLUSION
BRIAN AZZARELLO, writer
EDUARDO RISSO, artist
PATRICIA MULVIHILL, colorist
DIGITAL CHAMELEON, separations
CLEM ROBINS, letters
DAVE JOHNSON, cover
JENNIFER LEE, ass't editor
AXEL ALONSO, editor

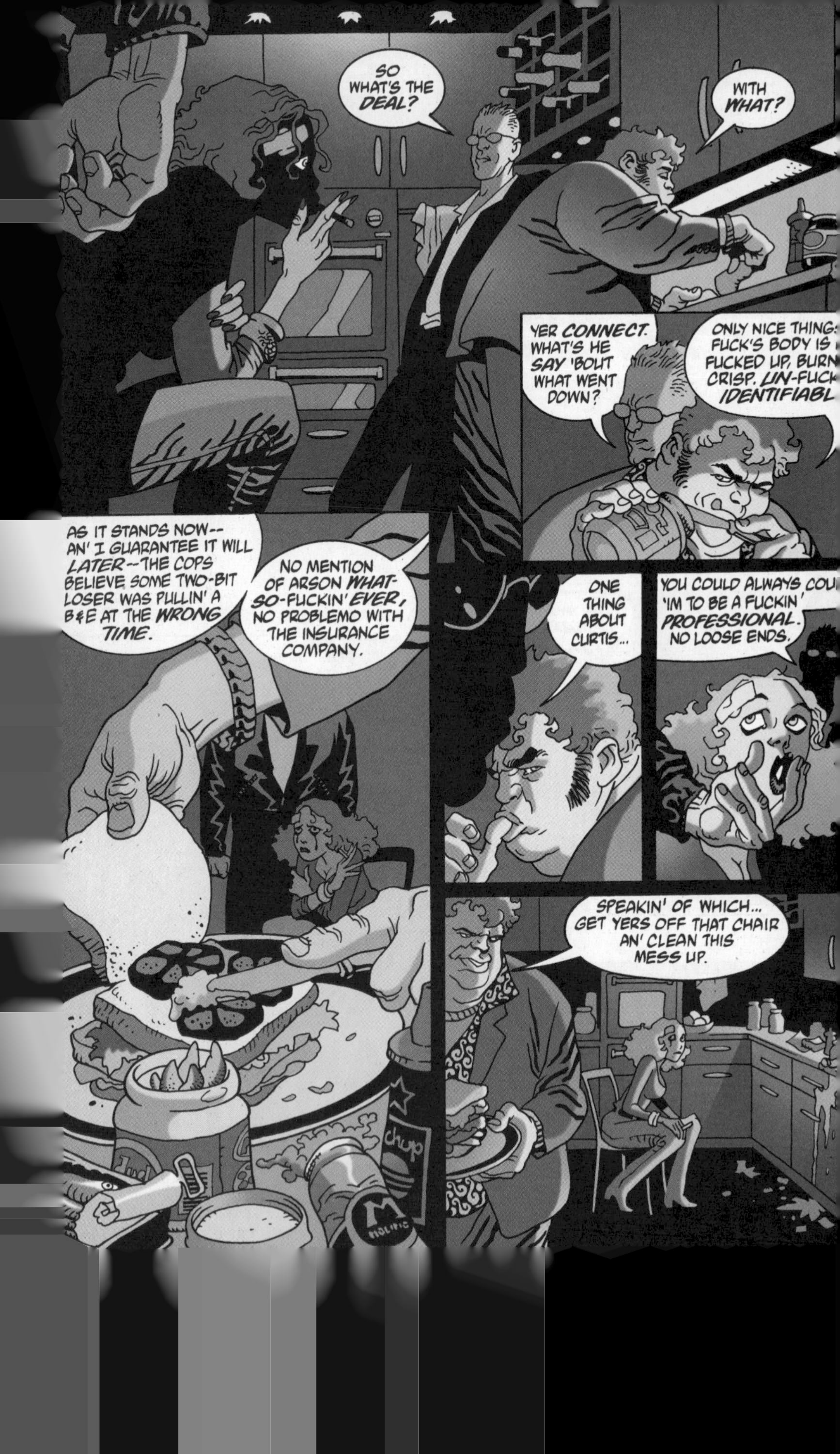

SO WHAT'S THE DEAL?
WITH WHAT?
YER CONNECT. WHAT'S HE SAY 'BOUT WHAT WENT DOWN?
ONLY NICE THING: FUCK'S BODY IS FUCKED UP, BURN CRISP. UN-FUCK IDENTIFIABL
AS IT STANDS NOW-- AN' I GUARANTEE IT WILL LATER--THE COPS BELIEVE SOME TWO-BIT LOSER WAS PULLIN' A B&E AT THE WRONG TIME.
NO MENTION OF ARSON WHAT-SO-FUCKIN' EVER, NO PROBLEMO WITH THE INSURANCE COMPANY.
ONE THING ABOUT CURTIS...
YOU COULD ALWAYS COU 'IM TO BE A FUCKIN' PROFESSIONAL. NO LOOSE ENDS.
SPEAKIN' OF WHICH... GET YERS OFF THAT CHAIR AN' CLEAN THIS MESS UP.

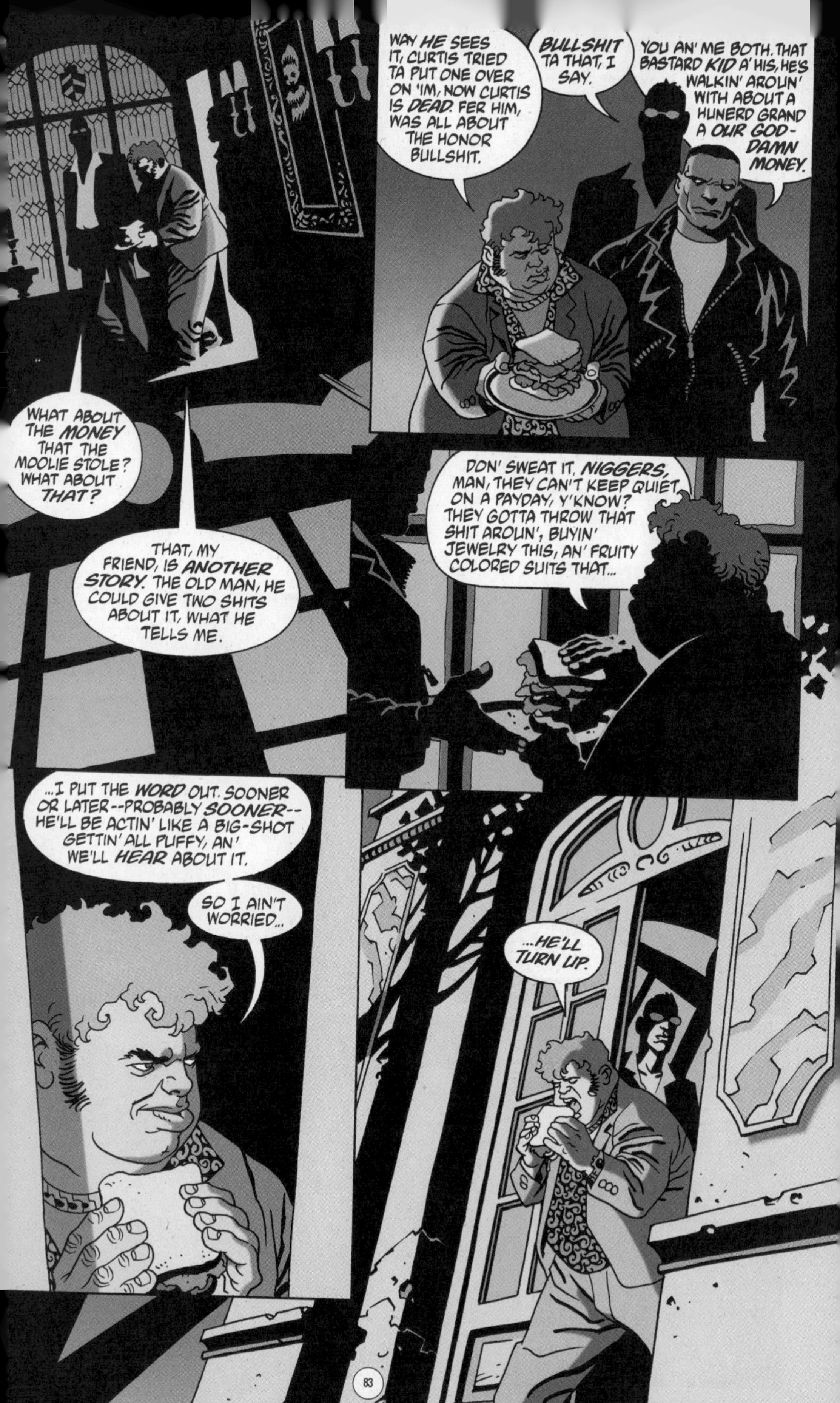
WAY HE SEES IT, CURTIS TRIED TA PUT ONE OVER ON 'IM, NOW CURTIS IS DEAD. FER HIM, WAS ALL ABOUT THE HONOR BULLSHIT.
BULLSHIT TA THAT, I SAY.
YOU AN' ME BOTH. THAT BASTARD KID A' HIS, HE'S WALKIN' AROUN' WITH ABOUT A HUNERD GRAND A OUR GOD-DAMN MONEY.
WHAT ABOUT THE MONEY THAT THE MOOLIE STOLE? WHAT ABOUT THAT?
THAT, MY FRIEND, IS ANOTHER STORY. THE OLD MAN, HE COULD GIVE TWO SHITS ABOUT IT, WHAT HE TELLS ME.
DON' SWEAT IT, NIGGERS, MAN, THEY CAN'T KEEP QUIET ON A PAYDAY, Y'KNOW? THEY GOTTA THROW THAT SHIT AROUN', BUYIN' JEWELRY THIS, AN' FRUITY COLORED SUITS THAT...
...I PUT THE WORD OUT. SOONER OR LATER--PROBABLY SOONER--HE'LL BE ACTIN' LIKE A BIG-SHOT GETTIN' ALL PUFFY, AN' WE'LL HEAR ABOUT IT.
SO I AIN'T WORRIED...
...HE'LL TURN UP.

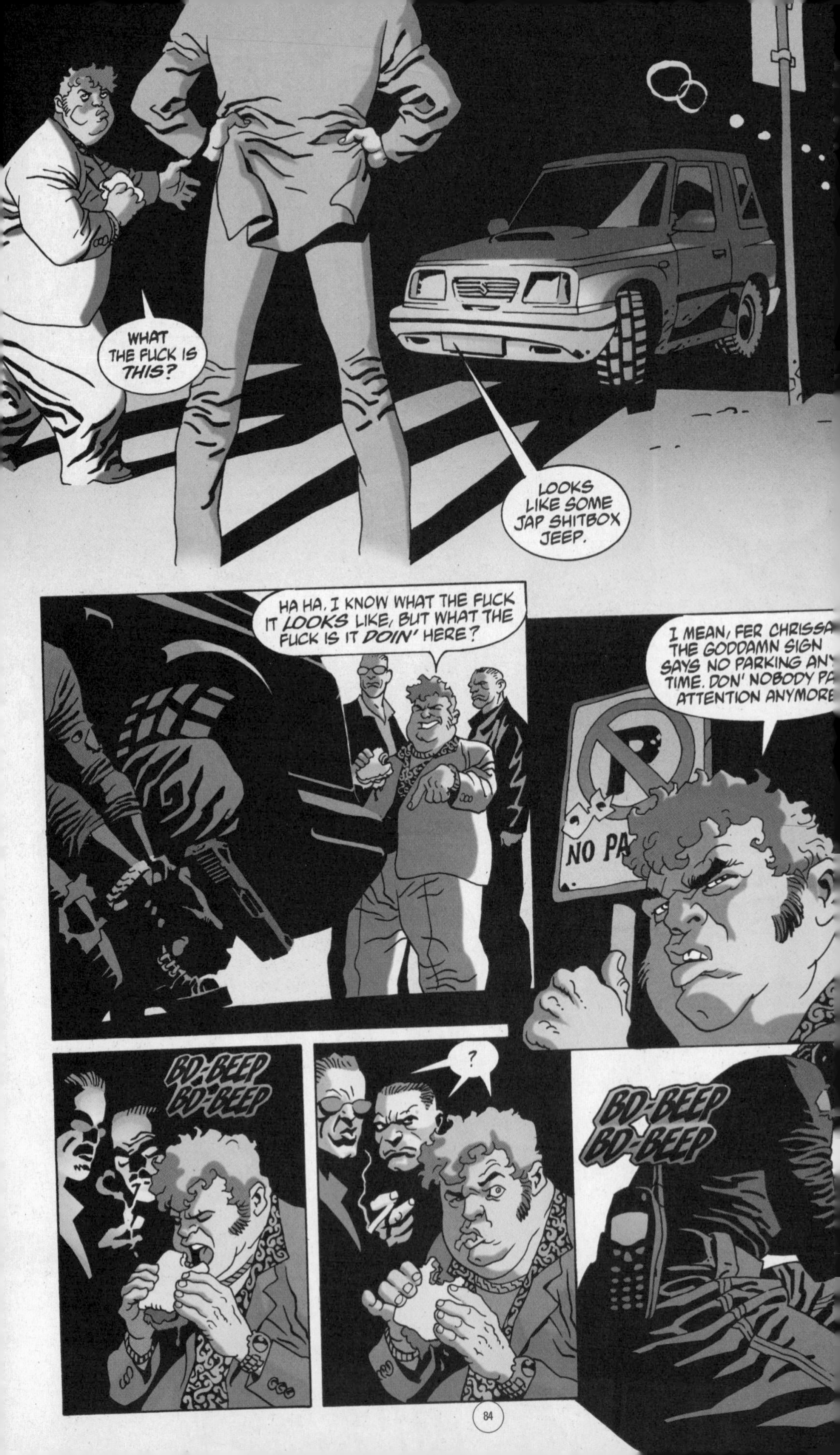

WHAT THE FUCK IS *THIS?*
LOOKS LIKE SOME JAP SHITBOX JEEP.
HA HA, I KNOW WHAT THE FUCK IT *LOOKS* LIKE, BUT WHAT THE FUCK IS IT *DOIN'* HERE?
I MEAN, FER CHRISSA THE GODDAMN SIGN SAYS NO PARKING ANY TIME. DON' NOBODY PA ATTENTION ANYMORE
NO PA
BD-BEEP BD-BEEP
?
BD-BEEP BD-BEEP

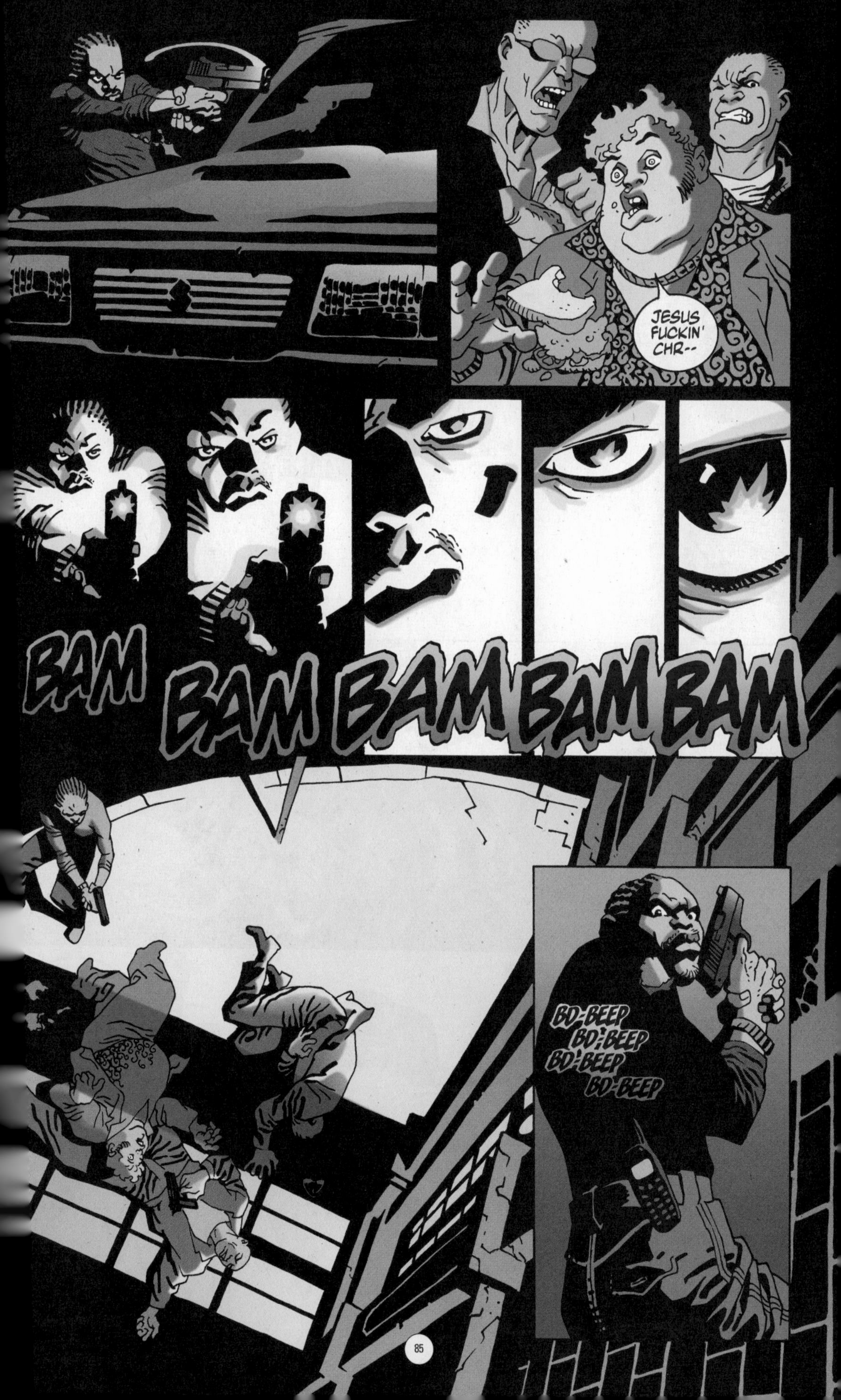
JESUS FUCKIN' CHR--
BAM
BAM BAM BAM BAM
BD-BEEP
BD-BEEP
BD-BEEP
BD-BEEP

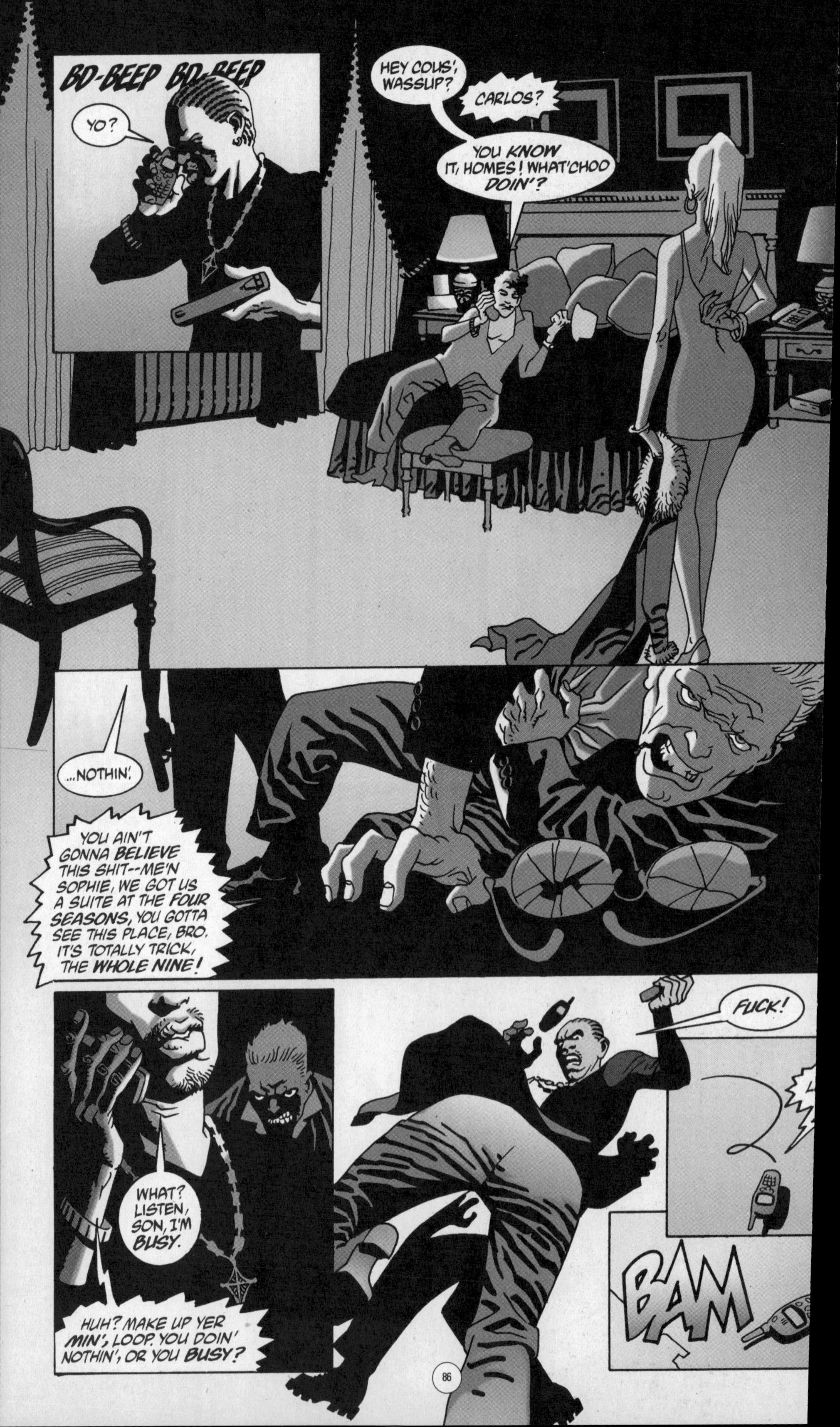
BD-BEEP BD-BEEP
YO?
HEY COUS', WASSUP?
CARLOS?
YOU KNOW IT, HOMES! WHAT'CHOO DOIN'?
...NOTHIN'.
YOU AIN'T GONNA BELIEVE THIS SHIT--ME'N SOPHIE, WE GOT US A SUITE AT THE FOUR SEASONS, YOU GOTTA SEE THIS PLACE, BRO. IT'S TOTALLY TRICK, THE WHOLE NINE!
WHAT? LISTEN, SON, I'M BUSY.
HUH? MAKE UP YER MIN', LOOP. YOU DOIN' NOTHIN', OR YOU BUSY?
FUCK!
BAM

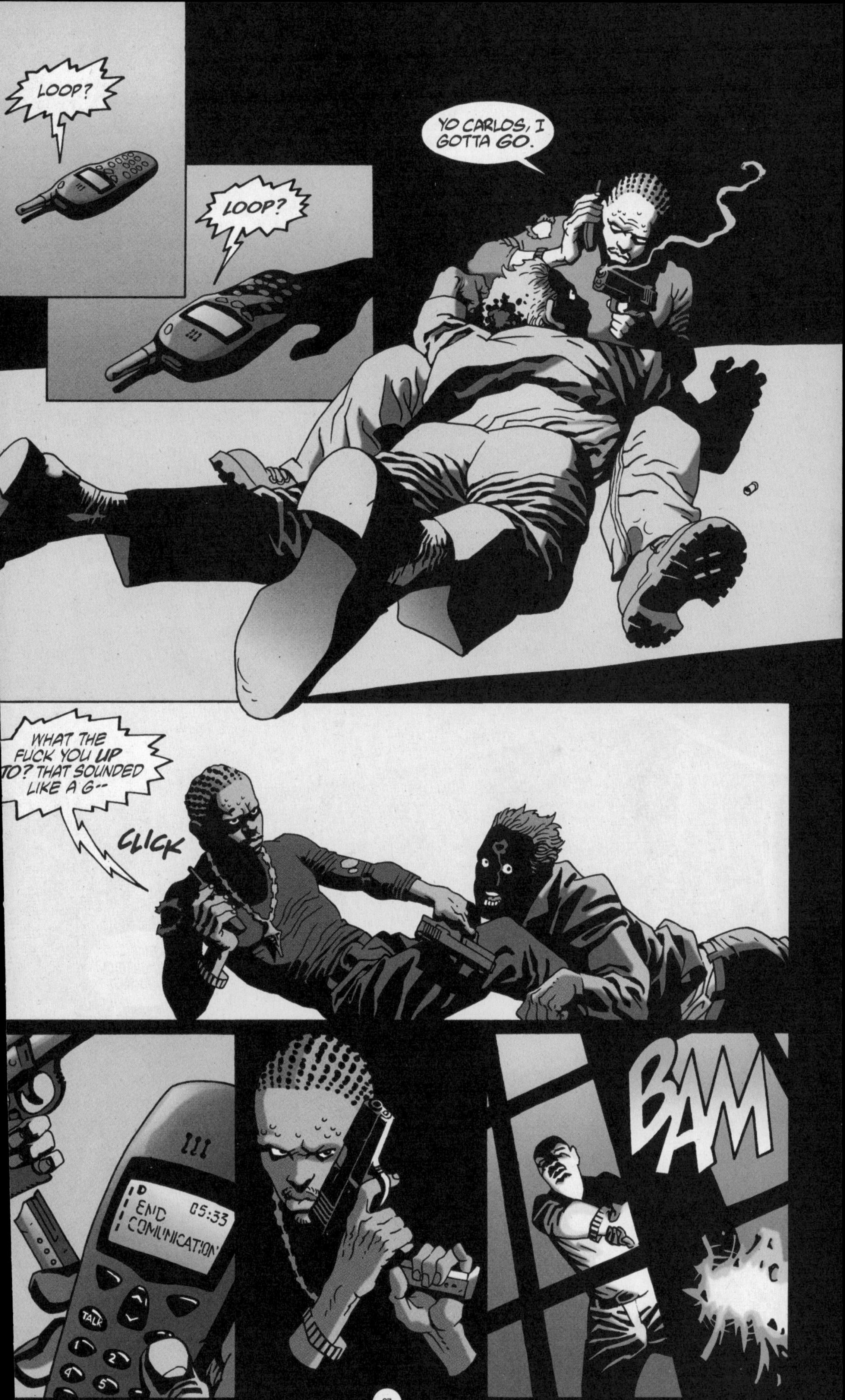
LOOP?
LOOP?
YO CARLOS, I GOTTA GO.
WHAT THE FUCK YOU UP TO? THAT SOUNDED LIKE A G--
CLICK
END 05:33
COMUNICATION
TALK
BAM

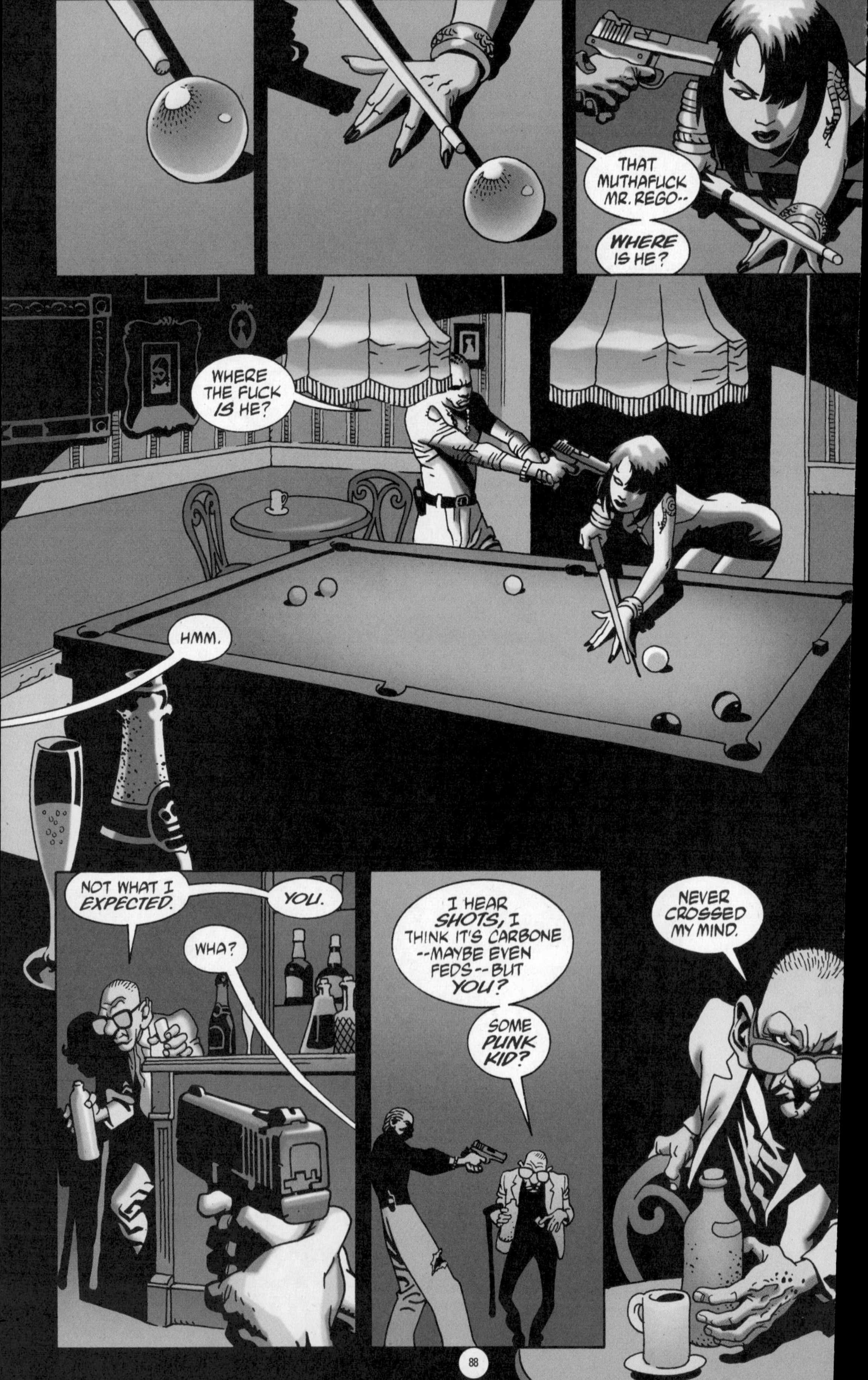
THAT MUTHAFUCK MR. REGO--
WHERE IS HE?
WHERE THE FUCK IS HE?
HMM.
NOT WHAT I EXPECTED.
YOU.
WHA?
I HEAR SHOTS, I THINK IT'S CARBONE --MAYBE EVEN FEDS--BUT YOU?
SOME PUNK KID?
NEVER CROSSED MY MIND.

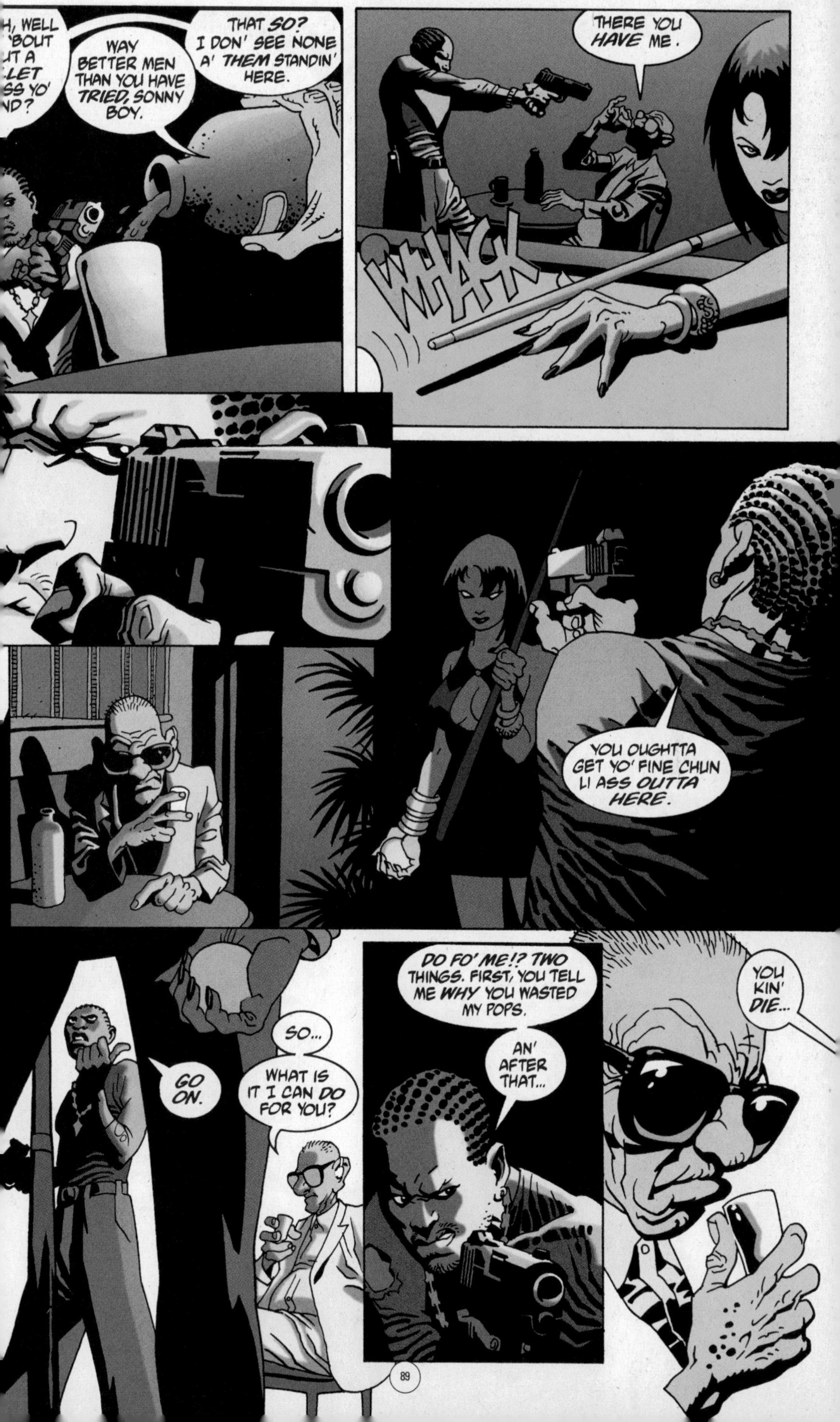
WAY BETTER MEN THAN YOU HAVE TRIED, SONNY BOY.
THAT SO? I DON' SEE NONE A' THEM STANDIN' HERE.
THERE YOU HAVE ME.
WHACK
YOU OUGHTTA GET YO' FINE CHUN LI ASS OUTTA HERE.
GO ON.
SO...
WHAT IS IT I CAN DO FOR YOU?
DO FO' ME!? TWO THINGS. FIRST, YOU TELL ME WHY YOU WASTED MY POPS.
AN' AFTER THAT...
YOU KIN' DIE...

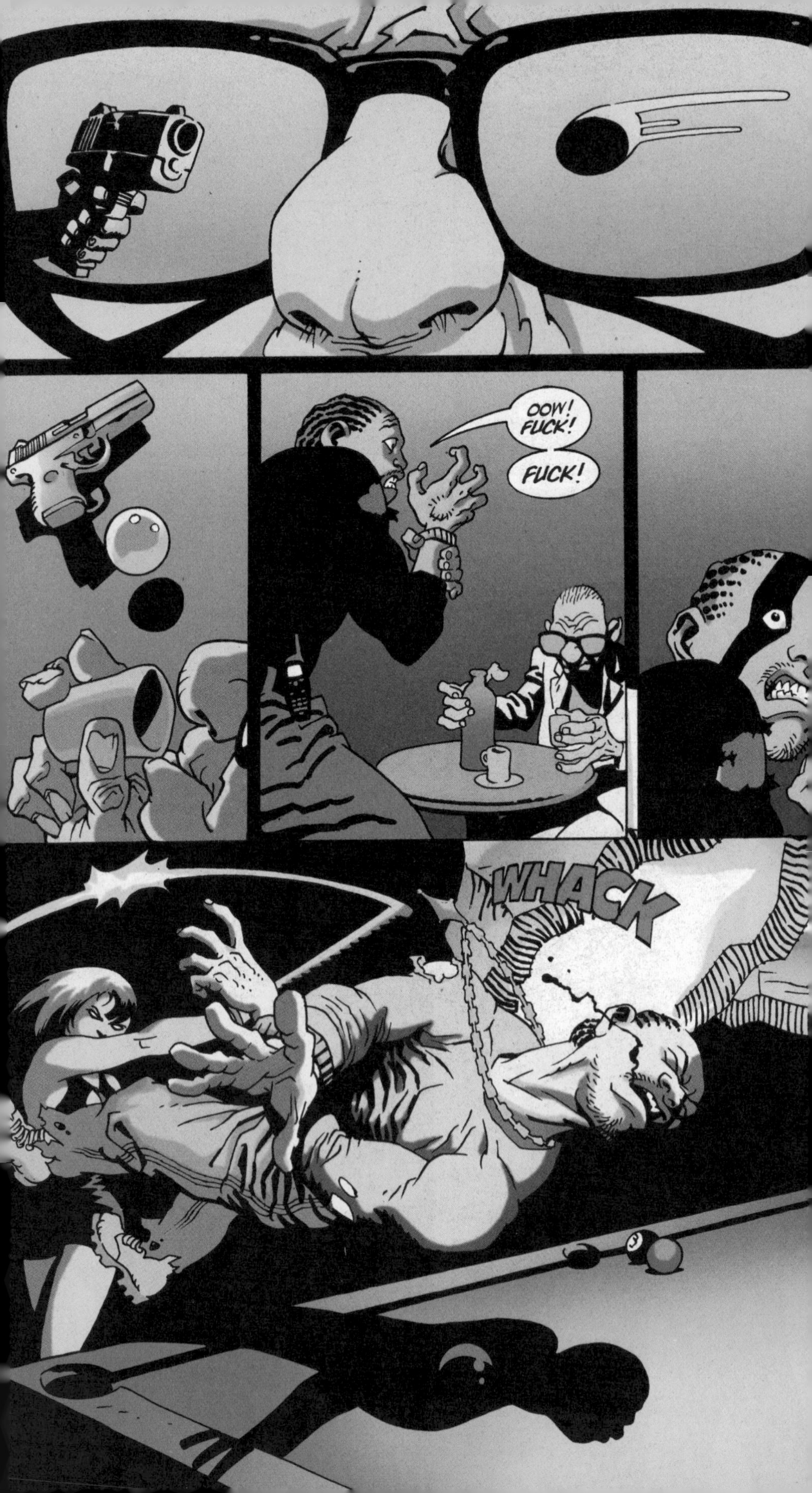
OOW! FUCK!
FUCK!
WHACK

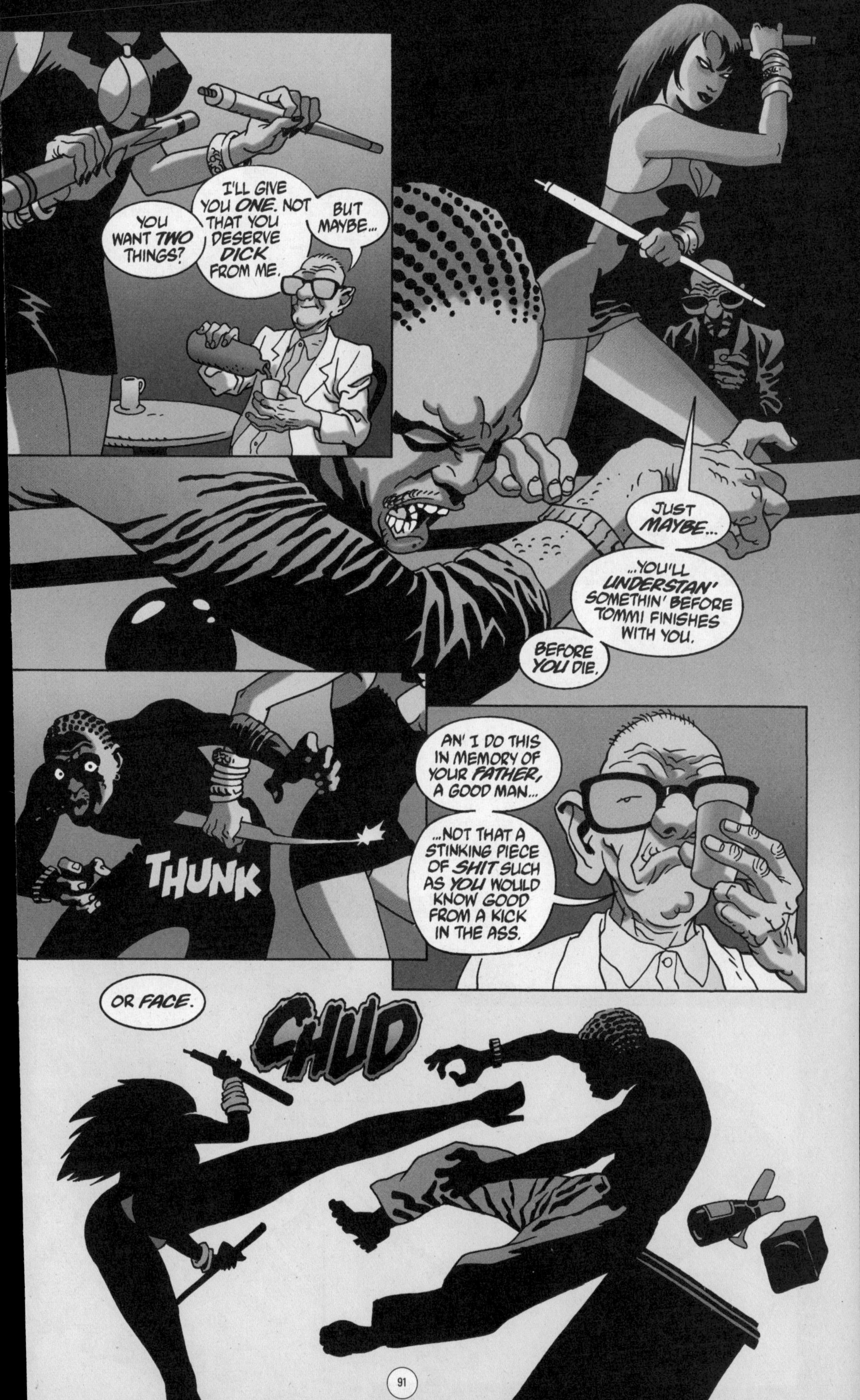

YOU WANT TWO THINGS?
I'LL GIVE YOU ONE. NOT THAT YOU DESERVE DICK FROM ME.
BUT MAYBE...
JUST MAYBE...
...YOU'LL UNDERSTAN' SOMETHIN' BEFORE TOMMI FINISHES WITH YOU.
BEFORE YOU DIE.
THUNK
AN' I DO THIS IN MEMORY OF YOUR FATHER, A GOOD MAN...
...NOT THAT A STINKING PIECE OF SHIT SUCH AS YOU WOULD KNOW GOOD FROM A KICK IN THE ASS.
OR FACE.
CHUD

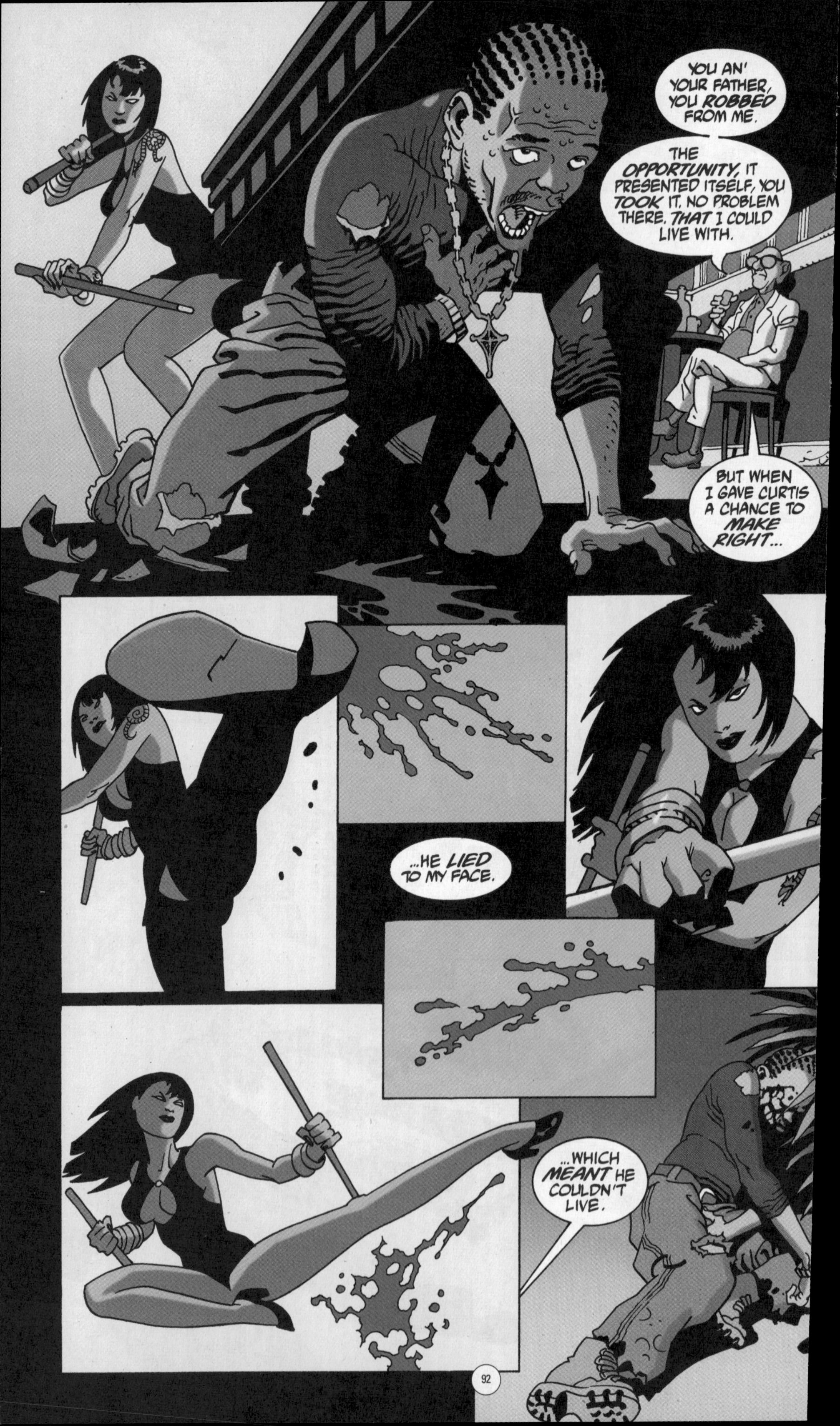
YOU AN' YOUR FATHER, YOU ROBBED FROM ME.
THE OPPORTUNITY, IT PRESENTED ITSELF, YOU TOOK IT. NO PROBLEM THERE. THAT I COULD LIVE WITH.
BUT WHEN I GAVE CURTIS A CHANCE TO MAKE RIGHT...
...HE LIED TO MY FACE.
...WHICH MEANT HE COULDN'T LIVE.

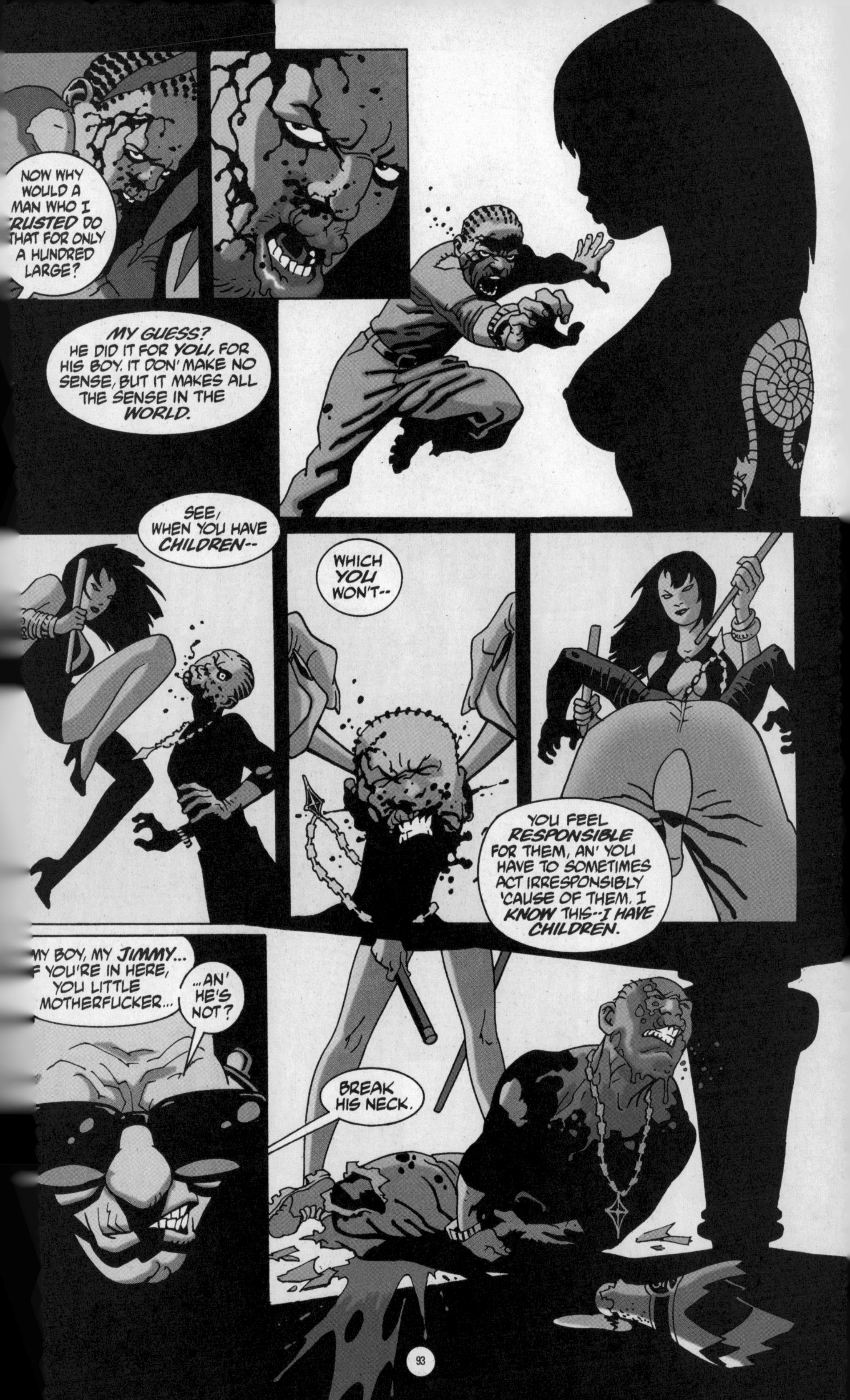

NOW WHY WOULD A MAN WHO I TRUSTED DO THAT FOR ONLY A HUNDRED LARGE?
MY GUESS? HE DID IT FOR YOU, FOR HIS BOY. IT DON' MAKE NO SENSE, BUT IT MAKES ALL THE SENSE IN THE WORLD.
SEE, WHEN YOU HAVE CHILDREN--
WHICH YOU WON'T--
YOU FEEL RESPONSIBLE FOR THEM, AN' YOU HAVE TO SOMETIMES ACT IRRESPONSIBLY 'CAUSE OF THEM. I KNOW THIS--I HAVE CHILDREN.
MY BOY, MY JIMMY... IF YOU'RE IN HERE, YOU LITTLE MOTHERFUCKER...
...AN' HE'S NOT?
BREAK HIS NECK.

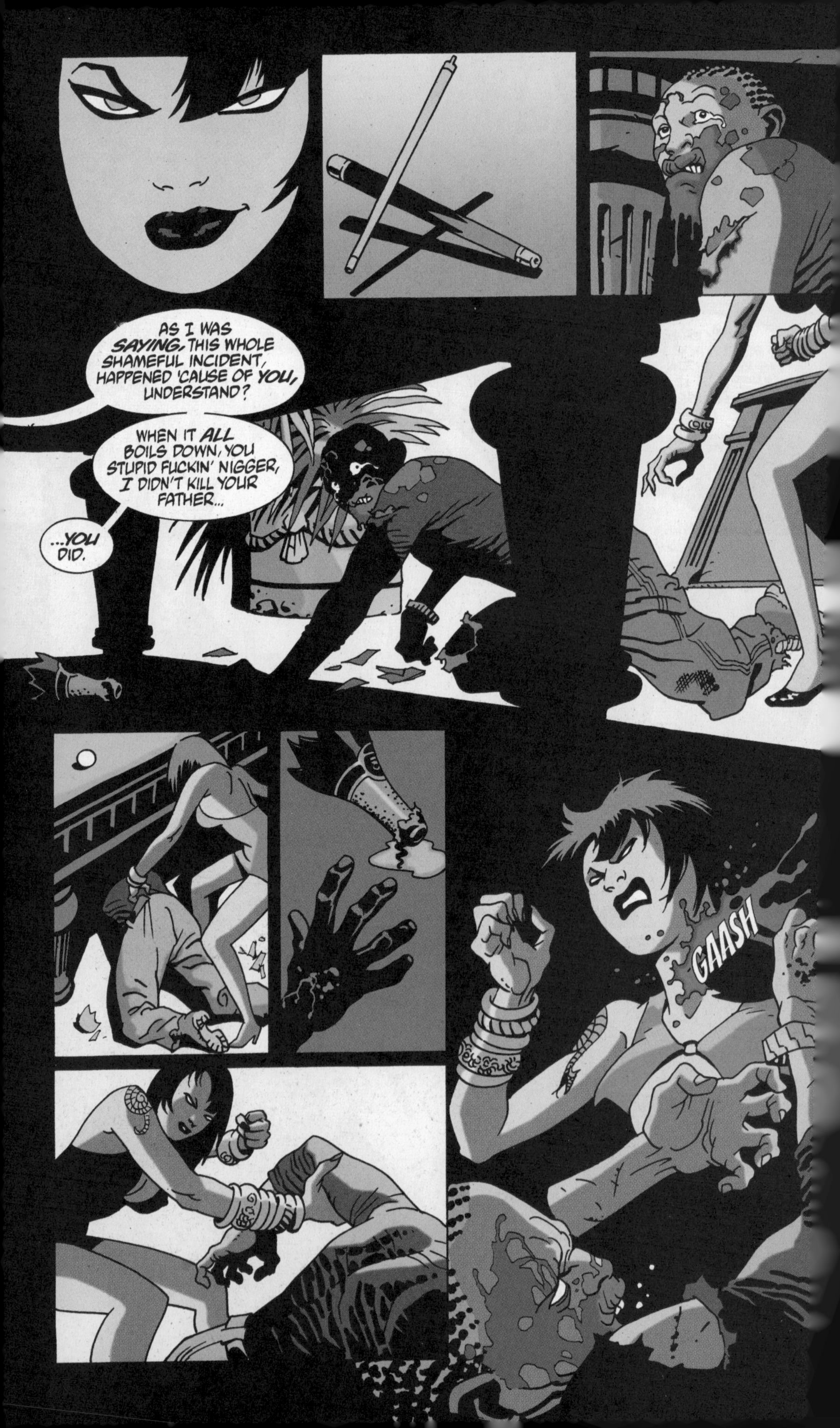
AS I WAS SAYING, THIS WHOLE SHAMEFUL INCIDENT, HAPPENED 'CAUSE OF YOU, UNDERSTAND?
WHEN IT ALL BOILS DOWN, YOU STUPID FUCKIN' NIGGER, I DIDN'T KILL YOUR FATHER...
...YOU DID.
GAASH

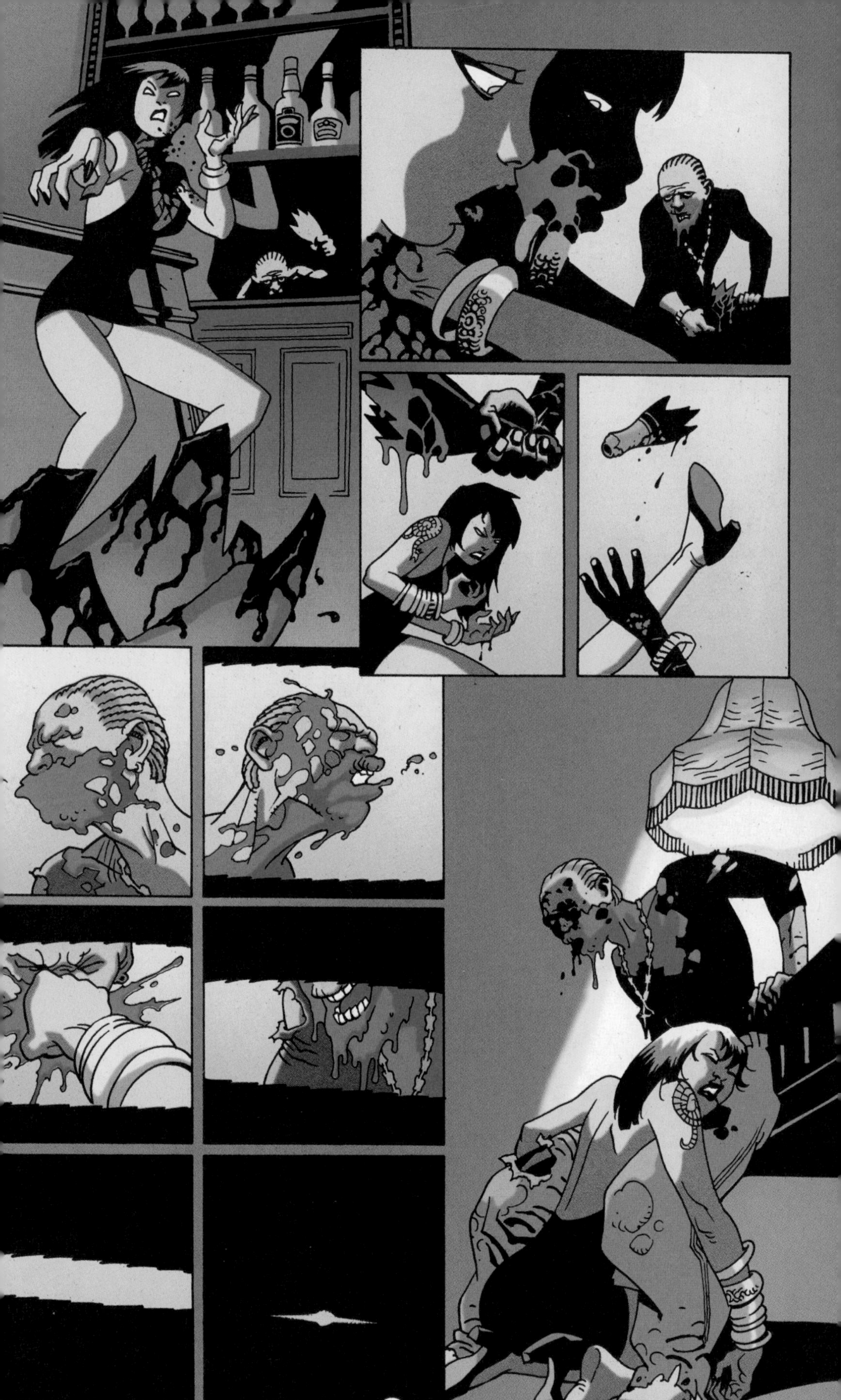

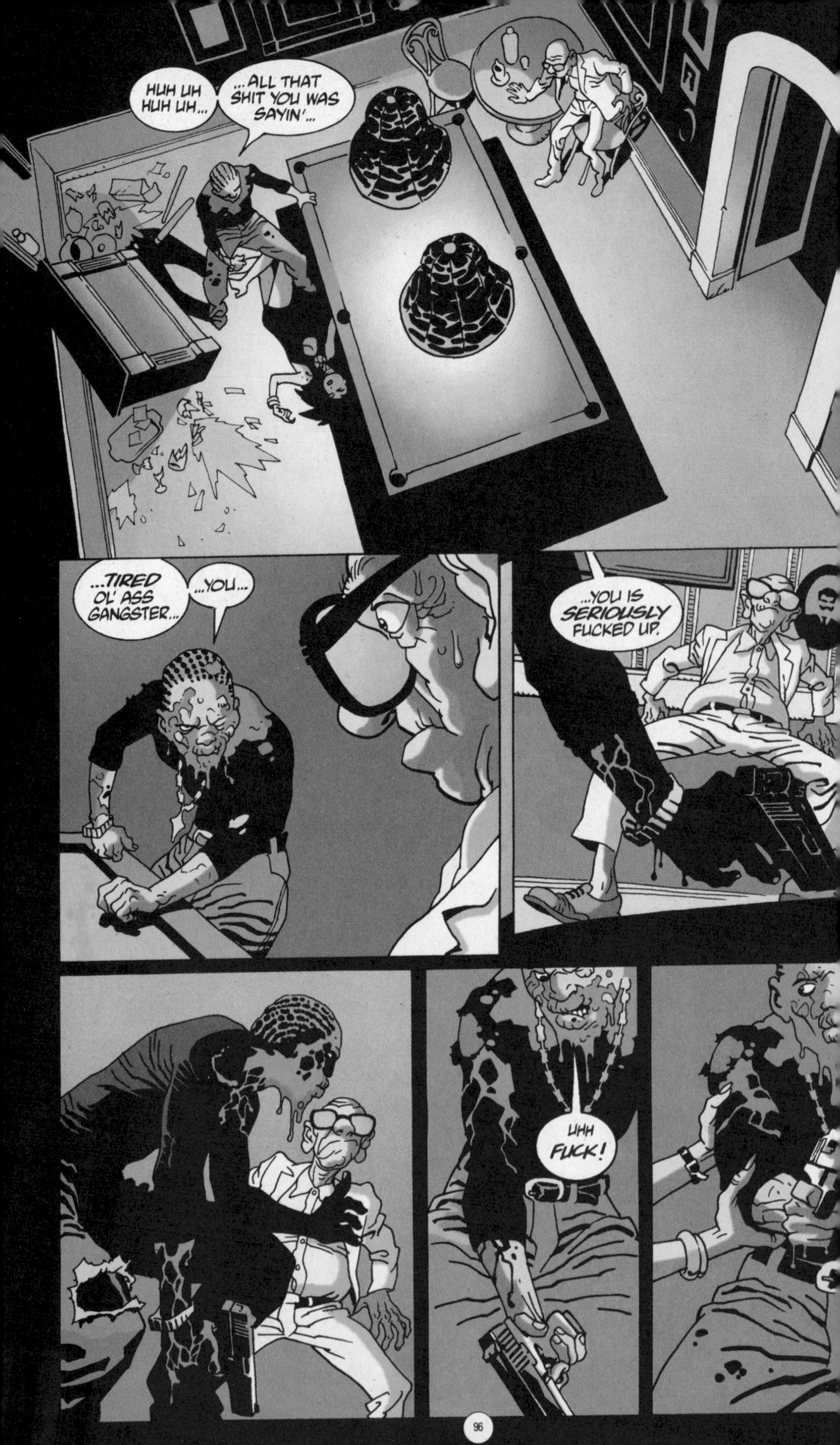
HUH UH HUH UH...
...ALL THAT SHIT YOU WAS SAYIN'...
...TIRED OL' ASS GANGSTER...
...YOU...
...YOU IS SERIOUSLY FUCKED UP.
UHH FUCK!

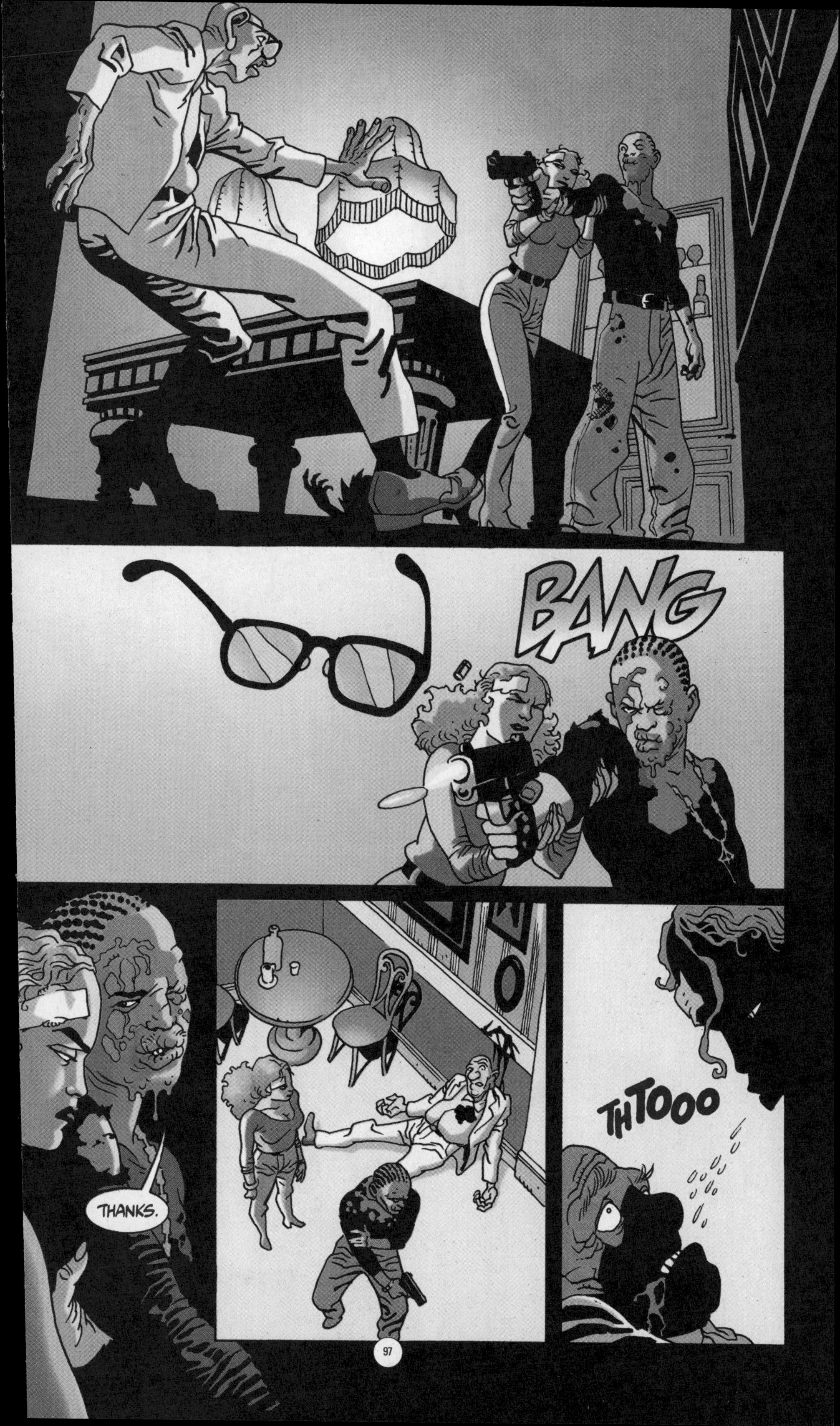
BANG
THANKS.
THTOOO

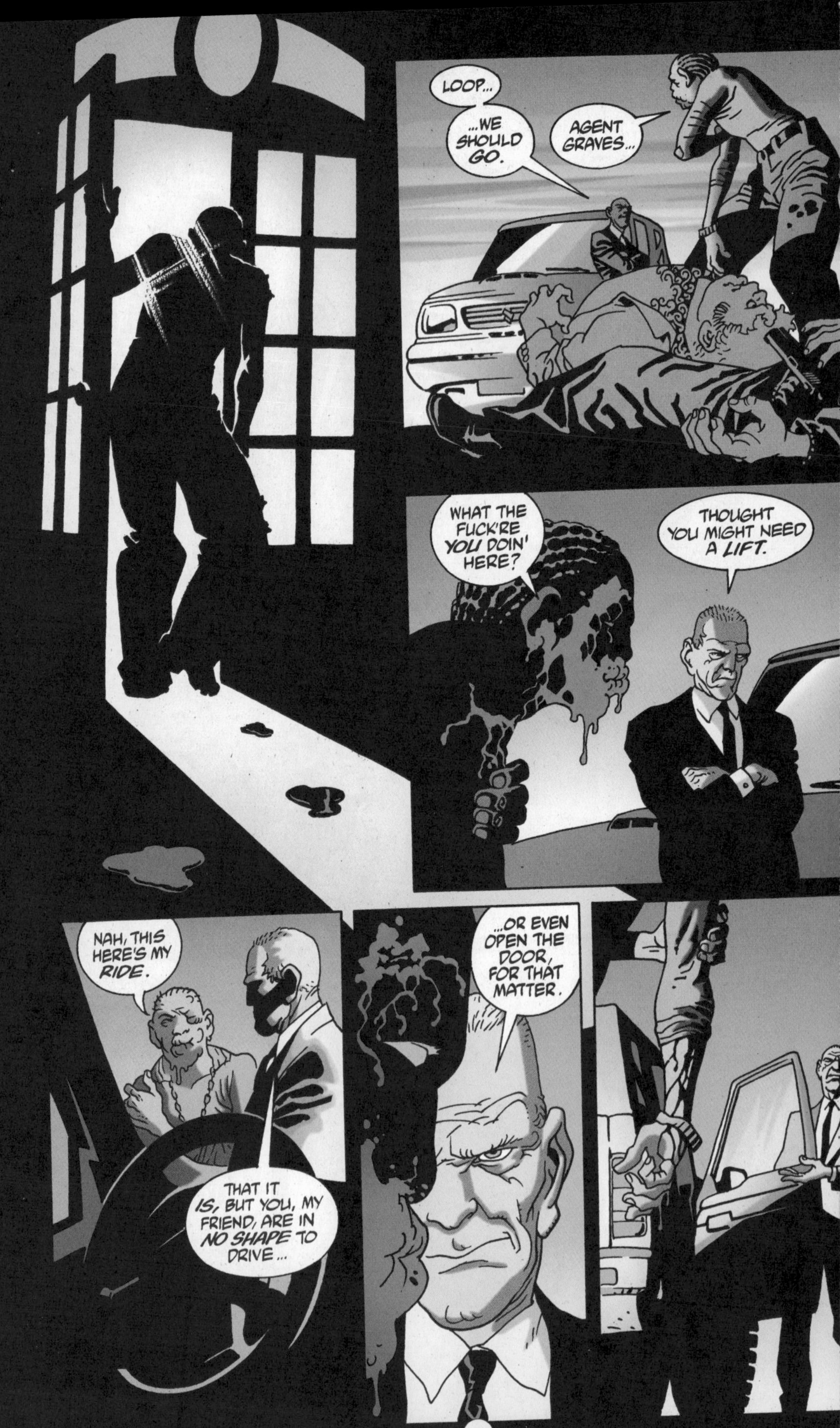

LOOP...
...WE SHOULD GO.
AGENT GRAVES...
WHAT THE FUCK'RE YOU DOIN' HERE?
THOUGHT YOU MIGHT NEED A LIFT.
NAH, THIS HERE'S MY RIDE.
THAT IT IS, BUT YOU, MY FRIEND, ARE IN NO SHAPE TO DRIVE...
...OR EVEN OPEN THE DOOR, FOR THAT MATTER.

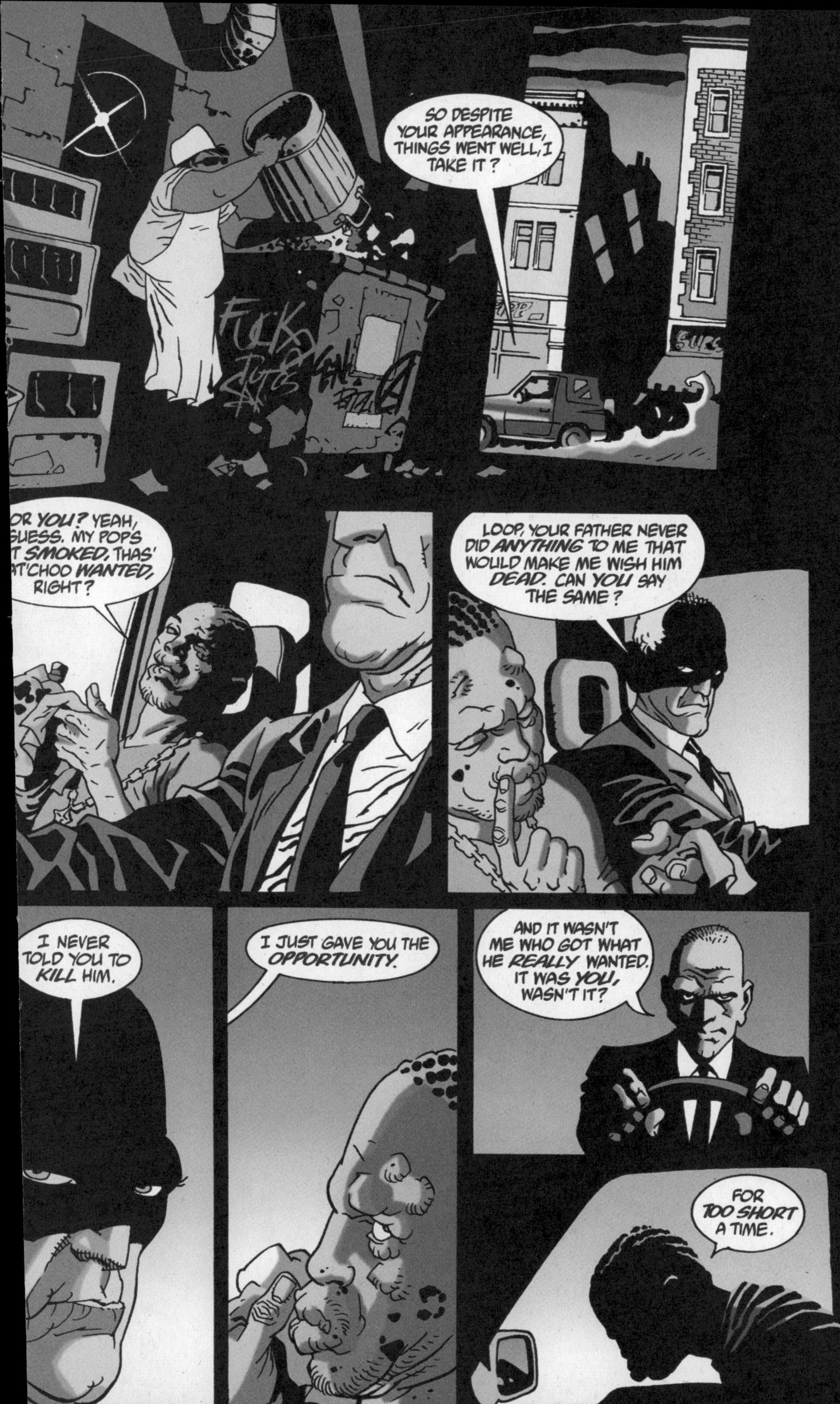
SO DESPITE YOUR APPEARANCE, THINGS WENT WELL, I TAKE IT?
OR YOU? YEAH, UESS. MY POP'S T SMOKED. THAS' AT'CHOO WANTED, RIGHT?
LOOP, YOUR FATHER NEVER DID ANYTHING TO ME THAT WOULD MAKE ME WISH HIM DEAD. CAN YOU SAY THE SAME?
I NEVER TOLD YOU TO KILL HIM.
I JUST GAVE YOU THE OPPORTUNITY.
AND IT WASN'T ME WHO GOT WHAT HE REALLY WANTED. IT WAS YOU, WASN'T IT?
FOR TOO SHORT A TIME.

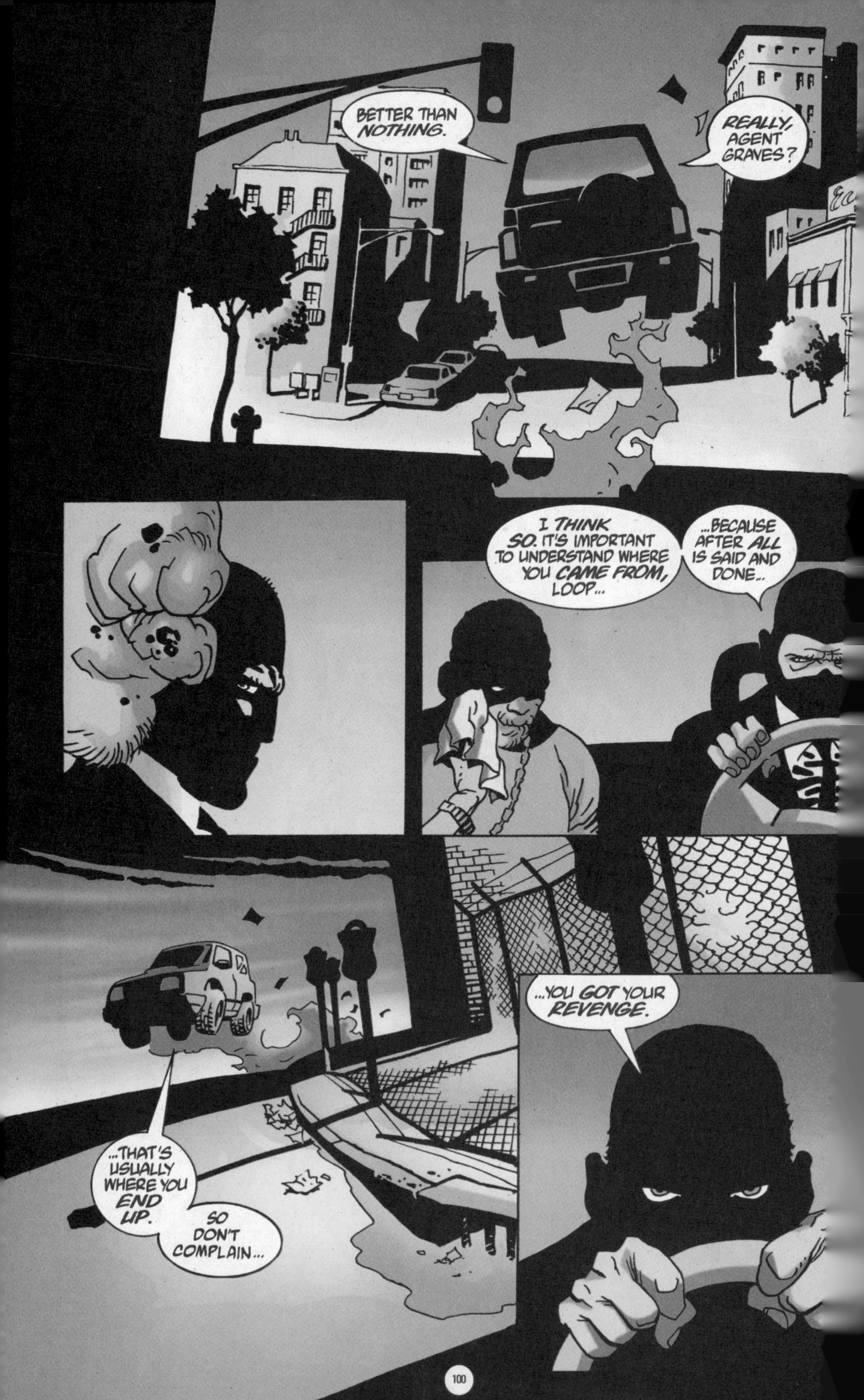

BETTER THAN NOTHING.
REALLY, AGENT GRAVES?
I THINK SO. IT'S IMPORTANT TO UNDERSTAND WHERE YOU CAME FROM, LOOP...
...BECAUSE AFTER ALL IS SAID AND DONE...
...THAT'S USUALLY WHERE YOU END UP.
SO DON'T COMPLAIN...
...YOU GOT YOUR REVENGE.

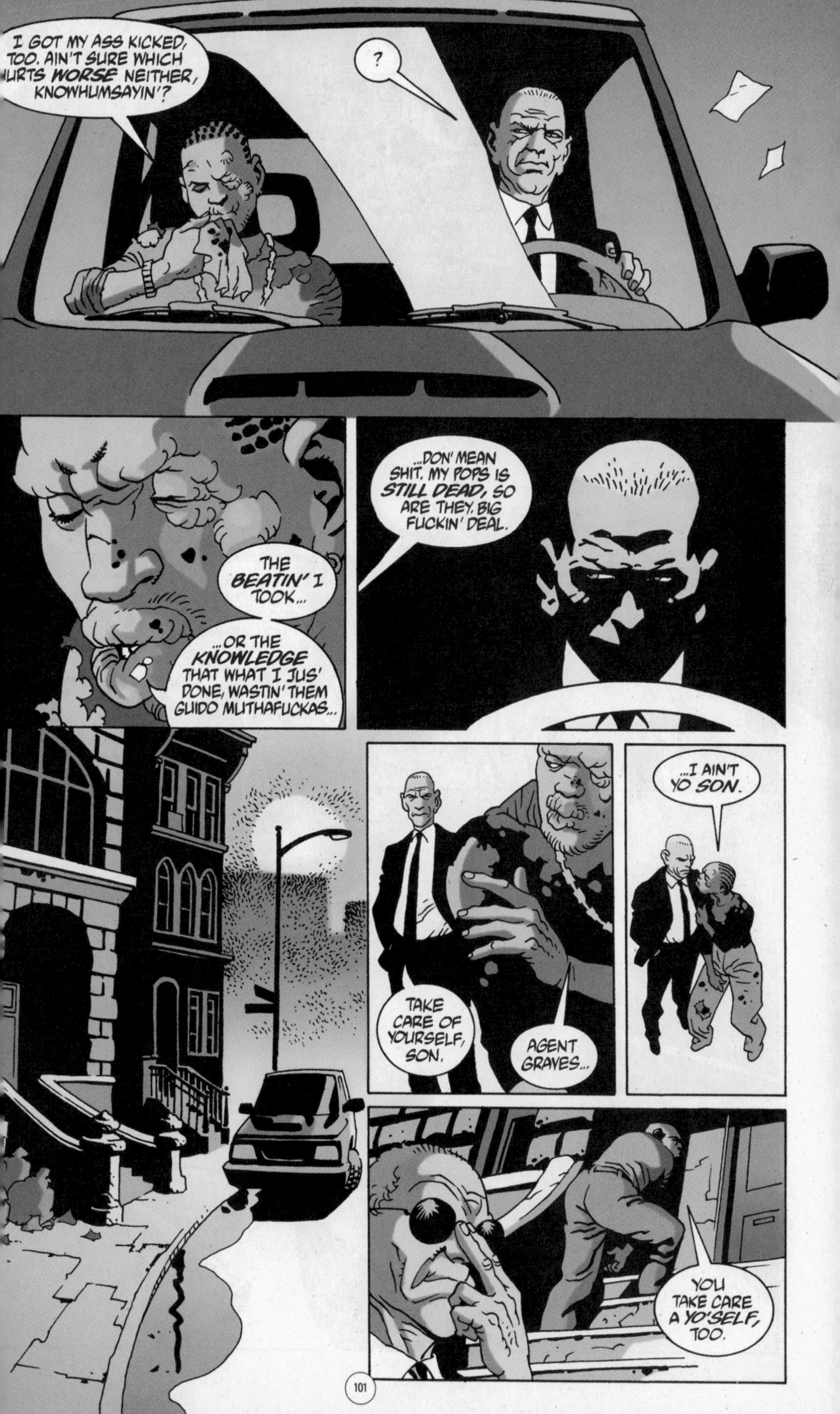
I GOT MY ASS KICKED, TOO. AIN'T SURE WHICH HURTS WORSE NEITHER, KNOWHUMSAYIN'?
?
THE BEATIN' I TOOK...
...OR THE KNOWLEDGE THAT WHAT I JUS' DONE, WASTIN' THEM GUIDO MUTHAFUCKAS...
...DON' MEAN SHIT. MY POPS IS STILL DEAD, SO ARE THEY. BIG FUCKIN' DEAL.
TAKE CARE OF YOURSELF, SON.
AGENT GRAVES...
...I AIN'T YO SON.
YOU TAKE CARE A YO'SELF, TOO.

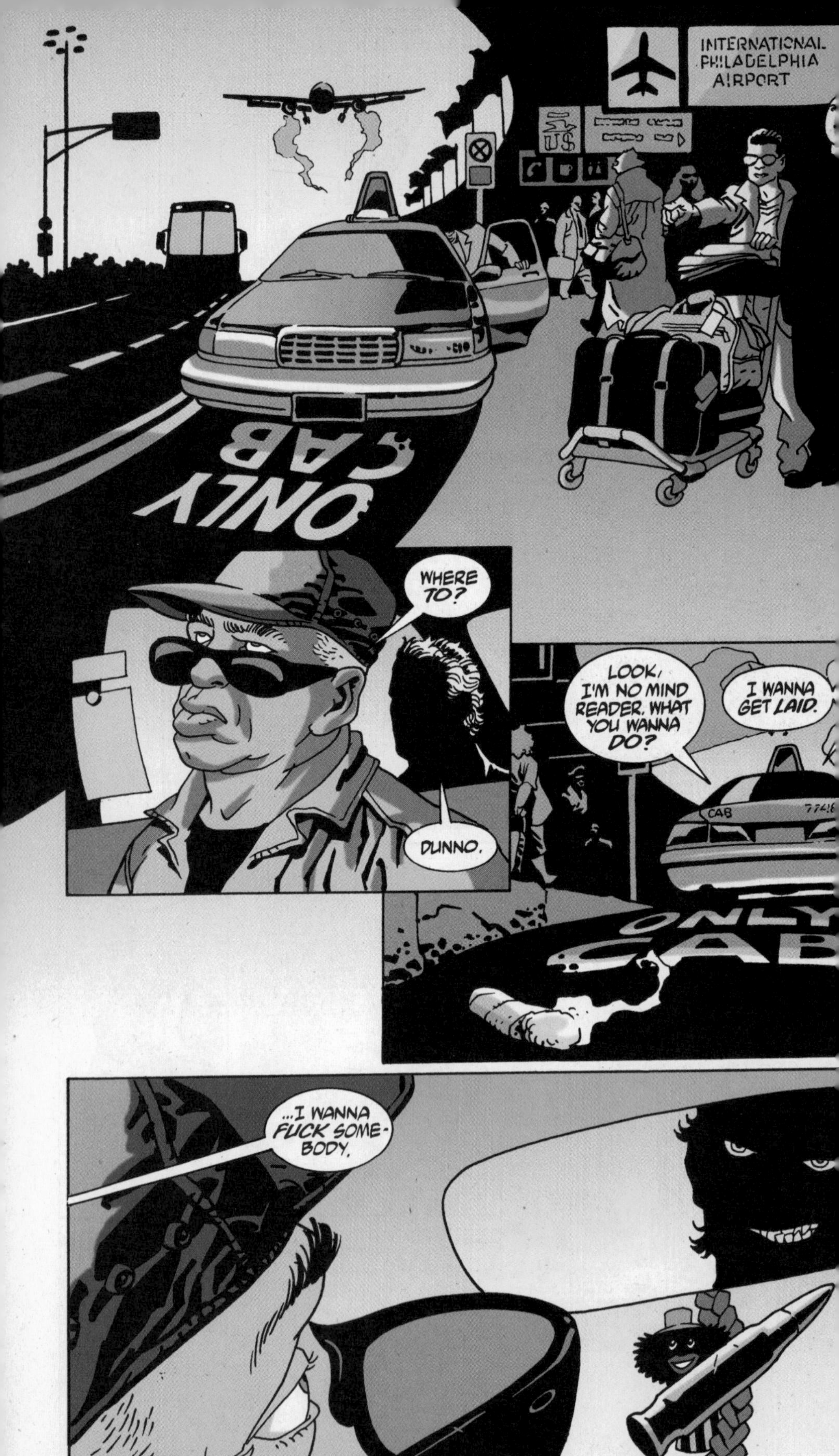
INTERNATIONAL PHILADELPHIA AIRPORT
CAB ONLY
WHERE TO?
DUNNO.
LOOK, I'M NO MIND READER. WHAT YOU WANNA DO?
I WANNA GET LAID.
CAB ONLY
...I WANNA FUCK SOME-BODY.

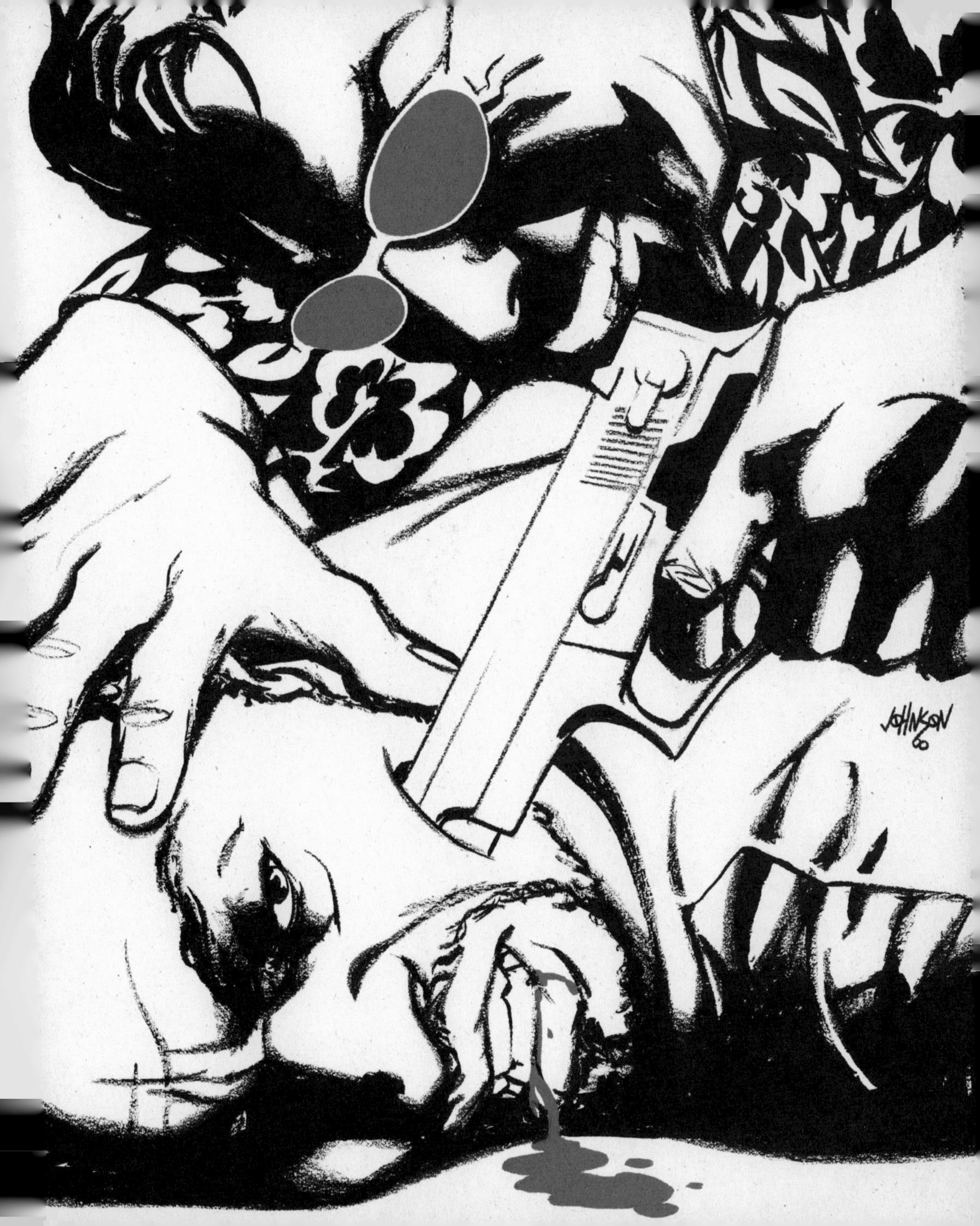
JOHNSON

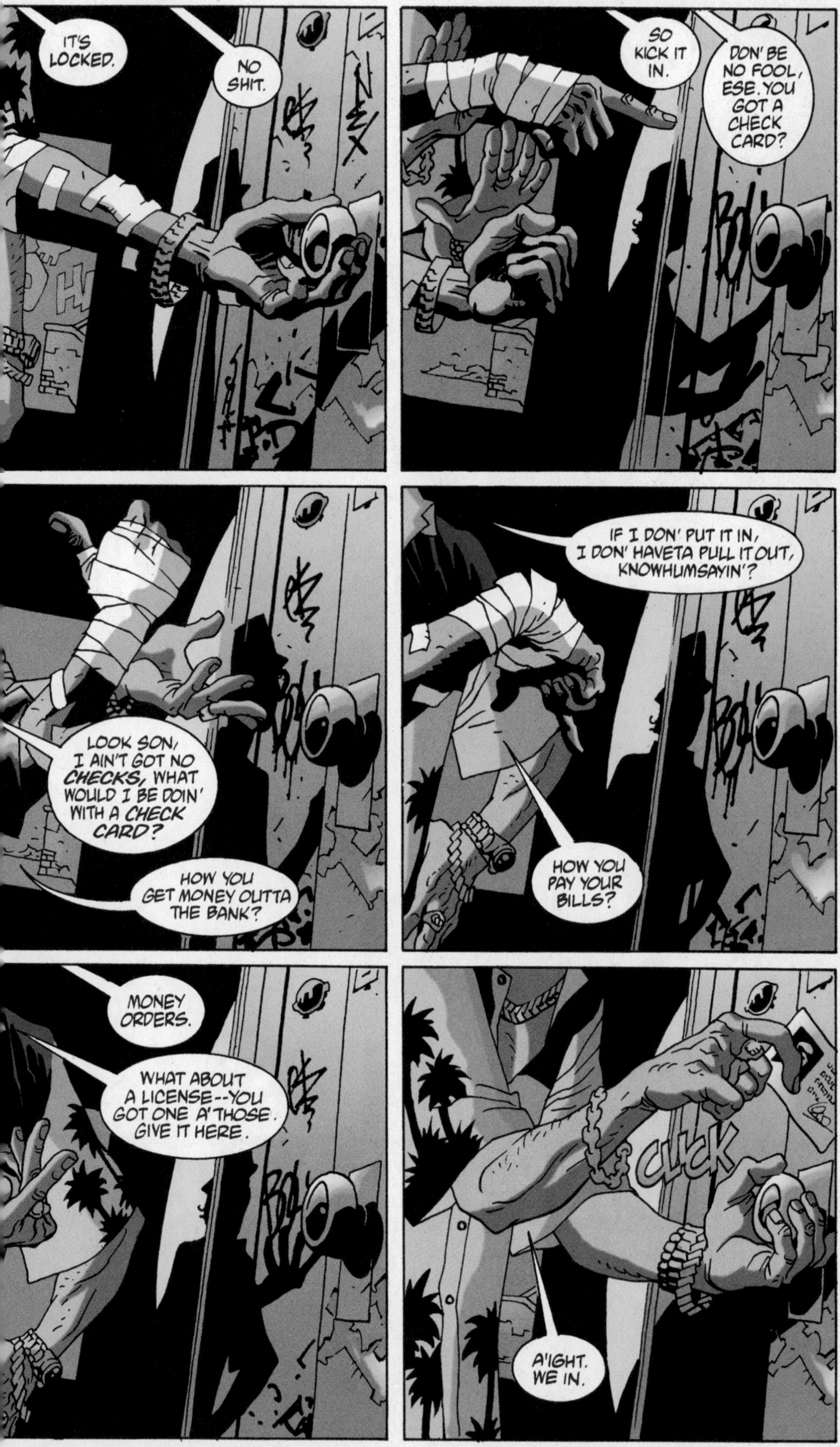

IT'S LOCKED.
NO SHIT.
SO KICK IT IN.
DON' BE NO FOOL, ESE. YOU GOT A CHECK CARD?
LOOK SON, I AIN'T GOT NO CHECKS, WHAT WOULD I BE DOIN' WITH A CHECK CARD?
HOW YOU GET MONEY OUTTA THE BANK?
IF I DON' PUT IT IN, I DON' HAVETA PULL IT OUT, KNOWHUMSAYIN'?
HOW YOU PAY YOUR BILLS?
MONEY ORDERS.
WHAT ABOUT A LICENSE--YOU GOT ONE A' THOSE. GIVE IT HERE.
CLICK
A'IGHT. WE IN.

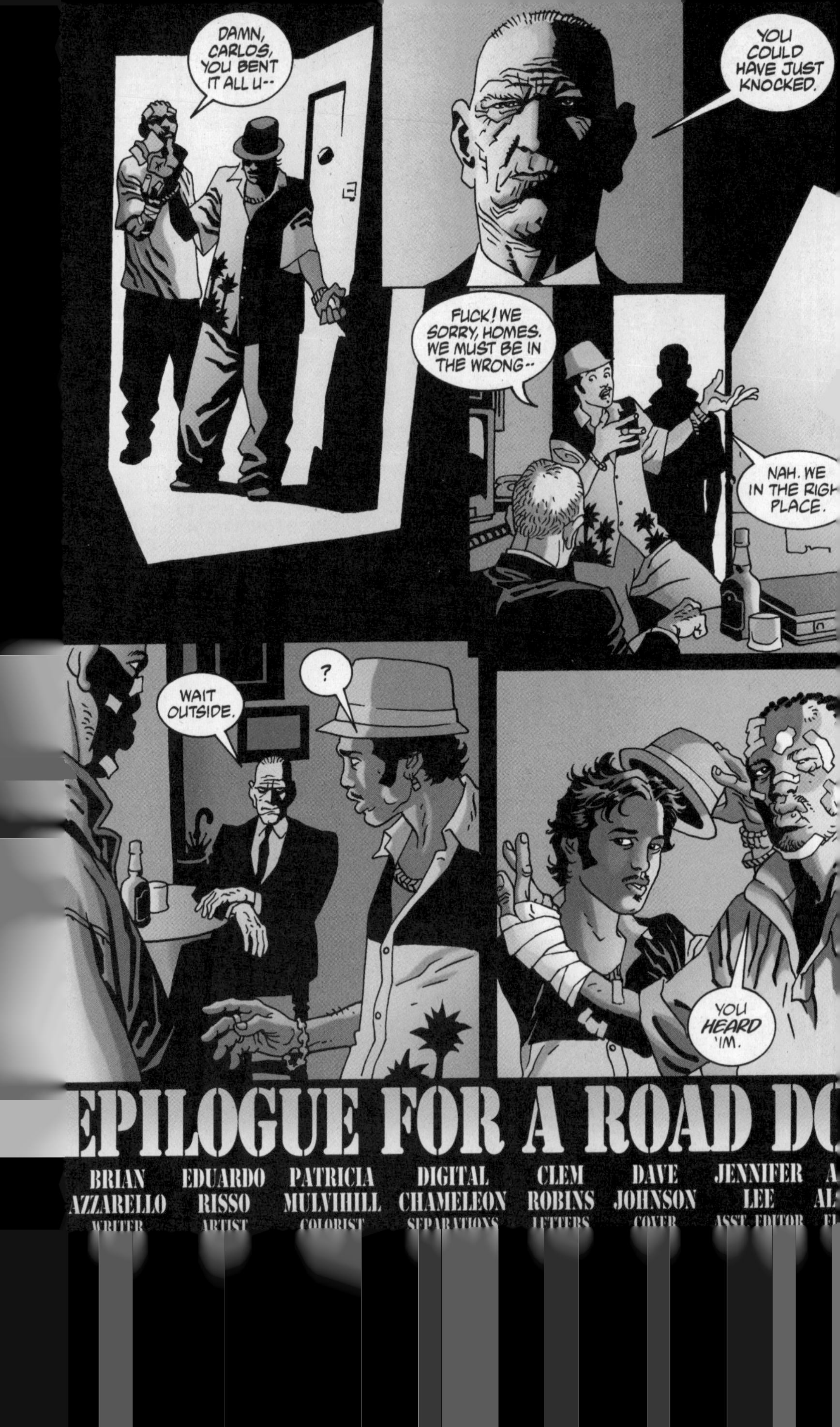
DAMN, CARLOS, YOU BENT IT ALL U--
YOU COULD HAVE JUST KNOCKED.
FUCK! WE SORRY, HOMES. WE MUST BE IN THE WRONG--
NAH. WE IN THE RIG
PLACE.
?
WAIT OUTSIDE.
YOU *HEARD* 'IM.

EPILOGUE FOR A ROAD DO

BRIAN AZZARELLO WRITER · EDUARDO RISSO ARTIST · PATRICIA MULVIHILL COLORIST · DIGITAL CHAMELEON SEPARATIONS · CLEM ROBINS LETTERS · DAVE JOHNSON COVER · JENNIFER LEE ASST. EDITOR

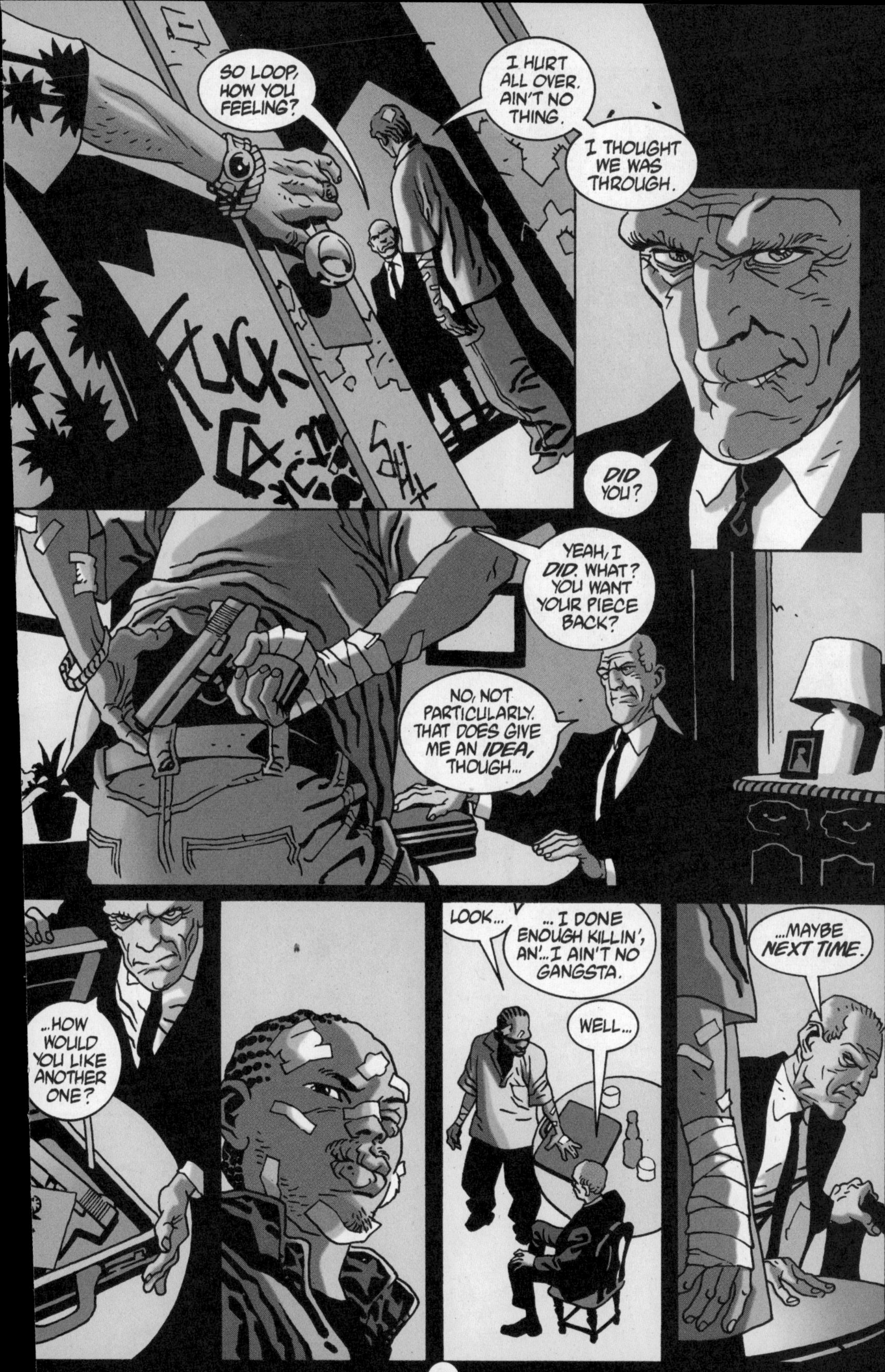
SO LOOP, HOW YOU FEELING?
I HURT ALL OVER. AIN'T NO THING.
I THOUGHT WE WAS THROUGH.
DID YOU?
YEAH, I DID. WHAT? YOU WANT YOUR PIECE BACK?
NO, NOT PARTICULARLY. THAT DOES GIVE ME AN IDEA, THOUGH...
...HOW WOULD YOU LIKE ANOTHER ONE?
LOOK...
... I DONE ENOUGH KILLIN', AN'...I AIN'T NO GANGSTA.
WELL...
...MAYBE NEXT TIME.

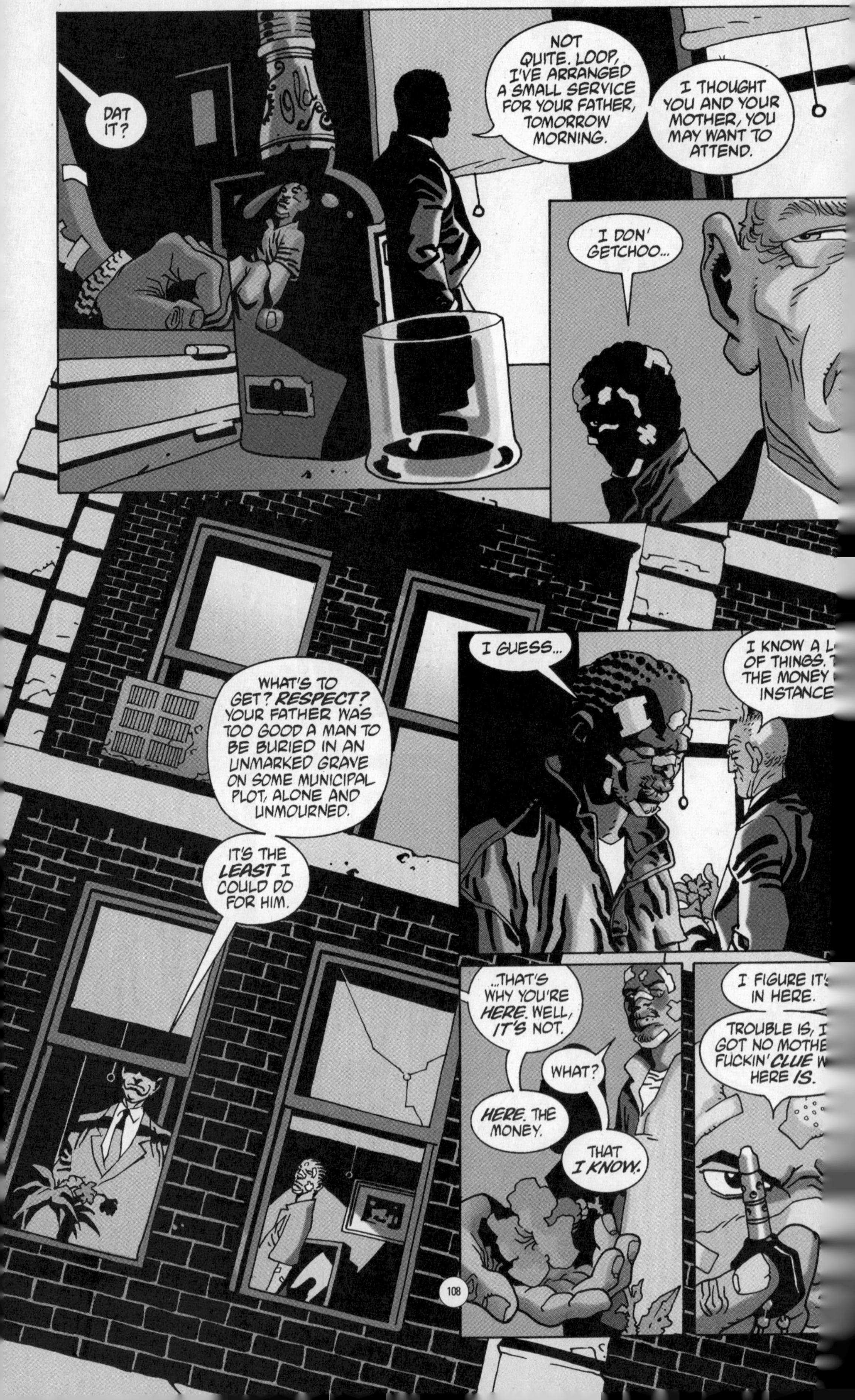

DAT IT?
NOT QUITE. LOOP, I'VE ARRANGED A SMALL SERVICE FOR YOUR FATHER, TOMORROW MORNING.
I THOUGHT YOU AND YOUR MOTHER, YOU MAY WANT TO ATTEND.
I DON' GETCHOO...
WHAT'S TO GET? RESPECT? YOUR FATHER WAS TOO GOOD A MAN TO BE BURIED IN AN UNMARKED GRAVE ON SOME MUNICIPAL PLOT, ALONE AND UNMOURNED.
IT'S THE LEAST I COULD DO FOR HIM.
I GUESS...
I KNOW A L OF THINGS. T THE MONEY INSTANCE
...THAT'S WHY YOU'RE HERE. WELL, IT'S NOT.
WHAT?
HERE. THE MONEY.
THAT I KNOW.
I FIGURE IT' IN HERE.
TROUBLE IS, I GOT NO MOTHE FUCKIN' CLUE W HERE IS.

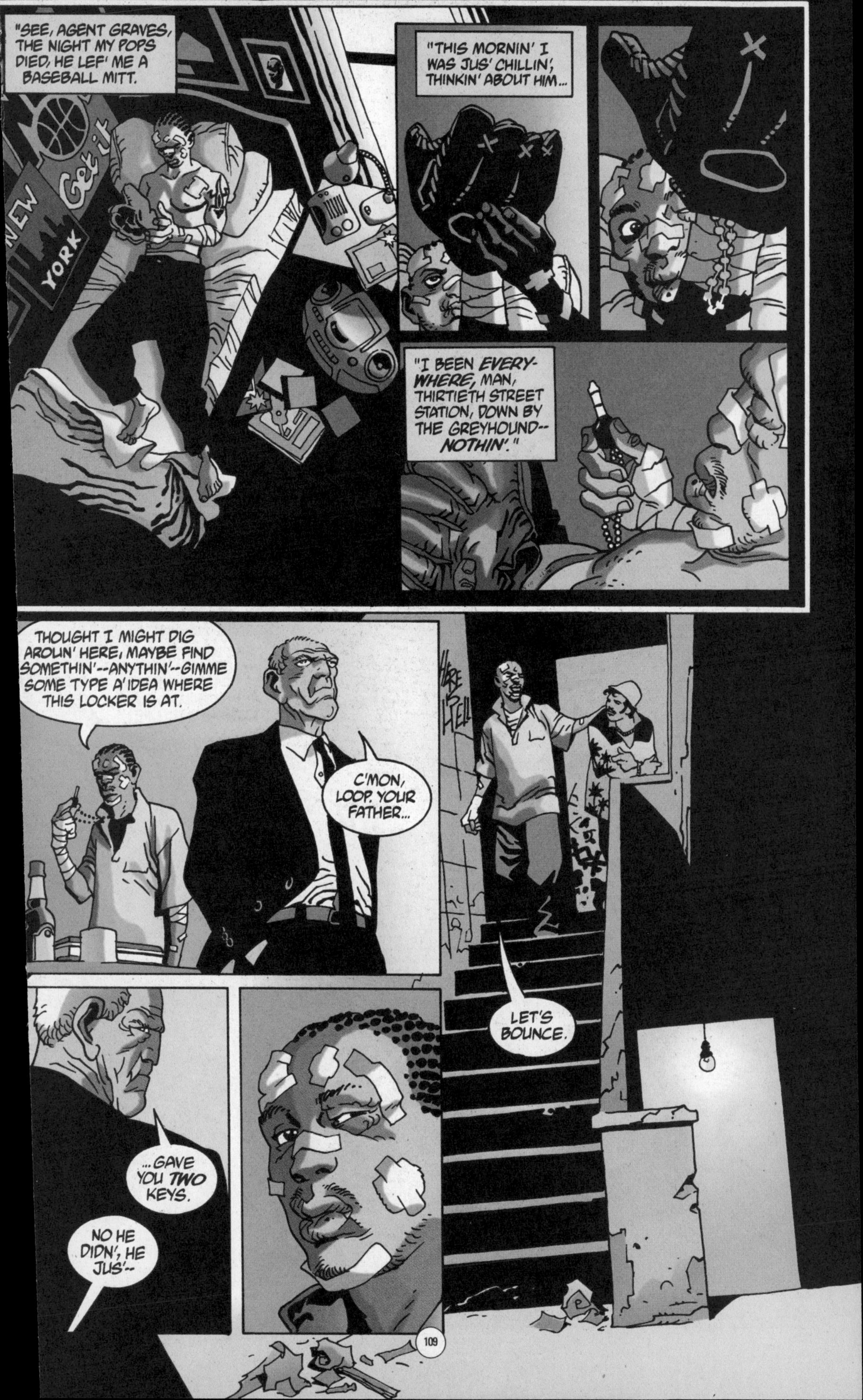
"SEE, AGENT GRAVES, THE NIGHT MY POPS DIED, HE LEF' ME A BASEBALL MITT.
"THIS MORNIN' I WAS JUS' CHILLIN', THINKIN' ABOUT HIM...
"I BEEN EVERY-WHERE, MAN, THIRTIETH STREET STATION, DOWN BY THE GREYHOUND-- NOTHIN'."
THOUGHT I MIGHT DIG AROUN' HERE, MAYBE FIND SOMETHIN'--ANYTHIN'--GIMME SOME TYPE A'IDEA WHERE THIS LOCKER IS AT.
C'MON, LOOP. YOUR FATHER...
LET'S BOUNCE.
...GAVE YOU TWO KEYS.
NO HE DIDN', HE JUS'--

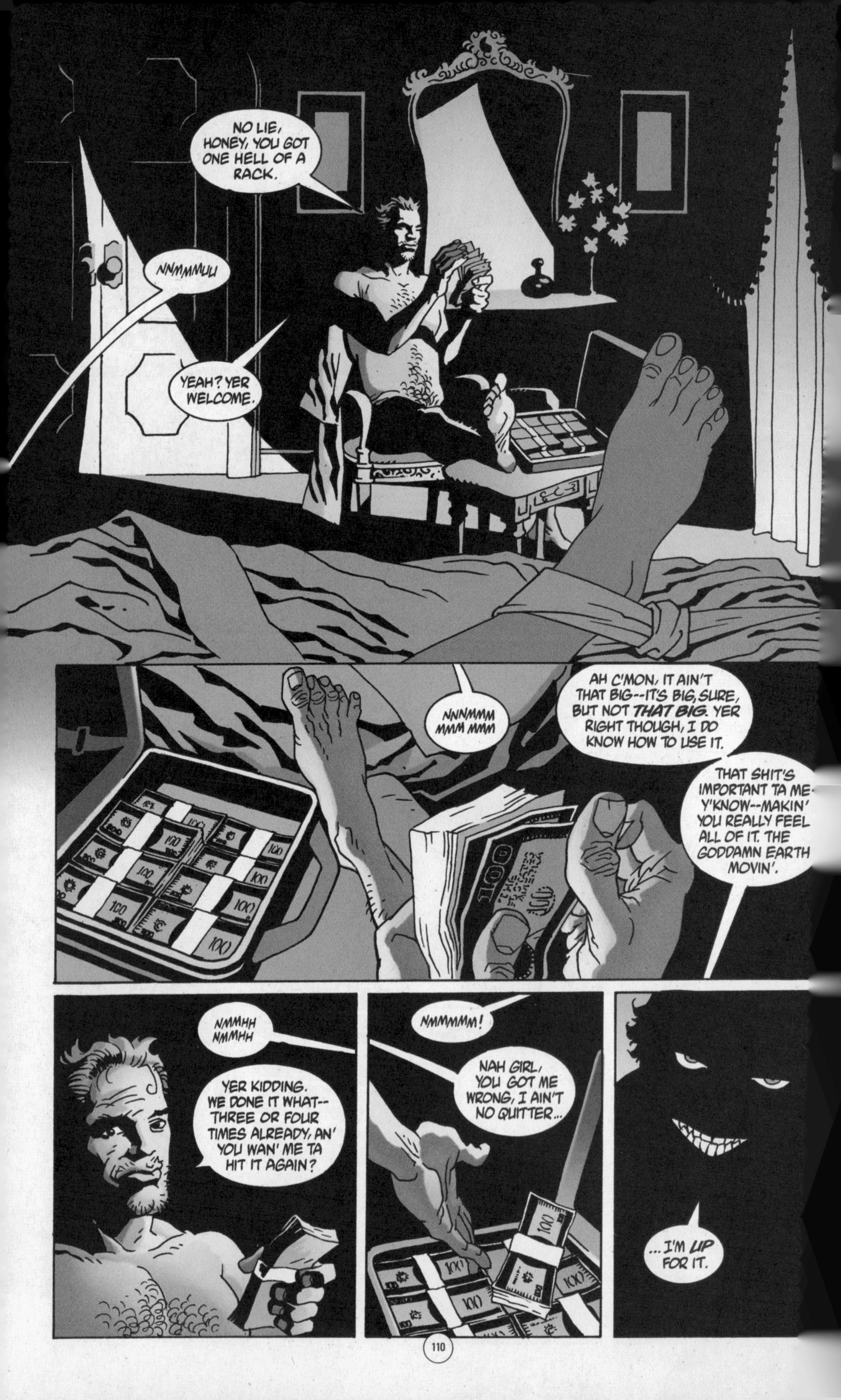
NO LIE, HONEY, YOU GOT ONE HELL OF A RACK.
NNMMMUU
YEAH? YER WELCOME.
NNNMMM MMM MMM
AH C'MON, IT AIN'T THAT BIG--IT'S BIG, SURE, BUT NOT THAT BIG. YER RIGHT THOUGH, I DO KNOW HOW TO USE IT.
THAT SHIT'S IMPORTANT TA ME Y'KNOW--MAKIN' YOU REALLY FEEL ALL OF IT. THE GODDAMN EARTH MOVIN'.
NMMHH NMMHH
YER KIDDING. WE DONE IT WHAT-- THREE OR FOUR TIMES ALREADY, AN' YOU WAN' ME TA HIT IT AGAIN?
NMMMMM!
NAH GIRL, YOU GOT ME WRONG, I AIN'T NO QUITTER...
...I'M UP FOR IT.

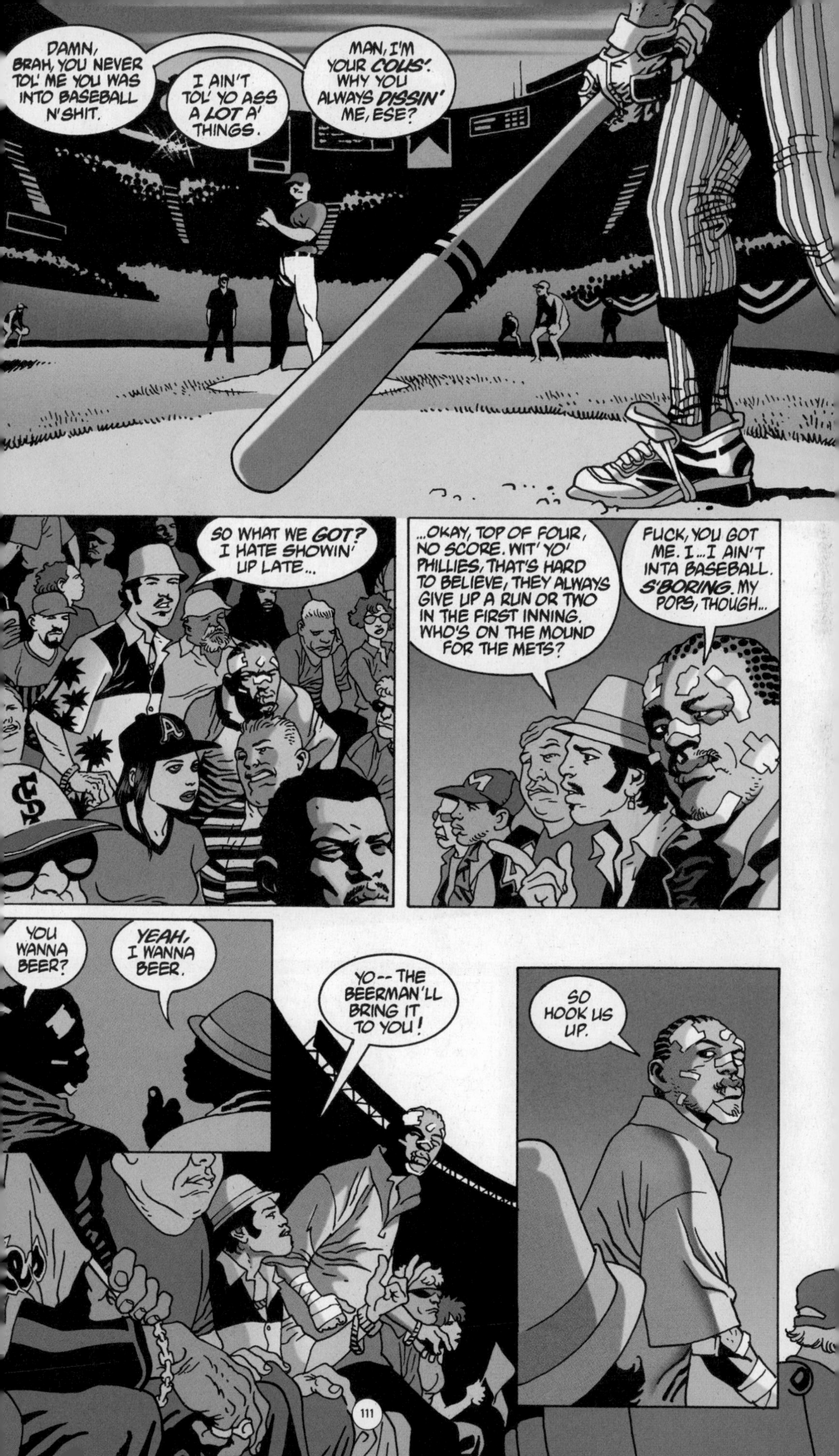

DAMN, BRAH, YOU NEVER TOL' ME YOU WAS INTO BASEBALL N'SHIT.
I AIN'T TOL' YO ASS A LOT A' THINGS.
MAN, I'M YOUR COUS'. WHY YOU ALWAYS DISSIN' ME, ESE?
SO WHAT WE GOT? I HATE SHOWIN' UP LATE...
...OKAY, TOP OF FOUR, NO SCORE. WIT' YO' PHILLIES, THAT'S HARD TO BELIEVE, THEY ALWAYS GIVE UP A RUN OR TWO IN THE FIRST INNING. WHO'S ON THE MOUND FOR THE METS?
FUCK, YOU GOT ME. I...I AIN'T INTA BASEBALL. S'BORING. MY POPS, THOUGH...
YOU WANNA BEER?
YEAH, I WANNA BEER.
YO-- THE BEERMAN'LL BRING IT TO YOU!
SO HOOK US UP.

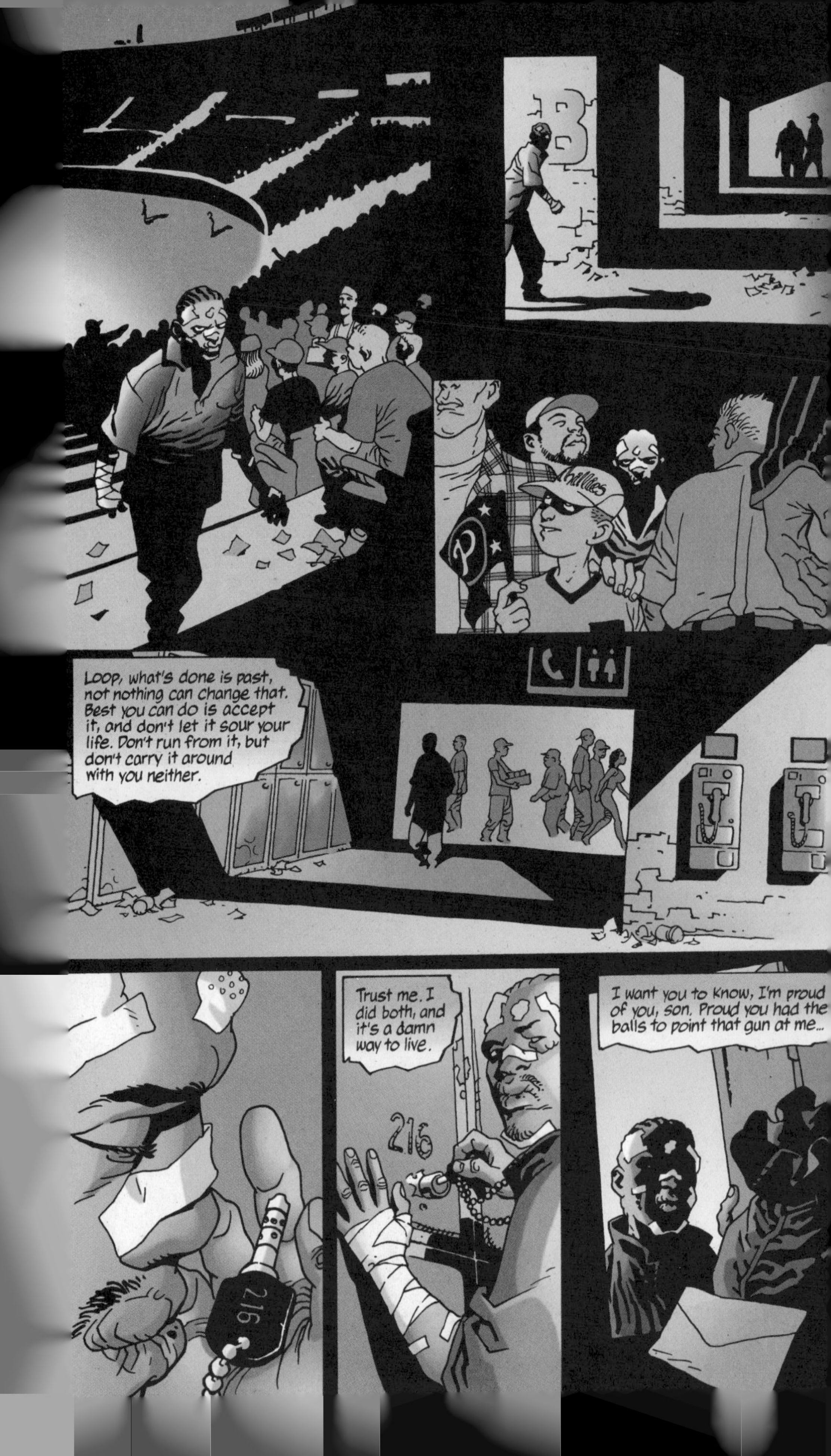
Phillies
Loop, what's done is past, not nothing can change that. Best you can do is accept it, and don't let it sour your life. Don't run from it, but don't carry it around with you neither.
216
Trust me. I did both, and it's a damn way to live.
216
I want you to know, I'm proud of you, son. Proud you had the balls to point that gun at me...

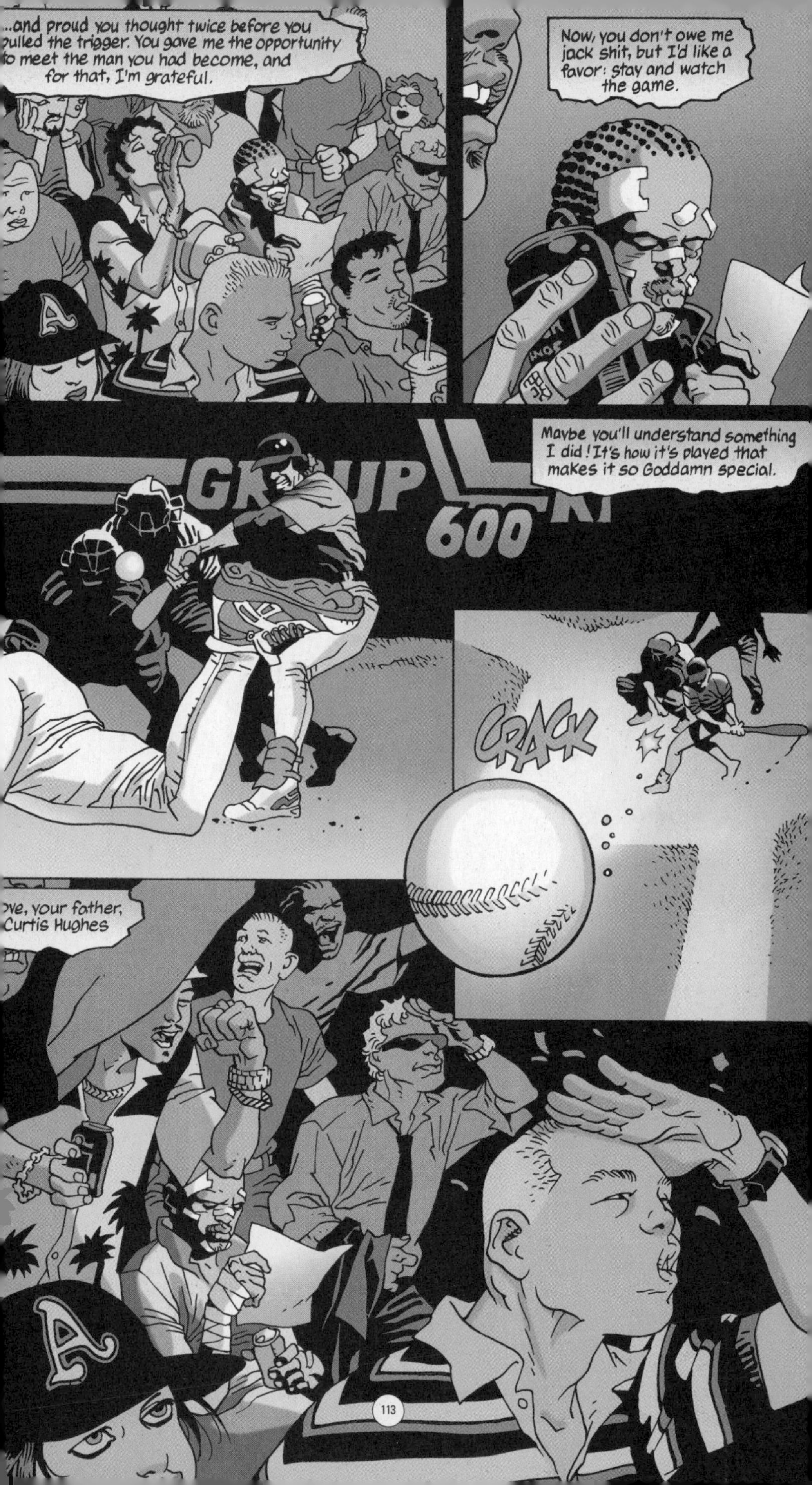
...and proud you thought twice before you pulled the trigger. You gave me the opportunity to meet the man you had become, and for that, I'm grateful.
Now, you don't owe me jack shit, but I'd like a favor: stay and watch the game.
Maybe you'll understand something I did! It's how it's played that makes it so Goddamn special.
600
CRACK
ove, your father, Curtis Hughes

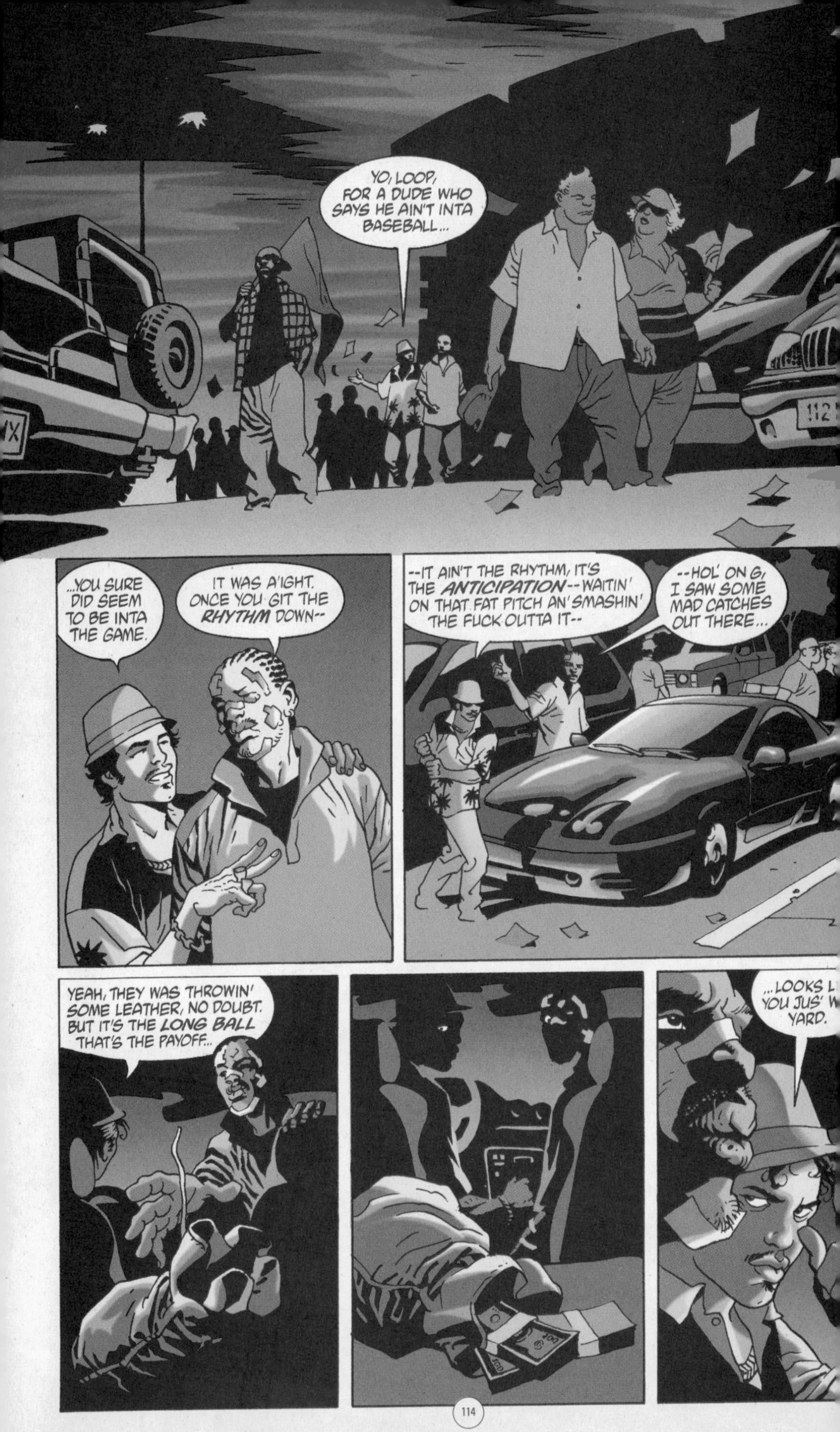

YO, LOOP, FOR A DUDE WHO SAYS HE AIN'T INTA BASEBALL...
...YOU SURE DID SEEM TO BE INTA THE GAME.
IT WAS A'IGHT. ONCE YOU GIT THE RHYTHM DOWN--
--IT AIN'T THE RHYTHM, IT'S THE ANTICIPATION--WAITIN' ON THAT FAT PITCH AN' SMASHIN' THE FUCK OUTTA IT--
--HOL' ON G, I SAW SOME MAD CATCHES OUT THERE...
YEAH, THEY WAS THROWIN' SOME LEATHER, NO DOUBT. BUT IT'S THE LONG BALL THAT'S THE PAYOFF...

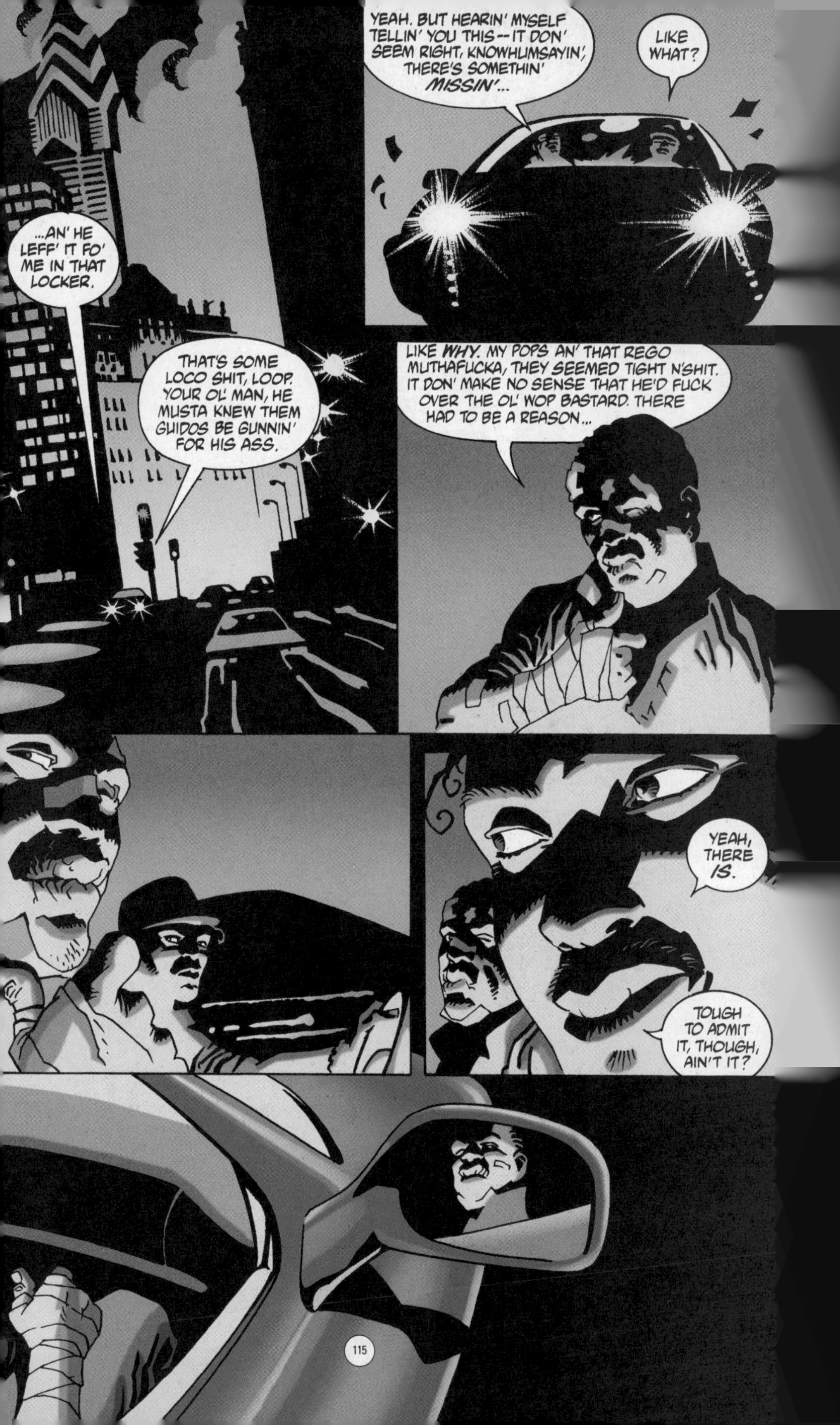

...AN' HE LEFF' IT FO' ME IN THAT LOCKER.
THAT'S SOME LOCO SHIT, LOOP. YOUR OL' MAN, HE MUSTA KNEW THEM GUIDOS BE GUNNIN' FOR HIS ASS.
YEAH. BUT HEARIN' MYSELF TELLIN' YOU THIS--IT DON' SEEM RIGHT, KNOWHUMSAYIN', THERE'S SOMETHIN' MISSIN'...
LIKE WHAT?
LIKE WHY. MY POPS AN' THAT REGO MUTHAFUCKA, THEY SEEMED TIGHT N'SHIT. IT DON' MAKE NO SENSE THAT HE'D FUCK OVER THE OL' WOP BASTARD. THERE HAD TO BE A REASON...
YEAH, THERE IS.
TOUGH TO ADMIT IT, THOUGH, AIN'T IT?

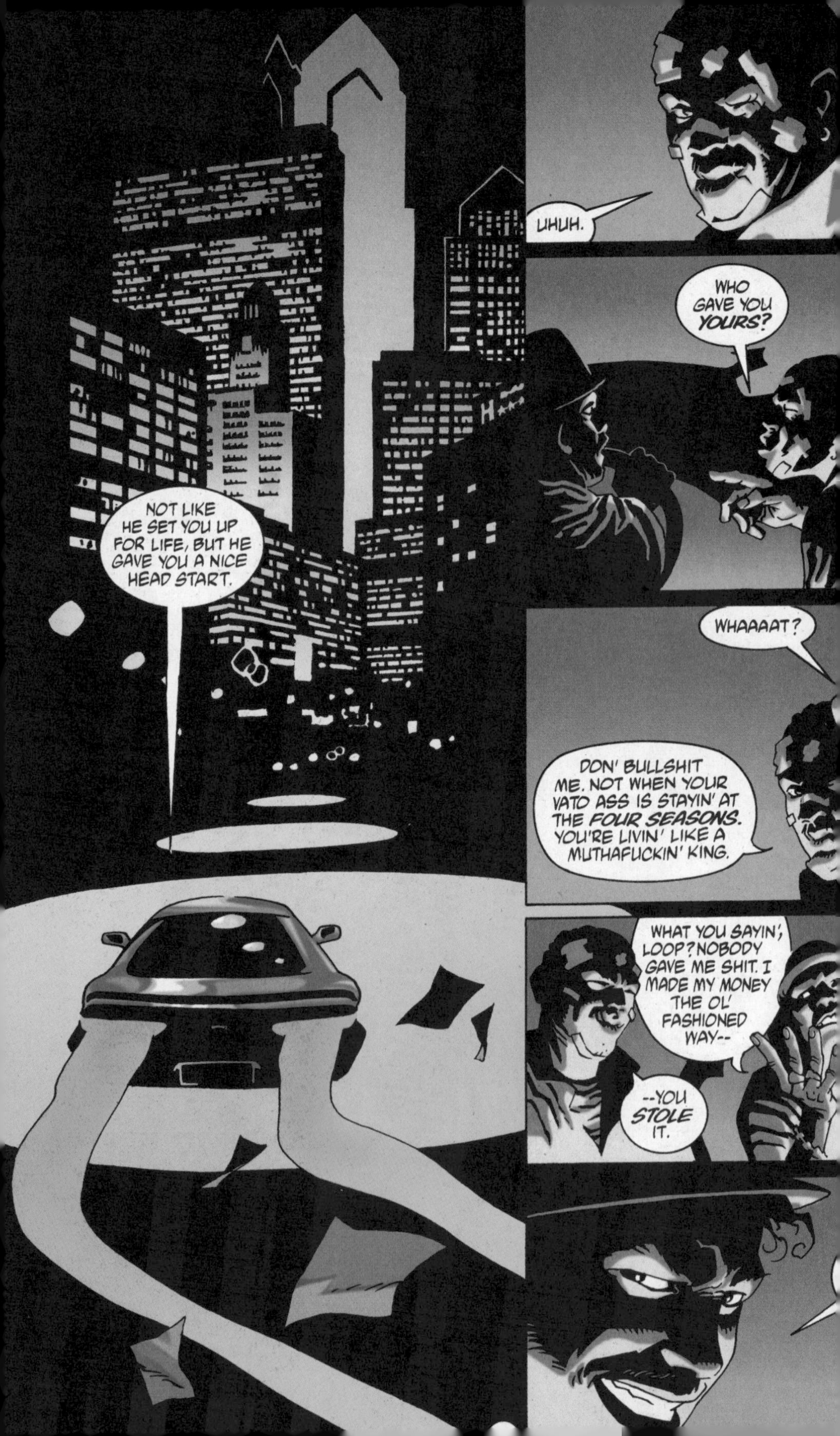

NOT LIKE HE SET YOU UP FOR LIFE, BUT HE GAVE YOU A NICE HEAD START.
UHUH.
WHO GAVE YOU YOURS?
WHAAAAT?
DON' BULLSHIT ME. NOT WHEN YOUR VATO ASS IS STAYIN' AT THE FOUR SEASONS. YOU'RE LIVIN' LIKE A MUTHAFUCKIN' KING.
WHAT YOU SAYIN', LOOP? NOBODY GAVE ME SHIT. I MADE MY MONEY THE OL' FASHIONED WAY--
--YOU STOLE IT.

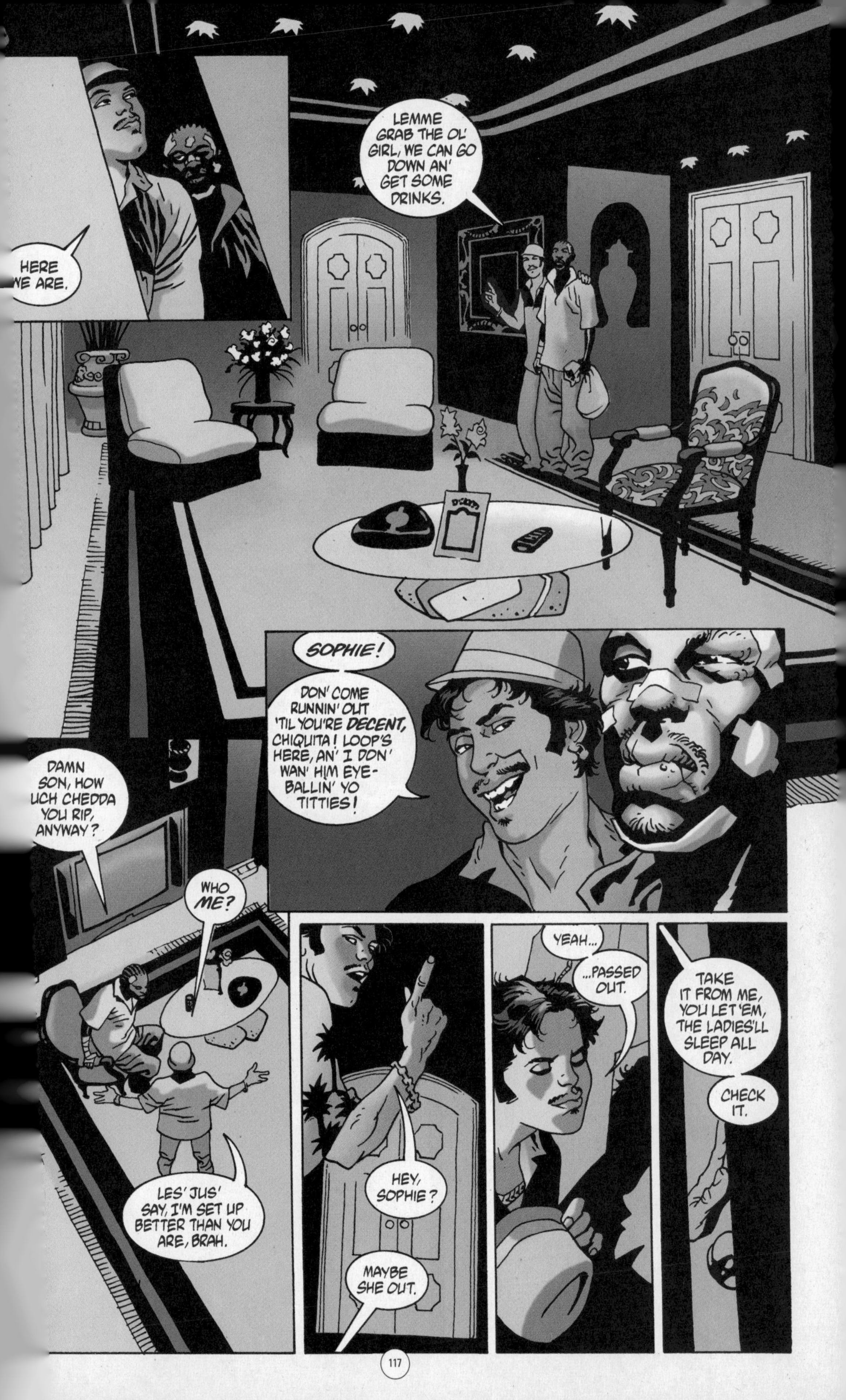

HERE WE ARE.
LEMME GRAB THE OL' GIRL, WE CAN GO DOWN AN' GET SOME DRINKS.
SOPHIE!
DON' COME RUNNIN' OUT 'TIL YOU'RE DECENT, CHIQUITA! LOOP'S HERE, AN' I DON' WAN' HIM EYE-BALLIN' YO TITTIES!
DAMN SON, HOW UCH CHEDDA YOU RIP, ANYWAY?
WHO ME?
LES' JUS' SAY, I'M SET UP BETTER THAN YOU ARE, BRAH.
HEY, SOPHIE?
MAYBE SHE OUT.
YEAH...
...PASSED OUT.
TAKE IT FROM ME, YOU LET 'EM, THE LADIES'LL SLEEP ALL DAY.
CHECK IT.

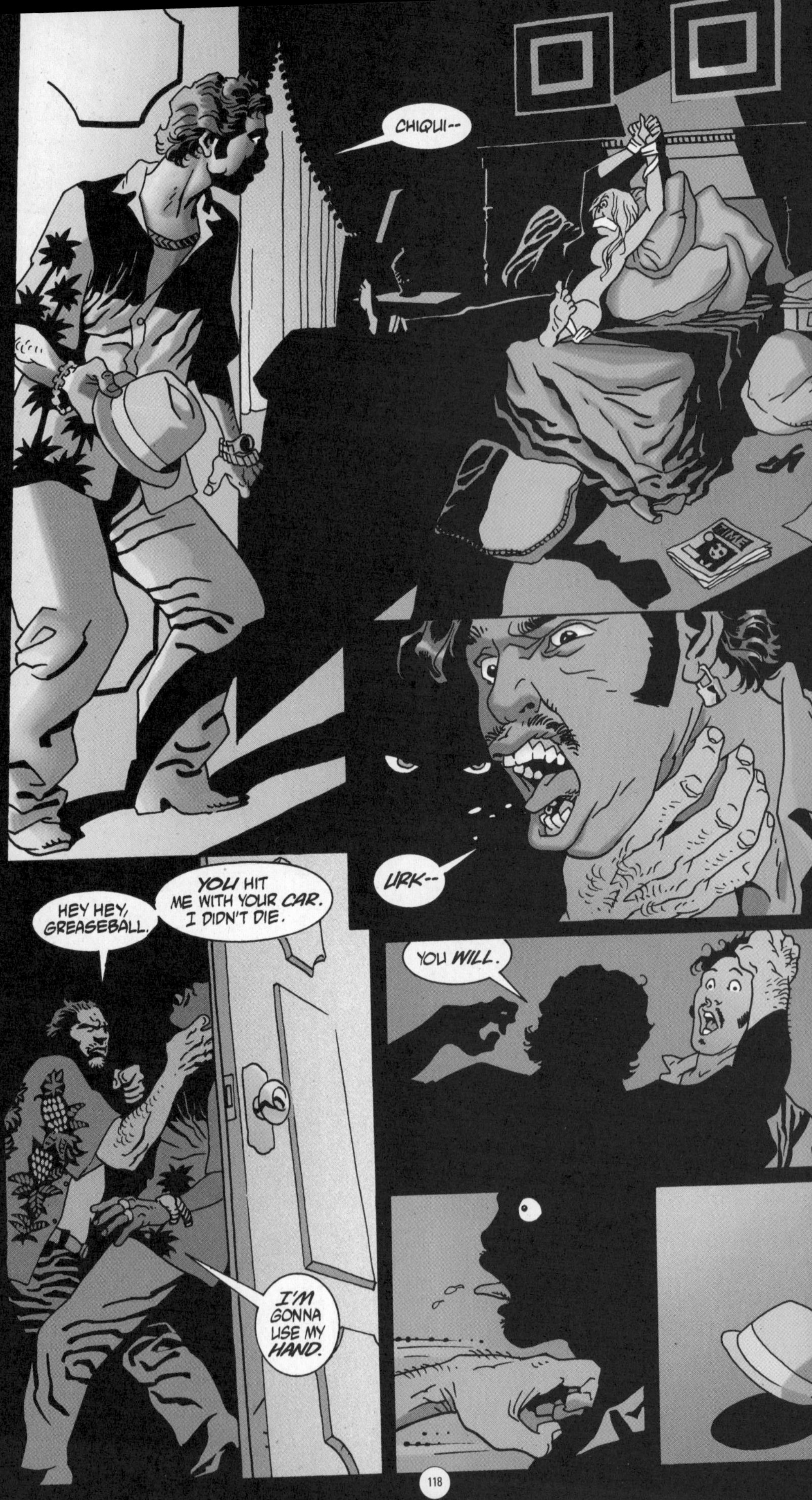
CHIQUI--
URK--
HEY HEY, GREASEBALL.
YOU HIT ME WITH YOUR CAR. I DIDN'T DIE.
I'M GONNA USE MY HAND.
YOU WILL.

THUMP

OKAY, HONEY. HERE'S THE STORY. YER DEAD BOY-FRIEND HERE, HE WAS PIMPIN' YER ASS.

HE WALKED IN, FOUND YOU IN ALL YOUR FIRM YOUNG GLORY GETTIN' IT ON WITH SOME ROUGH TRADE--

--THAT WOULD BE ME--

--AN' HE FREAKED. SO'D YER TRICK. END OF STORY.

NO, YOU CAN'T IDENTIFY THE MAN, 'CAUSE YOU WAS REAL HIGH.

DO IT.

GOOD GIRL. YOU TELL THE HEAT ANY MORE THAN THAT, AN' GUESS WHAT?

...YER DEAD.

THANKS FOR THE RIDE.

RIGHT.

119

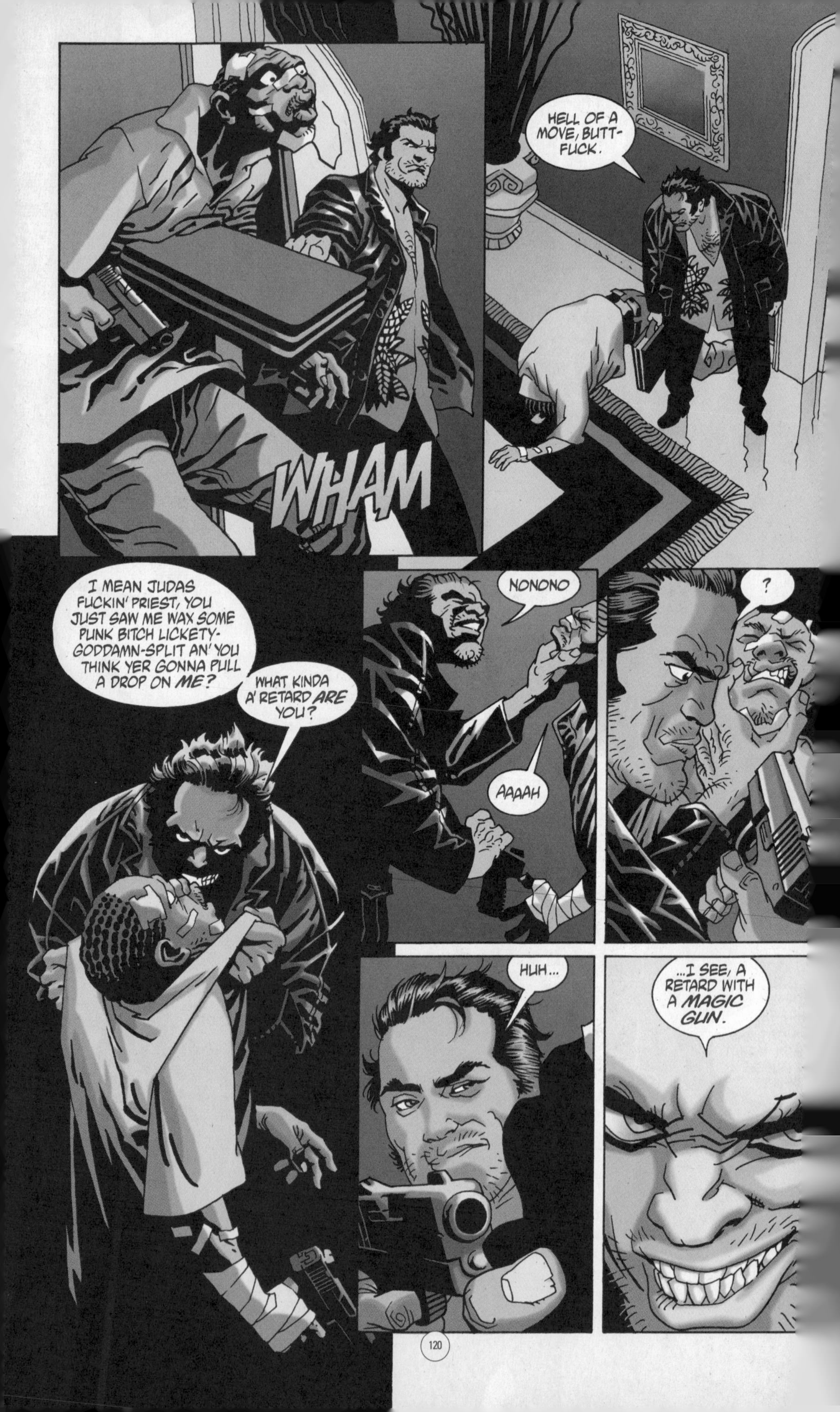
WHAM
HELL OF A MOVE, BUTT-FUCK.
I MEAN JUDAS FUCKIN' PRIEST, YOU JUST SAW ME WAX SOME PUNK BITCH LICKETY-GODDAMN-SPLIT AN' YOU THINK YER GONNA PULL A DROP ON ME?
WHAT KINDA A' RETARD ARE YOU?
NONONO
AAAAH
?
HUH...
...I SEE, A RETARD WITH A MAGIC GUN.

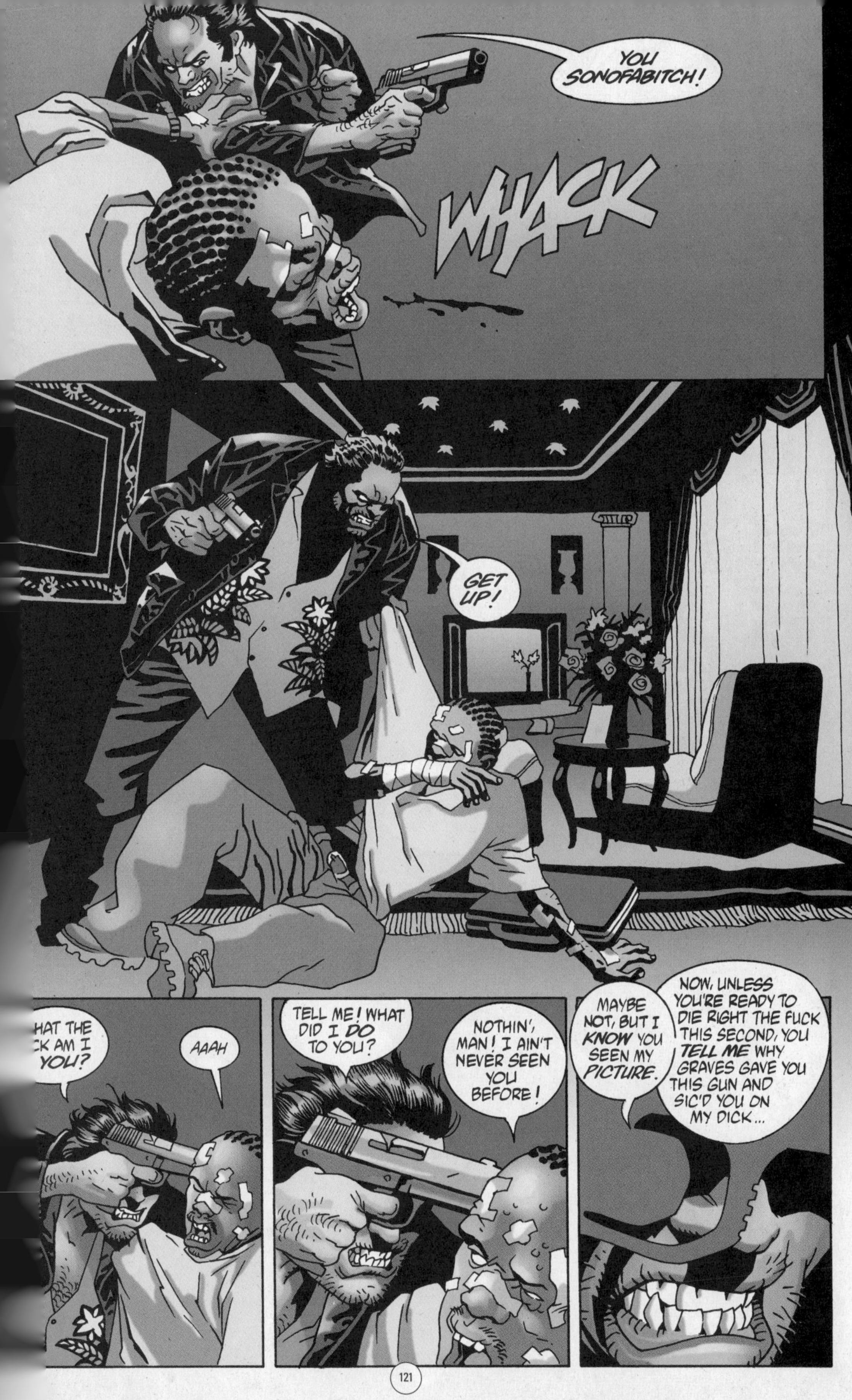
YOU SONOFABITCH!
WHACK
GET UP!
HAT THE
CK AM I
YOU?
AAAH
TELL ME! WHAT DID I DO TO YOU?
NOTHIN', MAN! I AIN'T NEVER SEEN YOU BEFORE!
MAYBE NOT, BUT I KNOW YOU SEEN MY PICTURE.
NOW, UNLESS YOU'RE READY TO DIE RIGHT THE FUCK THIS SECOND, YOU TELL ME WHY GRAVES GAVE YOU THIS GUN AND SIC'D YOU ON MY DICK...

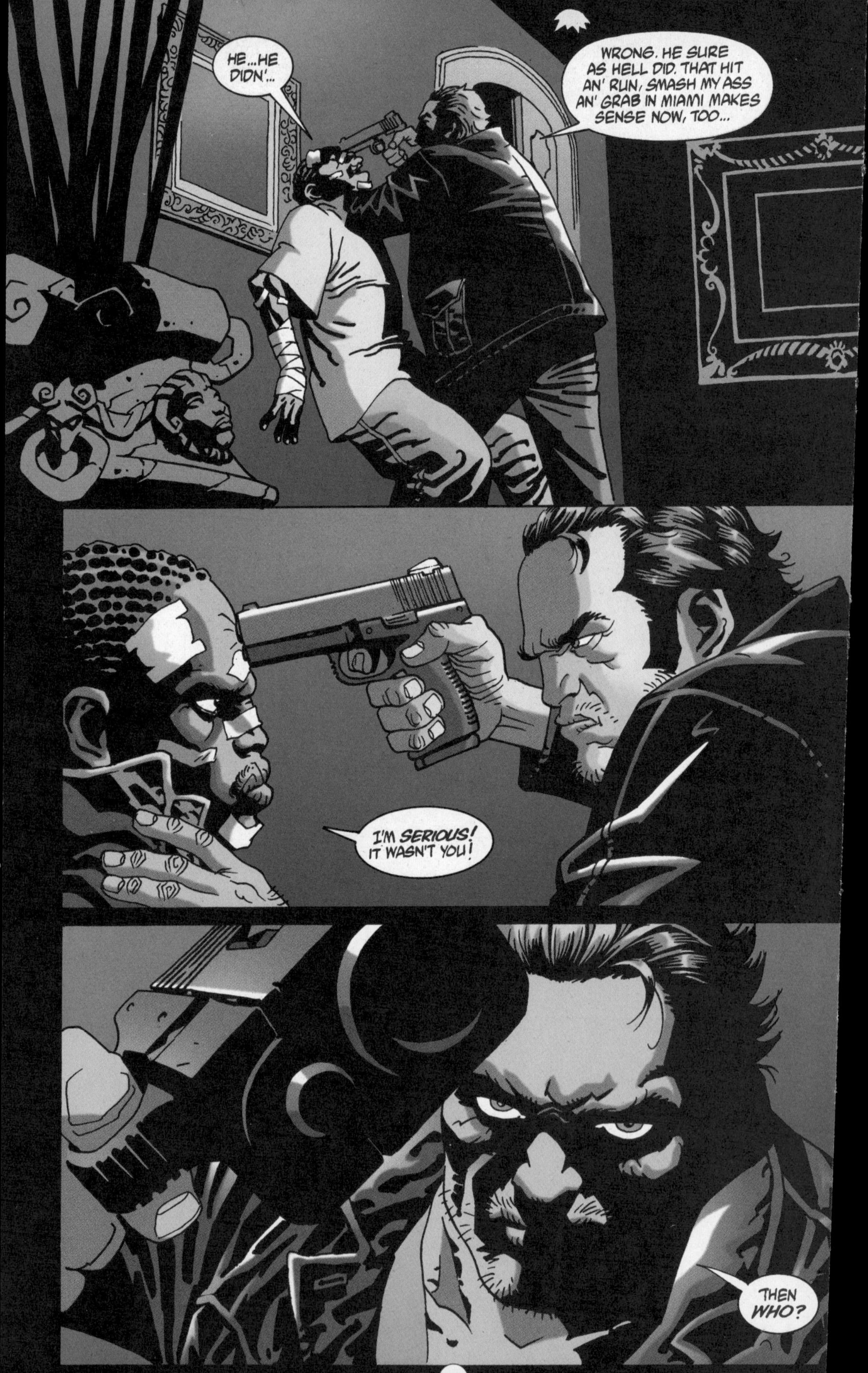
HE...HE DIDN'...
WRONG. HE SURE AS HELL DID. THAT HIT AN' RUN, SMASH MY ASS AN' GRAB IN MIAMI MAKES SENSE NOW, TOO...
I'M *SERIOUS!* IT WASN'T YOU!
THEN *WHO?*

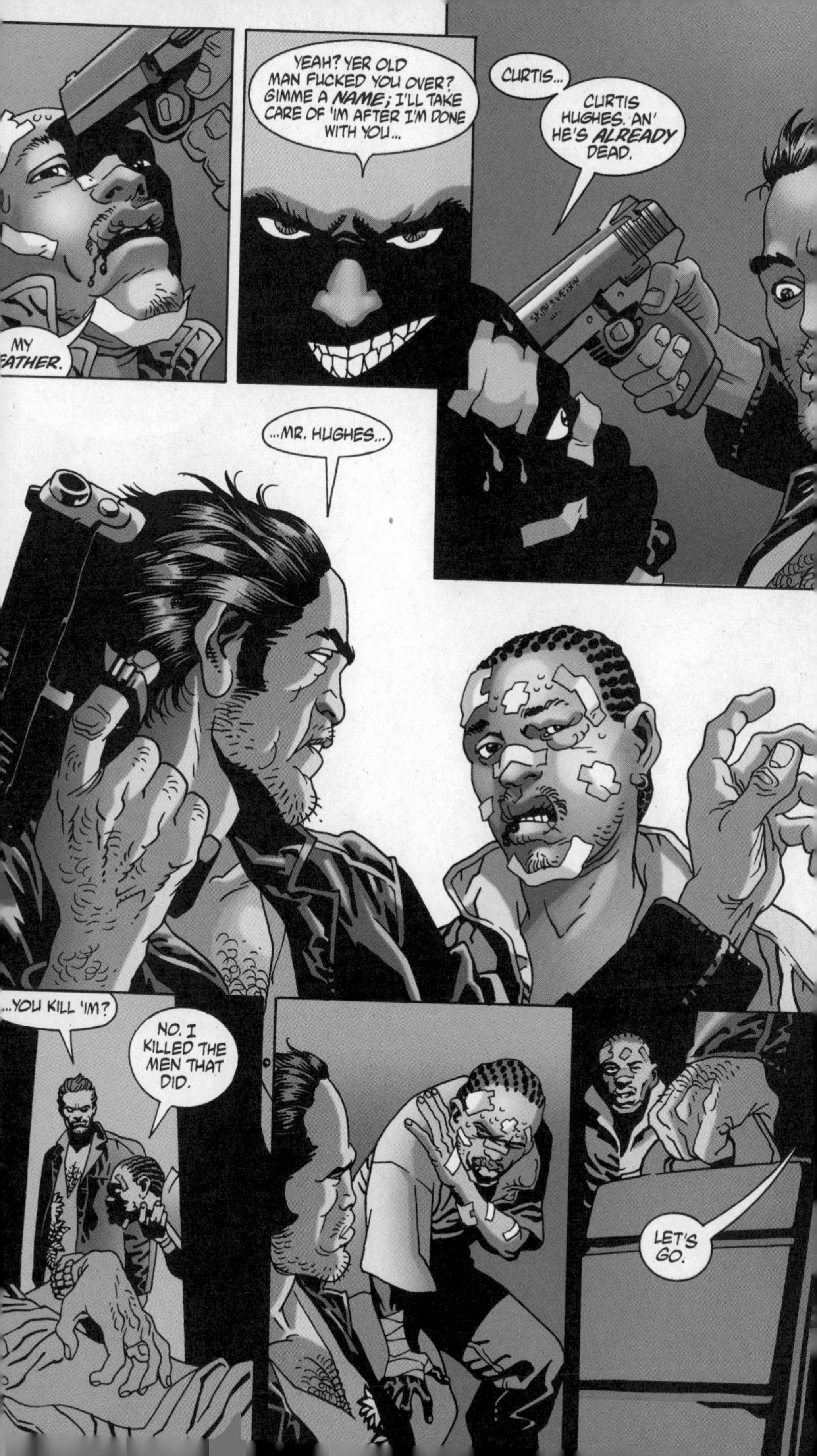
MY FATHER.
YEAH? YER OLD MAN FUCKED YOU OVER? GIMME A *NAME*; I'LL TAKE CARE OF 'IM AFTER I'M DONE WITH YOU...
CURTIS...
CURTIS HUGHES. AN' HE'S *ALREADY* DEAD.
...MR. HUGHES...
...YOU KILL 'IM?
NO. I KILLED THE MEN THAT DID.
LET'S GO.

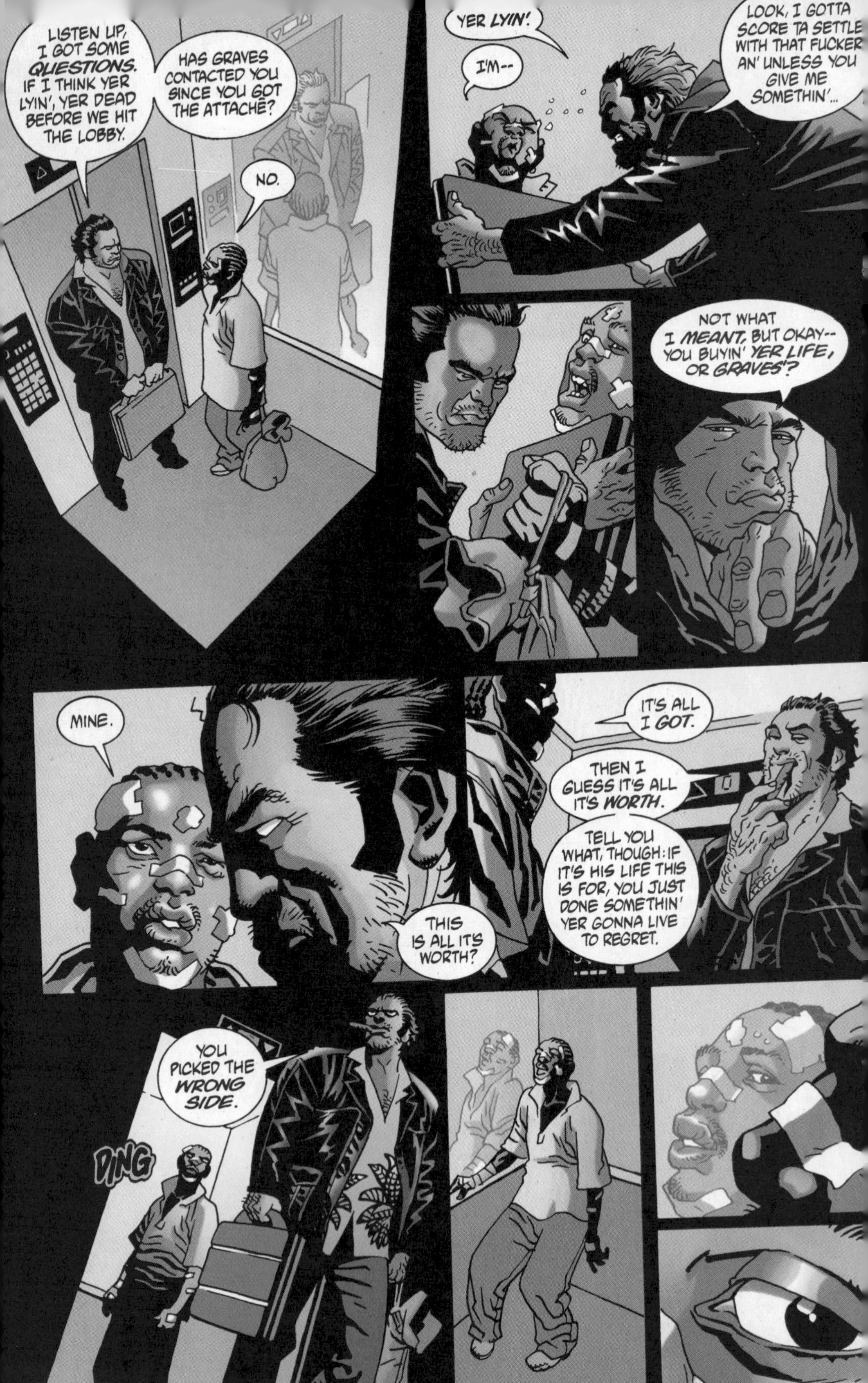
LISTEN UP, I GOT SOME QUESTIONS. IF I THINK YER LYIN', YER DEAD BEFORE WE HIT THE LOBBY.
HAS GRAVES CONTACTED YOU SINCE YOU GOT THE ATTACHÉ?
NO.
YER LYIN'.
I'M--
LOOK, I GOTTA SCORE TA SETTLE WITH THAT FUCKER AN' UNLESS YOU GIVE ME SOMETHIN'...
NOT WHAT I MEANT, BUT OKAY-- YOU BUYIN' YER LIFE, OR GRAVES'?
MINE.
THIS IS ALL IT'S WORTH?
IT'S ALL I GOT.
THEN I GUESS IT'S ALL IT'S WORTH.
TELL YOU WHAT, THOUGH: IF IT'S HIS LIFE THIS IS FOR, YOU JUST DONE SOMETHIN' YER GONNA LIVE TO REGRET.
YOU PICKED THE WRONG SIDE.
DING

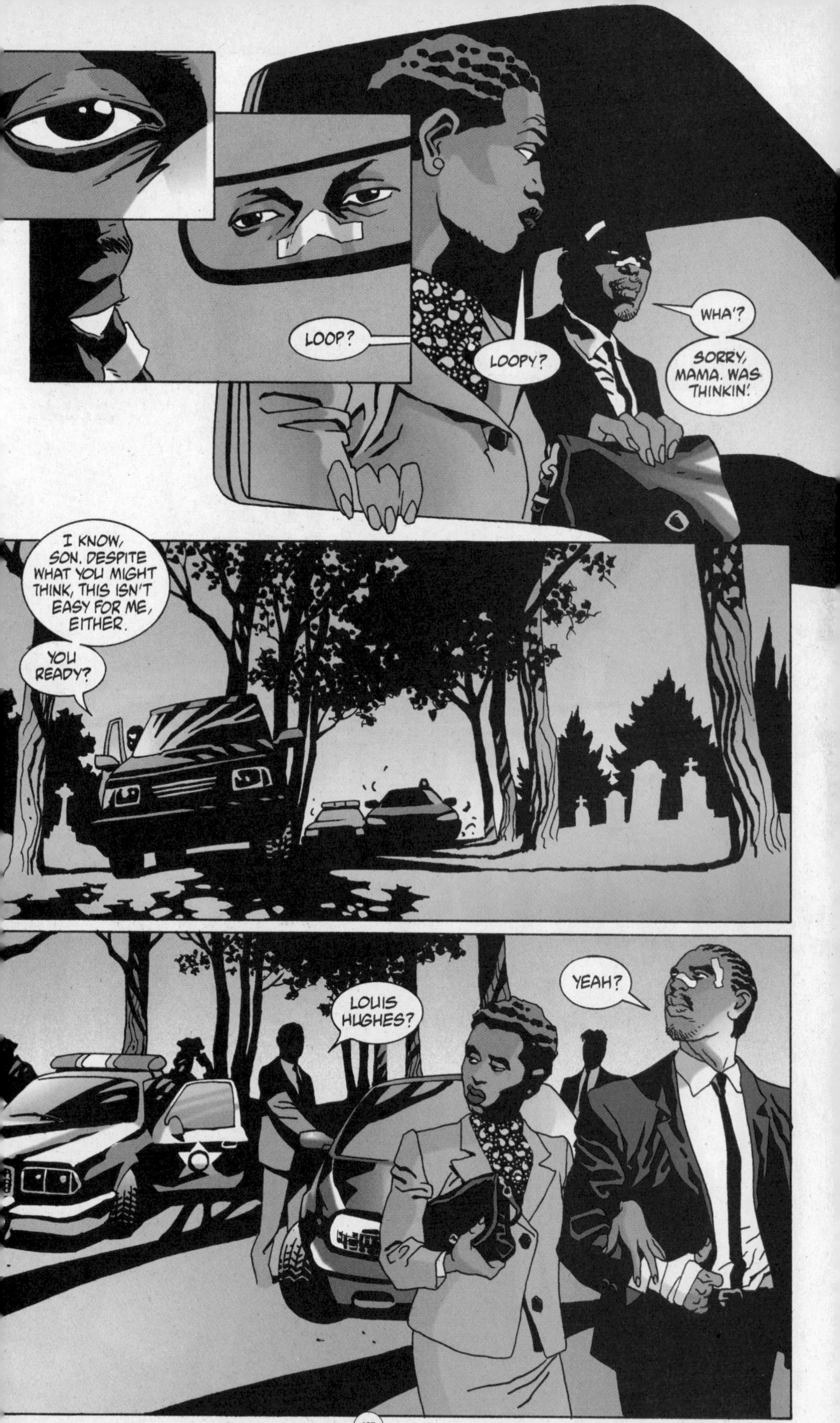
LOOP?
LOOPY?
WHA'?
SORRY, MAMA. WAS THINKIN'.
I KNOW, SON. DESPITE WHAT YOU MIGHT THINK, THIS ISN'T EASY FOR ME, EITHER.
YOU READY?
YEAH?
LOUIS HUGHES?

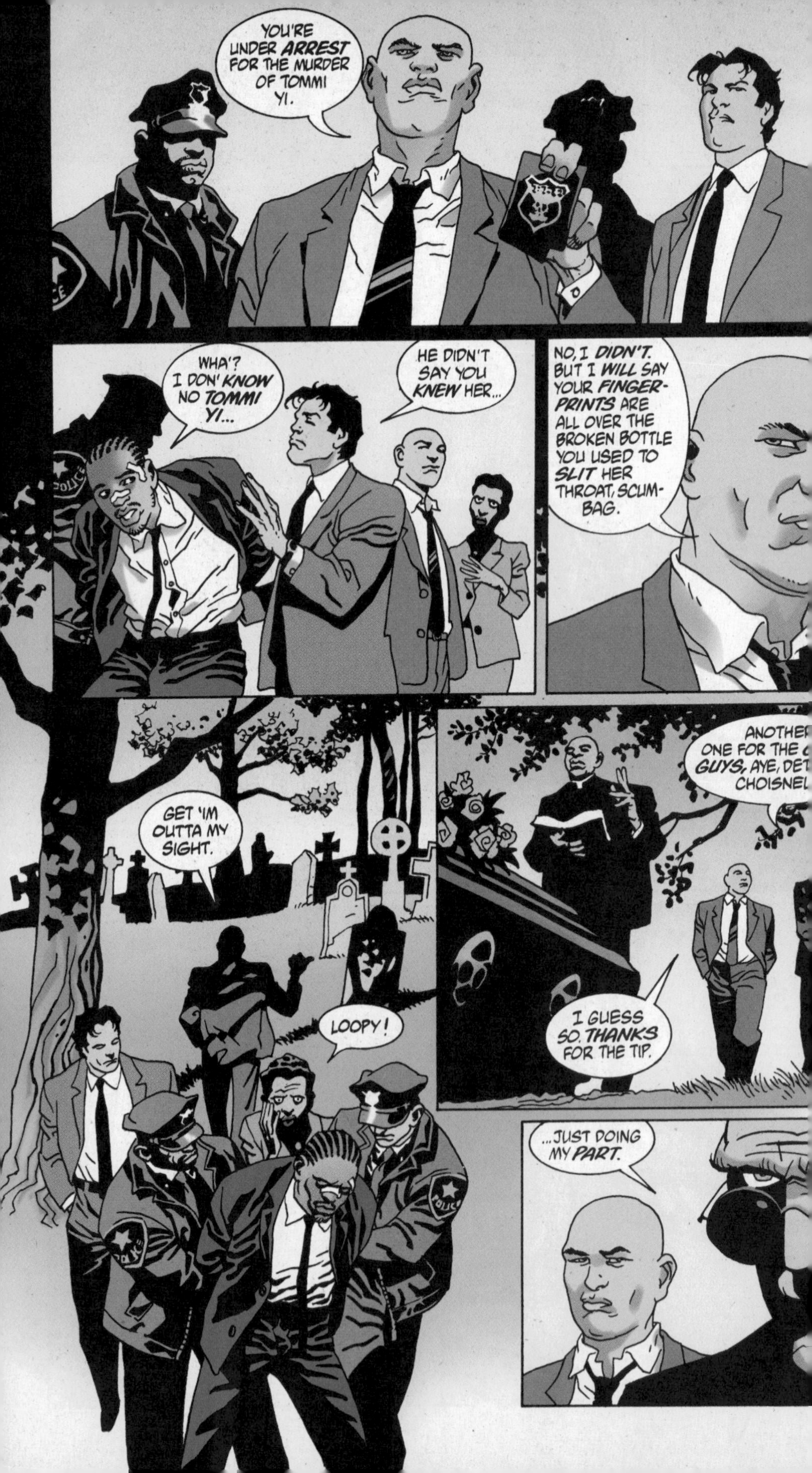

YOU'RE UNDER ARREST FOR THE MURDER OF TOMMI YI.
WHA'? I DON' KNOW NO TOMMI YI...
HE DIDN'T SAY YOU KNEW HER...
NO, I DIDN'T. BUT I WILL SAY YOUR FINGER-PRINTS ARE ALL OVER THE BROKEN BOTTLE YOU USED TO SLIT HER THROAT, SCUM-BAG.
GET 'IM OUTTA MY SIGHT.
LOOPY!
ANOTHE ONE FOR THE GUYS, AYE, DET CHOISNE
I GUESS SO. THANKS FOR THE TIP.
...JUST DOING MY PART.

aphic novels

IE AT MIDNIGHT
e Baker

L YOUR BOYFRIEND
nt Morrison/Philip Bond/
sraeli

NZ INSANA
istopher Fowler/
n Bolton

. PUNCH
Gaiman/Dave McKean

STERY PLAY
nt Morrison/Jon J Muth

L ME, DARK
l Edward Wagner/
t Williams/John Ney Rieber

KIC GUMBO
ia Lunch/Ted McKeever

LS
McGreal/S.J. Phillips/
illarrubia/R. Guay

Y I HATE SATURN
Baker

J ARE HERE
Baker

collections

100 BULLETS:
FIRST SHOT, LAST CALL
Brian Azzarello/Eduardo Risso

BLACK ORCHID
Neil Gaiman/Dave McKean

THE BOOKS OF FAERIE
Bronwyn Carlton/
John Ney Rieber/Peter Gross

THE BOOKS OF FAERIE:
AUBERON'S TALE
B. Carlton/J.N. Rieber/
P. Gross/M. Buckingham/
various

THE BOOKS OF MAGIC
N. Gaiman/J. Bolton/
S. Hampton/C. Vess/
P. Johnson

THE BOOKS OF MAGIC:
BINDINGS
John Ney Rieber/Gary Amaro/
Peter Gross

THE BOOKS OF MAGIC:
SUMMONINGS
J.N. Rieber/P. Gross/
P. Snejbjerg/G. Amaro/
D. Giordano

THE BOOKS OF MAGIC:
RECKONINGS
J.N. Rieber/P. Snejbjerg/
P. Gross/J. Ridgway

THE BOOKS OF MAGIC:
TRANSFORMATIONS
John Ney Rieber/Peter Gross

THE BOOKS OF MAGIC:
GIRL IN THE BOX
John Ney Rieber/Peter Gross/
Peter Snejbjerg

BREATHTAKER
Mark Wheatley/Marc Hempel

THE COMPLEAT
MOONSHADOW
J.M. DeMatteis/Jon J Muth

DEATH: THE HIGH COST OF
LIVING
Neil Gaiman/Chris Bachalo/
Mark Buckingham

DEATH: THE TIME OF
YOUR LIFE
N. Gaiman/C. Bachalo/
M. Buckingham/M. Pennington

DOG MOON
Robert Hunter/
Timothy Truman

DOOM PATROL: CRAWLING
FROM THE WRECKAGE
Grant Morrison/
Richard Case/various

THE DREAMING: BEYOND
THE SHORES OF NIGHT
Various writers and artists

THE DREAMING: THROUGH
THE GATES OF HORN
AND IVORY
Various writers and artists

ENIGMA
Peter Milligan/Duncan Fegredo

HELLBLAZER:
ORIGINAL SINS
Jamie Delano/John Ridgway/
various

HELLBLAZER: DANGEROUS
HABITS
Garth Ennis/William Simpson/
various

HELLBLAZER: FEAR AND
LOATHING
Garth Ennis/Steve Dillon

HELLBLAZER: TAINTED
LOVE
Garth Ennis/Steve Dillon

HELLBLAZER:
DAMNATION'S FLAME
G. Ennis/S. Dillon/
W. Simpson/P. Snejbjerg

HOUSE OF SECRETS:
FOUNDATIONS
Steven T. Seagle/
Teddy Kristiansen

THE INVISIBLES:
BLOODY HELL IN AMERICA
Grant Morrison/Phil Jimenez/
John Stokes

THE INVISIBLES:
COUNTING TO NONE
Grant Morrison/Phil Jimenez/
John Stokes

THE INVISIBLES: SAY YOU
WANT A REVOLUTION
G. Morrison/S. Yeowell/
J. Thompson/D. Cramer

HE INVISIBLES: KISSING MR. QUIMPER
G. Morrison/C. Weston/
. Reis/various

MICHAEL MOORCOCK'S MULTIVERSE
M. Moorcock/W. Simonson/
J. Ridgway/M. Reeve

MERCY
J.M. DeMatteis/Paul Johnson

NEIL GAIMAN & CHARLES VESS' STARDUST
Neil Gaiman/Charles Vess

NEIL GAIMAN'S MIDNIGHT DAYS
N. Gaiman/T. Kristiansen/
S. Bissette/J. Totleben/
M. Mignola/various

NEVADA
S. Gerber/P. Winslade/
S. Leialoha/D. Giordano

PREACHER: GONE TO TEXAS
Garth Ennis/Steve Dillon

PREACHER: UNTIL THE END OF THE WORLD
Garth Ennis/Steve Dillon

PREACHER: PROUD AMERICANS
Garth Ennis/Steve Dillon

PREACHER: ANCIENT HISTORY
G. Ennis/S. Pugh/C. Ezquerra/
R. Case

PREACHER: DIXIE FRIED
Garth Ennis/Steve Dillon

PREACHER: SALVATION
Garth Ennis/Steve Dillon

PREACHER: WAR IN THE SUN
Garth Ennis/Steve Dillon/
Peter Snejbjerg

THE SYSTEM
Peter Kuper

SWAMP THING: SAGA OF THE SWAMP THING
Alan Moore/Steve Bissette/
John Totleben

SWAMP THING: LOVE AND DEATH
A. Moore/S. Bissette/
J. Totleben/S. McManus

SWAMP THING: ROOTS
Jon J Muth

TERMINAL CITY
Dean Motter/Michael Lark

TRANSMETROPOLITAN: BACK ON THE STREET
Warren Ellis/Darick Robertson/
various

TRANSMETROPOLITAN: LUST FOR LIFE
Warren Ellis/Darick Robertson/
various

TRANSMETROPOLITAN: YEAR OF THE BASTARD
Warren Ellis/Darick Robertson/
Rodney Ramos

TRUE FAITH
Garth Ennis/Warren Pleece

UNCLE SAM
Steve Darnall/Alex Ross

UNKNOWN SOLDIER
Garth Ennis/Kilian Plunkett

V FOR VENDETTA
Alan Moore/David Lloyd

VAMPS
Elaine Lee/William Simpson

WITCHCRAFT
J. Robinson/P. Snejbjerg/
M. Zulli/S. Yeowell/
T. Kristiansen

the Sandman library

THE SANDMAN: PRELUDES & NOCTURNES
N. Gaiman/S. Kieth/
M. Dringenberg/M. Jones

THE SANDMAN: THE DOLL'S HOUSE
N. Gaiman/M. Dringenberg/
M. Jones/C. Bachalo/
M. Zulli/S. Parkhouse

THE SANDMAN: DREAM COUNTRY
N. Gaiman/K. Jones/C. Vess/
C. Doran/M. Jones

THE SANDMAN: THE DREAM HU
Neil Gaiman/Yosh

THE SANDMAN: MISTS
N. Gaiman/K. Jo
M. Dringenberg/
various

THE SANDMAN: OF YOU
Neil Gaiman/Sha
various

THE SANDMAN: FABLES AND RE
Neil Gaiman/vari

THE SANDMAN:
Neil Gaiman/Jill
Vince Locke

THE SANDMAN:
Neil Gaiman/vari

THE SANDMAN: THE KINDLY ON
N. Gaiman/M. He
various

THE SANDMAN:
N. Gaiman/M. Zu
C. Vess

DUSTCOVERS-T SANDMAN COVE
Dave McKean/Nei

THE SANDMAN
Hy Bender